THE HIGH SCHOOL ALGEBRA TUTOR

SECOND EDITION

Staff of Research and Education Association
Dr. M. Fogiel, Chief Editor

Research and Education Association
61 Ethel Road West
Piscataway, New Jersey 08854

THE HIGH SCHOOL ALGEBRA TUTOR®

Revised Edition of
THE HIGH SCHOOL ALGEBRA PROBLEM SOLVER®

Printed in the United States of America

Library of Congress Catalog Card Number 94-69648

International Standard Book Number 0-87891-564-8

THE HIGH SCHOOL TUTOR is a registered trademark of Research & Education Association, Piscataway, New Jersey 08854

WHAT THIS BOOK IS FOR

For as long as algebra has been taught in high schools, students have found this subject difficult to understand and learn. Despite the publication of hundreds of textbooks in this field, each one intended to provide an improvement over previous textbooks, students continue to remain perplexed, and the subject is often taken in class only to meet school/departmental requirements for a selected course of study.

In a study of the problem, REA found the following basic reasons underlying students' difficulties with algebra taught in schools:

(a) No systematic rules of analysis have been developed which students may follow in a step-by-step manner to solve the usual problems encountered. This results from the fact that the numerous different conditions and principles which may be involved in a problem, lead to many possible different methods of solution. To prescribe a set of rules to be followed for each of the possible variations, would involve an enormous number of rules and steps to be searched through by students, and this task would perhaps be more burdensome than solving the problem directly with some accompanying trial and error to find the correct solution route.

(b) Textbooks currently available will usually explain a given principle in a few pages written by a professional who has an insight in the subject matter that is not shared by students. The explanations are often written in an abstract manner which leaves the students confused as to the application of the principle. The explanations given are not sufficiently detailed and extensive to make the student aware of the wide range of applications and different aspects of the principle being studied. The numerous possible variations of principles and their applications are usually not discussed, and it is left for the students to discover these for themselves while doing the exercises. Accordingly, the average student is expected to rediscover that which has been long known and practiced, but not published or explained extensively.

(c) The examples usually following the explanation of a topic are too few in number and too simple to enable the student to obtain a thorough grasp of the principles involved. The explanations do not provide sufficient basis to enable a student to solve problems that may be subsequently assigned for homework or given on examinations.

The examples are presented in abbreviated form which leaves out much material between steps, and requires that students derive the omitted material themselves. As a result, students find the examples difficult to understand--contrary to the purpose of the examples.

Examples are, furthermore, often worded in a confusing manner. They do not state the problem and then present the solution. Instead, they pass through a general discussion, never revealing what is to be solved for.

Examples, also, do not always include diagrams/graphs, wherever appropriate, and students do not obtain the training to draw diagrams or graphs to simplify and organize their thinking.

(d) Students can learn the subject only by doing the exercises themselves and reviewing them in class, to obtain experience in applying the principles with their different ramifications.

In doing the exercise by themselves, students find that they are required to devote considerably more time to algebra than to other subjects of comparable credits, because they are uncertain with regard to the selection and application of the theorems and principles involved. It is also often necessary for students to discover those "tricks" not revealed in their texts (or review books), that make it possible to solve problems easily. Students must usually resort to methods of trial-and-error to discover these "tricks", and as a result they find that they may sometimes spend several hours in solving a single problem.

(e) When reviewing the exercises in classrooms, instructors usually request students to take turns in writing solutions on the boards and explaining them to the class. Students often find it difficult to explain in a manner that holds the interest of the class, and enables the class to follow the material written on the boards. The remaining students seated in the class are, furthermore, too occupied with copying the material from the boards, to listen to the oral explanations and concentrate on the methods of solution.

This book is intended to aid students in algebra in overcoming the difficulties described, by supplying detailed illustrations of the solution methods which are usually not apparent to students. The solution methods are illustrated by problems selected from those that are most often assigned for class work and given on examinations. The problems are arranged in order of complexity to enable students to learn and understand a particular topic by reviewing the problems in sequence. The problems are illustrated with detailed step-by- step explanations, to save the students the large amount of time that is often needed to fill in the gaps that are usually found between steps of illustrations in textbooks or review/outline books.

The staff of REA considers algebra a subject that is best learned by allowing students to view the methods of analysis and solution techniques themselves. This approach to learning the subject matter is similar to that practiced in various scientific laboratories, particularly in the medical fields.

In using this book, students may review and study the illustrated problems at their own pace; they are not limited to the time allowed for explaining problems on the board in class.

When students want to look up a particular type of problem and solution, they can readily locate it in the book by referring to the index which has been extensively prepared. It is also possible to locate a particular type of problem by glancing at just the material within the boxed portions. To facilitate rapid scanning of the problems, each problem has a heavy border around it. Furthermore, each problem is identified with a number immediately above the problem at the right-hand margin.

To obtain maximum benefit from the book, students should

familiarize themselves with the section, "How To Use This Book," located in the front pages.

To meet the objectives of this book, staff members of REA have selected problems usually encountered in assignments and examinations, and have solved each problem meticulously to illustrate the steps which are usually difficult for students to comprehend. Special gratitude is expressed to them for their efforts in this area, as well as to the numerous contributors who devoted brief periods of time to this work.

Gratitude is also expressed to the many persons involved in the difficult task of typing the manuscript with its endless changes, and to the REA art staff who prepared the numerous detailed illustrations together with the layout and physical features of the book.

The difficult task of coordinating the efforts of all persons was carried out by Carl Fuchs. His conscientious work deserves much appreciation. He also trained and supervised art and production personnel in the preparation of the book for printing.

Finally, special thanks are due to Helen Kaufmann for her unique talents to render those difficult border-line decisions and constructive suggestions related to the design and organization of the book.

Max Fogiel, **Ph.D.**
Program Director

HOW TO USE THIS BOOK

This book can be an invaluable aid to students in algebra as a supplement to their textbooks. The book is subdivided into 29 chapters, each dealing with a separate topic. The subject matter is developed beginning with fundamental algebraic laws and operations and extending through systems of equations and applied problems.

TO LEARN AND UNDERSTAND A TOPIC THOROUGHLY

1. Refer to your class text and read there the section pertaining to the topic. You should become acquainted with the principles discussed there. These principles, however, may not be clear to you at that time.

2. Then locate the topic you are looking for by referring to the "Table of Contents" in front of this book, "The High School Algebra Problem Solver".

3. Turn to the page where the topic begins and review the problems under each topic, in the order given. For each topic, the problems are arranged in order of complexity, from the simplest to the more difficult. Some problems may appear similar to others, but each problem has been selected to illustrate a different point or solution method.

To learn and understand a topic thoroughly and retain its contents, it will generally be necessary for students to review the problems several times. Repeated review is essential in order to gain experience in recognizing the principles that should be applied, and to select the best solution technique.

TO FIND A PARTICULAR PROBLEM

To locate one or more problems related to a particular subject matter, refer to the index. In using the index, be certain to note that the numbers given there refer to problem numbers, not to page numbers. This arrangement of the index is intended to facilitate finding a problem more rapidly, since two or more problems may appear on a page.

If a particular type of problem cannot be found readily, it is recommended that the student refer to the "Table of Contents" in the front pages, and then turn to the chapter which is applicable to the problem being sought. By scanning or glancing at the material that is boxed, it will generally be possible to find problems related to the one being sought, without consuming considerable time. After the problems have been located, the solutions can be reviewed and studied in detail. For this purpose of locating problems rapidly, students should acquaint themselves with the organization of the book as found in the "Table of Contents".

In preparing for an exam, locate the topics to be covered on the exam in the "Table of Contents," and then review the problems under those topics several times. This should equip the students with what might be needed for the exam.

CONTENTS

CHAPTER 1

FUNDAMENTAL ALGEBRAIC LAWS AND OPERATIONS

● PROBLEM 1-1

Find the sum 8 + (- 3).

<u>Solution:</u> The sum of 8 + (- 3) can be obtained by using facts from arithmetic and the associative law:

$$8 + (- 3) = (5 + 3) + (- 3)$$

Use the associative law of addition (a + b) + c = a + (b + c):

$$= 5 + [3 + (- 3)]$$

Using the additive inverse property, a + (- a) = 0:

$$= 5 + 0$$

Using the additive identity property, a + 0 = a

$$= 5.$$

● PROBLEM 1-2

Evaluate 2 - {5 + (2 - 3) + [2 - (3 - 4)]}

<u>Solution:</u> When working with a group of nested parentheses, we evaluate the innermost parenthesis first.

Thus, 2 - {5 + (2 - 3) + [2 - (3 - 4)]}

$$= 2 - \{5 + (2 - 3) + [2 - (- 1)]\}$$

$$= 2 - \{5 + (- 1) + [2 + 1]\}$$

$$= 2 - \{5 + (-1) + 3\}$$

$$= 2 - \{4 + 3\}$$

$$= 2 - 7$$

$$= -5.$$

● **PROBLEM 1-3**

Simplify $4[-2(3 + 9) \div 3] + 5$.

<u>Solution:</u>   To simplify means to find the simplest expression. We perform the operations within the innermost grouping symbols first.   That is $3 + 9 = 12$.

Thus, $4[-2(3 + 9) \div 3] + 5 = 4[-2(12) \div 3] + 5$

Next we simplify within the brackets:

$$= 4[-24 \div 3] + 5$$

$$= 4 \cdot (-8) + 5$$

We now perform the multiplication, since multiplication is done before addition:

$$= -32 + 5$$

$$= -27$$

Hence, $4[-2(3 + 9) \div 3] + 5 = -27$.

● **PROBLEM 1-4**

Simplify the following expressions, removing the parentheses.

1) $a + (b - c)$

2) $ax - (by - c)$

3) $2 - (-x + y)$.

<u>Solution:</u> 1) Place a factor of 1 between the + (plus) sign and the term in the parenthesis. This procedure does not change the value of the entire expression. Hence, $a + (b-c) = a + 1(b-c)$

$$= a + 1(b) + 1(-c) \text{ distributing}$$
$$= a + b - c$$

2) Again, place a factor of 1 between the - (minus) sign and the term in the parenthesis. Again, this procedure does not change the value of the entire expression. Hence,

$$ax - (by - c) = ax - 1(by - c)$$

$$= ax - 1(by) - 1(-c) \text{ distributing}$$

2

$$= ax - by + c$$

3) Again, place a factor of 1 between the - (minus) sign and the term in parenthesis. Again, this procedure does not change the value of the entire expression. Hence,

$$2 - (-x + y) = 2 - 1(-x + y)$$
$$= 2 - 1(-x) - 1(y) \text{ distributing}$$
$$= 2 + x - y$$

● **PROBLEM 1-5**

Evaluate $3s - [5t + (2s - 5)]$

Solution: We always evaluate the expression within the innermost parentheses first, when working with a group of nested parentheses. Thus,

$$3s - [5t + (2s - 5)] = 3s - [5t + 2s - 5]$$
$$= 3s - 5t - 2s + 5$$
$$= 3s - 2s - 5t + 5$$
$$= s - 5t + 5.$$

● **PROBLEM 1-6**

Simplify: $3a - 2\{3a - 2[1 - 4(a - 1)] + 5\}$.

Solution: When working with several sets of brackets and, or parentheses, we work from the inside out. That is, we use the law of distribution throughout the expression, starting from the innermost parentheses, and working our way out. Hence in this case we have: $2\{3a - 2[1 - 4(a - 1)] + 5\}$ and we note that $(a - 1)$ is the innermost parenthesis, so our first step is to distribute the (-4). Thus, we obtain:

$$3a - 2[3a - 2(1 - 4a + 4) + 5].$$

We now find that $(1 - 4a + 4)$ is in our innermost parentheses. Combining terms we obtain:

$$(1 - 4a + 4) = (5 - 4a) \ ;$$

hence, $3a - 2[3a - 2(1 - 4a + 4) + 5] = 3a - 2[3a - 2(5 - 4a) + 5]$
and since $(5 - 4a)$ is in the innermost parentheses we distribute the (-2), obtaining:

$$3a - 2(3a - 10 + 8a + 5).$$

We are now left with the terms in our last set of parentheses,

(3a - 10 + 8a + 5).Combining like terms we obtain:

$\qquad$ (3a - 10 + 8a + 5) = (11a - 5)

hence, $\qquad$ 3a - 2(3a - 10 + 8a + 5) = 3a - 2(11a - 5) .

Distributing the (-2), $\quad$ = 3a - 22a + 10

combining terms, $\qquad$ = -19a + 10 .

Hence $\qquad$ 3a - 2{3a - 2[1 - 4(a - 1)] + 5} = -19a + 10 .

● **PROBLEM 1-7**

(a) Add, 3a + 5a

(b) Factor, 5ac + 2bc.

Solution: (a) To add 3a + 5a, factor out the common factor a. Then,

$\qquad$ 3a + 5a = (3 + 5)a = 8a.

(b) To factor 5ac + 2bc, factor out the common factor c. Then,

$\qquad$ 5ac + 2bc = (5a + 2b)c.

● **PROBLEM 1-8**

Express each of the following as a single term.

$\quad$ (a) $3x^2 + 2x^2 - 4x^2$ $\quad$ (b) $5axy^2 - 7axy^2 - 3xy^2$

Solution: (a) Factor x^2 in the expression.

$$3x^2 + 2x^2 - 4x^2 = (3 + 2 - 4)x^2 = 1x^2 = x^2.$$

(b) Factor xy^2 in the expression and then factor a.

$$5axy^2 - 7axy^2 - 3xy^2 = (5a - 7a - 3)xy^2$$
$$= [(5-7)a - 3]xy^2$$
$$= (-2a - 3)xy^2.$$

● **PROBLEM 1-9**

Use the field properties to derive the equation x = 5 from the equation 5x - 3 = 2(x + 6).

Solution: $\qquad$ 5x - 3 = 2(x + 6) $\qquad$ Given

$\qquad\qquad\qquad$ 5x - 3 = 2x + 12 $\qquad$ distributive property of multiplication over addition

$$(5x - 3) + (-2x) = 2x + 12 + (-2x) \qquad \text{Additive Property } (-2x)$$
$$3x - 3 = 12 \qquad \text{Simplifying}$$
$$(3x - 3) + 3 = 12 + 3 \qquad \text{additive property } (+3)$$
$$3x = 15 \qquad \text{Simplifying}$$
$$\tfrac{1}{3} \cdot (3x) = \tfrac{1}{3} \cdot 15 \qquad \text{Multiplicative Property } (\tfrac{1}{3})$$
$$x = 5 \qquad \text{Simplifying}$$

We could also derive $5x - 3 = 2(x + 6)$ from $x = 5$ by reversing the steps in the solution. Let us see if 5 will make the equation $5x - 3 = 2(x + 6)$ true.

$$5(5) - 3 \overset{?}{=} 2(5 + 6)$$

$$22 = 22$$

Two equations are equivalent if and only if they have the same solution set. Since $5x - 3 = 2(x + 6)$ and $x = 5$ have the same solution set, $\{5\}$, the two equations are equivalent.

● **PROBLEM** 1-10

Approximate:

$$A = \frac{\pi \times \sqrt{2} \times 2.17}{(6.83)^2 + (1.07)^2}$$

Solution: We use the following approximate values:

$$\pi = 3.1416 \cong 3$$
$$\sqrt{2} = 1.414 \cong 1.5$$
$$2.17 \cong 2$$
$$(6.83)^2 \cong 7^2 = 49 \cong 50$$
$$(1.07)^2 \cong 1^2 = 1$$

Then,

$$A \cong \frac{3 \times 1.5 \times 2}{50 + 1} = \frac{9}{51} \cong \frac{10}{50} = .2$$

● **PROBLEM** 1-11

Evaluate $p = \dfrac{(a - b)(ab + c)}{(cb - 2a)}$

when $a = +2$, $b = -\tfrac{1}{2}$, and $c = -3$.

Solution: Inserting the given values of a, b, and c

$$p = \frac{[+ 2 - (- \tfrac{1}{2})][(+2)(- \tfrac{1}{2}) + (- 3)]}{[(- 3)(- \tfrac{1}{2}) - 2(+ 2)]}$$

$$= \frac{[+ 2 + \tfrac{1}{2}][- 1 - 3]}{[+ 1\tfrac{1}{2} - 4]}$$

$$= \frac{(2\tfrac{1}{2})(- 4)}{- (2\tfrac{1}{2})}$$

The 2½ in the numerator cancels the 2½ in the denominator.

$$p = \frac{- 4}{- 1}$$

Multiplying numerator and denominator by - 1

$$p = \frac{+ 4}{+ 1}$$

$$p = + 4.$$

CHAPTER 2

LEAST COMMON MULTIPLE AND GREATEST COMMON DIVISOR

● **PROBLEM** 2-1

Find the least common multiple (lcm) of 15 and 18.

Solution: Some of the integers divisible by 15 are

15,30,45,60,75,90,105,...

Some of the integers divisible by 18 are

18,36,54,72,90,108,...

The smallest positive integer divisible by both 15 and 18 is 90. Thus,

lcm{15,18} = 90

Another method for finding lcm{15,18} is the following:
Factor 15 and 18 into their prime factors.

15 = 3·5

18 = 2·3·3

Now, take the different factors of the two numbers and multiply them together. The exponent to be used for each factor is the highest number of times that the factor appears in either number (15 or 18). The product obtained will be the lcm{15,18}. Hence:

lcm{15,18} = $2^1 \cdot 3^2 \cdot 5^1$ = 2(9)(5) = 90.

● **PROBLEM** 2-2

Find the Least Common Multiple, LCM, of 26, 39, and 66.

Solution: Write each number as the product of primes:

26 = 2(13), 39 = 3(13), 66 = 2(3)(11)

The LCM is obtained by using the greatest power of

7

each prime, only once, to form a product. Thus,

$$LCM = 2(3)(11)(13)$$

$$= 858.$$

Find the Least Common Multiple, LCM, of 12, 18, 21, 25 and 35.

<u>Solution:</u> We want to express each number as a product of prime factors:

$$12 = 2^2(3), \quad 18 = 2(3^2), \quad 21 = 3(7),$$

$$25 = 5^2, \quad 35 = 5(7)$$

Find the LCM by retaining the highest power of each distinct factor and multiplying them together, making sure to use each factor only once regardless of the number of times it appears. Thus,

$$LCM = (2^2)(3^2)(5^2)(7) = (4)(9)(25)(7)$$

$$= 6300$$

Find the greatest common divisor $\{15,28\}$.

<u>Solution:</u> If 15 and 28 are factored completely into their respective prime factors, $15 = 3 \cdot 5$ and $28 = 2 \cdot 2 \cdot 7$

Since 1 divides every integer, and since 15 and 28 possess no common prime factors, it follows that

$$gcd\{15,28\} = 1.$$

If the gcd of two integers is 1, then the two integers are said to be relatively prime. Since $gcd\{15,28\} = 1$, the integers 15 and 28 are relatively prime.

Find the greatest common divisor and the least common multiple of 16 and 12.

<u>Solution:</u> Factor the two given numbers into their prime factors.

$$12 = 2 \cdot 2 \cdot 3$$

8

$$16 = 2 \cdot 2 \cdot 2 \cdot 2$$

The greatest common divisor of 16 and 12, or gcd{12,16}, is the largest number which divides both 16 and 12, (largest common factor).

$$\frac{12}{16} = \frac{2 \cdot 2 \cdot 3}{2 \cdot 2 \cdot 2 \cdot 2} = \frac{(4)(3)}{(4)(2)(2)}$$

Hence, gcd{12,16} = 4 .

The least common multiple of 16 and 12, or lcm{12,16}, is obtained in the following way. Take the different factors of the two numbers and multiply them together. The exponent to be used for each factor is the highest number of times that the factor appears in either number (12 or 16). The product obtained will be the lcm{12,16}. Hence:

$$\text{lcm}\{16,12\} = 2^4 \cdot 3^1 = (16)(3) = 48 .$$

● **PROBLEM 2-6**

Find the greatest common divisor of 24 and 40. Also, find the least common multiple of 24 and 40.

Solution: To find the greatest common divisor of 24 and 40, or gcd{24,40}, we write down the set of all positive integers which divide both 24 and 40. Thus we obtain the two sets

$$\{1,2,3,4,6,8,12,24\} \text{ for } 24$$
$$\{1,2,4,5,8,10,20,40\} \text{ for } 40$$

Those integers dividing both 24 and 40 are in the intersection of these two sets. Thus,

$$\{1,2,3,4,6,8,12,24\} \cap \{1,2,4,5,8,10,20,40\} = \{1,2,4,8\}$$

The largest element in this last set is 8. Thus,

$$8 = \text{gcd}\{24,40\} .$$

Another method for finding the gcd{24,40} is called the factoring technique. Factor the two given numbers into their prime factors.

$$24 = 2 \cdot 2 \cdot 2 \cdot 3$$
$$40 = 2 \cdot 2 \cdot 2 \cdot 5$$

The greatest common divisor of any two numbers is the largest number which divides both of those numbers. Therefore,

$$\frac{24}{40} = \frac{2 \cdot 2 \cdot 2 \cdot 3}{2 \cdot 2 \cdot 2 \cdot 5} = \frac{(8)(3)}{(8)(5)} . \quad \text{Hence,}$$

$$\text{gcd} \{24,40\} = 8 .$$

The following technique is the definition for finding the least common multiple of 24 and 40, or lcm {24,40}. To find the lcm{24,40}, we write down the set of all positive integer multiples of both 24 and 40. Then we obtain

$$\{24,48,72,96,120,144,168,192,216,240,264,\ldots\} \text{ for } 24$$

$$\{40,80,120,160,200,240,280,\ldots\} \qquad \text{for } 40$$

The integers which are multiples of both 24 and 40; that is, common multiples of 24 and 40, are in the intersection of these two sets. This is the set $\{120, 240, ...\}$. The smallest element of this set is 120. Hence, lcm$\{24,40\}$ = 120. Another method for finding the lcm$\{24,40\}$ is called the factoring technique. Factor the two given numbers into their prime factors.

$$24 = 2 \cdot 2 \cdot 2 \cdot 3$$
$$40 = 2 \cdot 2 \cdot 2 \cdot 5$$

Now, take the different factors of the two numbers and multiply them together. The exponent to be used for each factor is the highest number of times that the factor appears in either number (24 or 40). The produce obtained will be the lcm$\{24,40\}$. Hence:

$$\text{lcm}\{24,40\} = 2^3 \cdot 3^1 \cdot 5^1 = (8)(3)(5) = (24)(5) = 120.$$

CHAPTER 3

SETS AND SUBSETS

● **PROBLEM 3-1**

If a = { 1, 2, 3, 4, 5} and b = { 2, 3, 4, 5, 6}, find a ∪ b.

Solution: The symbol ∪ is used to denote the union of sets. Thus a ∪ b (which is read "the union of a and b') is the set of all elements that are in either a or b or both. In this problem, if,

then   a = { 1, 2, 3, 4, 5} and b = { 2, 3, 4, 5, 6},

a ∪ b = { 1, 2, 3, 4, 5, 6}.

● **PROBLEM 3-2**

If a = { 1, 2, 3, 4, 5) and b = { 2, 3, 4, 5, 6}, find a ∩ b.

Solution: The intersection of two sets a and b is the set of all elements that belong to both a and b; that is, all elements common to a and b. In this problem, if

a = { 1, 2, 3, 4, 5} and b = { 2, 3, 4, 5, 6},

then
a ∩ b = { 2, 3, 4, 5}.

● **PROBLEM 3-3**

Show that (A ∩ B) ∩ C = A ∩ (B ∩ C).

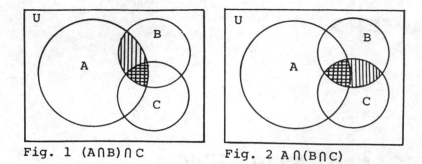

Fig. 1 (A∩B)∩C   Fig. 2 A∩(B∩C)

__Solution:__ In Figure 1 the vertically shaded area represents
A ∩ B, and the horizontally shaded area represents the
points common to the set (A ∩ B) and the set C, that is
(A ∩ B) ∩ C. Similarly, in Figure 2, the vertically shaded
area represents B ∩ C, and the horizontally shaded area
represents the points common to the set (B ∩ C) and the
set A, that is A ∩ (B ∩ C). Since the two horizontally
shaded areas in the two figures are the same,

$$(A \cap B) \cap C = A \cap (B \cap C).$$

● **PROBLEM 3-4**

If U = { 1, 2, 3, 4, 5} and A = { 2, 4}, find A'.

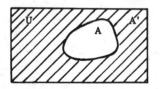

__Solution:__ The complement of a set A in U is the set of all
elements of U that do not belong to A. The symbol A' (or,
sometimes, $\bar{A}$, ⌐A, or Å) denotes the complement of A in U.
The figure gives a representation of A', the complement of
A in U. In this problem, since,

U = { 1, 2, 3, 4, 5}

and

A = { 2, 4},

A' = { 1, 3, 5}.

● **PROBLEM 3-5**

U = {1,2,3,4,5,6,7,8,9,10}, P = {2,4,6,8,10}, Q = {1,2,3,4,5}.
Find (a) $\bar{P}$ and (b) $\bar{Q}$.

12

<u>Solution:</u> $\bar{P}$ and $\bar{Q}$ are the complements of P and Q respectively. That is, $\bar{P}$ is the set of all elements in the universal set, U, that are not elements of P, and $\bar{Q}$ is the set of elements in U that are not in Q. Therefore,

(a) $\bar{P} = \{1,3,5,7,9\}$; (b) $\bar{Q} = \{6,7,8,9,10\}$

● **PROBLEM 3-6**

Show that the complement of the complement of a set is the set itself.

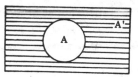

<u>Solution:</u> The complement of set A is given by A'. Therefore, the complement of the complement of a set is given by (A')'. This set, (A')', must be shown to be the set A; that is, that (A')' = A. In the figure the complement of the set A, or A', is the set of all points not in set A; that is, all points in the rectangle that are not in the circle. This is the shaded area in the figure. Therefore, this shaded area is A'. The complement of this set, or (A')', is the set of all points of the rectangle that are not in the shaded area; that is, all points in the circle, which is the set A. Therefore, the set (A')' is the same as set A; that is,

(A')' = A.

● **PROBLEM 3-7**

If a = { 1, 2, 3} and b = { 5, 6}, find a x b and b x a.

<u>Solution:</u> The Cartesian product of two sets a and b, denoted by a x b, is the set of all ordered pairs (x, y) such that x ε a and y ε b. In this problem, if a = { 1, 2, 3} and b = { 5, 6}, then the Cartesian product a x b is:

a x b = { (1, 5), (1, 6), (2,5), (2, 6), (3, 5),

(3, 6)}.

The Cartesian product b x a is the set of all ordered pairs (x, y) such that x ε b and y ε a. Hence, the Cartesian product b x a is:

b x a = { (5, 1), (5, 2), (5, 3), (6, 1), (6, 2),

(6, 3)}.

List all the subsets of C = {1,2}.

Solution: {1}, {2}, {1,2}, $\emptyset$, where $\emptyset$ is the empty set. Each set listed in the solution contains at least one element of the set C. The set {2,1} is identical to {1,2} and therefore is not listed. $\emptyset$ is included in the solution because $\emptyset$ is a subset of every set.

Find four proper subsets of P = {n: n ε I, -5 < n ≤ 5}.

Solution: P = {-4, -3, -2, -1, 0, 1, 2, 3, 4, 5}. All these elements are integers that are either less than or equal to 5 or greater than -5. A set A is a proper subset of P if every element of A is an element of B and in addition there is an element of B which is not in A.

(a) B = {-4, -2, 0, 2, 4} is a subset because each element of B is an integer greater than -5 but less than or equal to 5. B is a proper subset because 3 is an element of P but not an element of B. We can write 3 ε P but 3 $\notin$ B.

(b) C = {3} is a subset of P, since 3 ε P. However, 5 ε P but 5 $\notin$ C. Hence, C ⊂ P.

(c) D = {-4, -3, -2, -1, 1, 2, 3, 4, 5} is a proper subset of P, since each element of D is an element of P, but 0 ε P and 0 $\notin$ D.

(d) ϕ ⊂ P, since ϕ has no elements. Note that ϕ is the empty set. ϕ is a proper subset of every set except itself.

CHAPTER 4

ABSOLUTE VALUES

Solve for x when $|x - 7| = 3$.

Solution: This equation, according to the definition of absolute value, expresses the conditions that $x - 7$ must be 3 or -3, since in either case the absolute value is 3. If $x - 7 = 3$, we have $x = 10$; and if $x - 7 = -3$, we have $x = 4$. We see that there are two values of x which solve the equation.

Solve for x when $|3x + 2| = 5$.

Solution: First we write expressions which replace the absolute symbols in forms of equations that can be manipulated algebraically. Thus this equation will be satisfied if either

$$3x + 2 = 5 \quad \text{or} \quad 3x + 2 = -5.$$

Considering each equation separately, we find

$$x = 1 \quad \text{and} \quad x = -\frac{7}{3}.$$

Accordingly, the given equation has two solutions.

Solve for x when $|5x + 4| = -3$.

Solution: In examining the given equation, it is seen that the

15

absolute value of a number is set equal to a negative value. By definition of an absolute number, however, the number cannot be negative. Therefore the given equation has no solution.

Solve for x when $|5 - 3x| = -2$.

<u>Solution</u>: This problem has no solution, since the absolute value can never be negative and we need not proceed further.

Solve for x in $|2x - 6| = |4 - 5x|$.

<u>Solution</u>: There are four possibilities here. 2x - 6 and 4 - 5x can be either positive or negative. Therefore,

$$2x - 6 = 4 - 5x \qquad (1)$$
$$-(2x - 6) = 4 - 5x \qquad (2)$$
and
$$2x - 6 = -(4 - 5x) \qquad (3)$$
$$-(2x - 6) = -(4 - 5x) \qquad (4)$$

Equations (2) and (3) result in the same solution, as do equations (1) and (4). Therefore it is necessary to solve only for equations (1) and (2). This gives:

$$x = \frac{10}{7}, -\frac{2}{3}.$$

Solve for x when $|2x - 1| = |4x + 3|$.

<u>Solution</u>: Replacing the absolute sysmbols with equations that can be handled algebraically according to the conditions implied by the given equation, we have:

$$2x - 1 = 4x + 3 \quad \text{or} \quad 2x - 1 = -(4x + 3).$$

Solving the first equation, we have x =-2; solving the second, we obtain $x = -\frac{1}{3}$, thus giving us two solutions to the original equation. (We could also write: $-(2x - 1) = -(4x + 3)$, but this is equivalent to the first of the equations above.)

CHAPTER 5

OPERATIONS WITH FRACTIONS

● PROBLEM 5-1

Simplify $\dfrac{\frac{1}{2} + \frac{1}{3}}{\frac{1}{6}}$.

Solution: $\dfrac{\frac{1}{2} + \frac{1}{3}}{\frac{1}{6}}$ means $\left(\dfrac{1}{2} + \dfrac{1}{3}\right) \div \dfrac{1}{6}$

Since division by a fraction is equivalent to multiplication by its reciprocal:

$$\left(\frac{1}{2} + \frac{1}{3}\right) \div \frac{1}{6} = \left(\frac{1}{2} + \frac{1}{3}\right) \times 6$$

By the distributive law:

$$\left(\frac{1}{2} + \frac{1}{3}\right) \times 6 = \left(\frac{1}{2}\right)(6) + \left(\frac{1}{3}\right)(6)$$
$$= \frac{6}{2} + \frac{6}{3}$$
$$= 3 + 2$$
$$= 5$$

● PROBLEM 5-2

Simplify the following expression: $1 - \dfrac{1}{2 - \frac{1}{3}}$.

Solution: In order to combine the denominator, $2 - \dfrac{1}{3}$, we must convert 2 into thirds. $2 = 2 \cdot 1 = 2 \cdot \dfrac{3}{3} = \dfrac{6}{3}$. Thus

$$1 - \cfrac{1}{2 - \cfrac{1}{3}} = 1 - \cfrac{1}{\cfrac{6}{3} - \cfrac{1}{3}} = 1 - \cfrac{1}{\cfrac{5}{3}}$$

Since division by a fraction is equivalent to multiplication by that fraction's reciprocal

$$1 - \cfrac{1}{\cfrac{5}{3}} = 1 - (1)\left(\frac{3}{5}\right) = 1 - \frac{3}{5} = \frac{5}{5} - \frac{3}{5} = \frac{2}{5}$$

Therefore, $\qquad 1 - \cfrac{1}{2 - \cfrac{1}{3}} = \dfrac{2}{5}.$

● PROBLEM 5-3

Simplify the complex fraction $\qquad \cfrac{\dfrac{1}{2} + \dfrac{1}{3}}{\dfrac{1}{4} + \dfrac{1}{5}} .$

<u>Solution:</u> First simplify the expressions in the numerator and denominator by adding the fractions together according to the rule

$$\frac{a}{b} + \frac{c}{d} = \frac{ad + bc}{bd}$$

We now obtain $\dfrac{1}{2} + \dfrac{1}{3} = \dfrac{3 + 2}{6} = \dfrac{5}{6}$

$$\frac{1}{4} + \frac{1}{5} = \frac{4 + 5}{20} = \frac{9}{20}$$

therefore,

$$\cfrac{\dfrac{1}{2} + \dfrac{1}{3}}{\dfrac{1}{4} + \dfrac{1}{5}} = \cfrac{\dfrac{5}{6}}{\dfrac{9}{20}}$$

To divide this complex fraction invert the fraction in the denominator and multiply the resulting fraction by the fraction in the numerator:

$$\cfrac{\dfrac{1}{2} + \dfrac{1}{3}}{\dfrac{1}{4} + \dfrac{1}{5}} = \frac{5}{6} \times \frac{20}{9} = \frac{100}{54} = \frac{50}{27}$$

● PROBLEM 5-4

If $a = 4$ and $b = 7$ find the value of $\qquad \cfrac{a + \dfrac{a}{b}}{a - \dfrac{a}{b}} .$

Solution: By substitution, $\dfrac{a + \dfrac{a}{b}}{a - \dfrac{a}{b}} = \dfrac{4 + \dfrac{4}{7}}{4 - \dfrac{4}{7}}$.

In order to combine the terms we convert 4 into sevenths:

$$4 = 4 \cdot 1 = 4 \cdot \frac{7}{7} = \frac{28}{7} .$$

Thus, we have:

$$\frac{\dfrac{28}{7} + \dfrac{4}{7}}{\dfrac{28}{7} - \dfrac{4}{7}} = \frac{\dfrac{32}{7}}{\dfrac{24}{7}} .$$

Dividing by $\dfrac{24}{7}$ is equivalent to multiplying by $\dfrac{7}{24}$. Therefore,

$$\frac{4 + \dfrac{4}{7}}{4 - \dfrac{4}{7}} = \frac{32}{7} \cdot \frac{7}{24}$$

Now, the 7 in the numerator cancels with the 7 in the denominator.

Thus, we obtain: $\dfrac{32}{24}$, and dividing numerator and denominator by 8,

we obtain: $\dfrac{4}{3}$.

Therefore $\dfrac{a + \dfrac{a}{b}}{a - \dfrac{a}{b}} = \dfrac{4}{3}$ when a = 4 and b = 7.

● **PROBLEM 5-5**

Perform the indicated operation:

$$\frac{3a - 9b}{x - 5} \cdot \frac{xy - 5y}{ax - 3bx}$$

Solution: According to our definition of multiplication, we need only to write the product of the numerators over the product of the denominators. The only remaining step is that of reducing the fraction to lowest terms by factoring the numerator and denominator of the answer and simplifying the result.

$$\frac{3a - 9b}{x - 5} \cdot \frac{xy - 5y}{ax - 3bx} = \frac{(3a - 9b)(xy - 5y)}{(x - 5)(ax - 3bx)}$$

Factor out 3 from (3a - 9b) and y from (xy - 5y). Also, factor out x from ax - 3bx.

$$= \frac{3(a - 3b)y(x - 5)}{(x - 5)x(a - 3b)}$$

Group the same terms in numerator and the denominator.

$$= \frac{3y}{x} \cdot \frac{a - 3b}{a - 3b} \cdot \frac{x - 5}{x - 5}$$

19

Cancel like terms.

$$= \frac{3y}{x} \cdot 1 \cdot 1$$

$$= \frac{3y}{x}$$

This procedure could have been abbreviated in the following manner:

$$\frac{3a - 9b}{x - 5} \cdot \frac{xy - 5y}{ax - 3bx} = \frac{3(a - 3b)}{x - 5} \cdot \frac{y(x - 5)}{x(a - 3b)} = \frac{3y}{x}$$

● **PROBLEM 5-6**

Simplify $\dfrac{1 + \dfrac{1}{x}}{1 - \dfrac{1}{x}}$.

Solution: In order to eliminate the fractions in the numerator and de-nominator we multiply numerator and denominator by x.

$$\frac{1 + \frac{1}{x}}{1 - \frac{1}{x}} = \frac{x\left(1 + \frac{1}{x}\right)}{x\left(1 - \frac{1}{x}\right)} = \frac{x + \frac{x}{x}}{x - \frac{x}{x}} = \frac{x + 1}{x - 1} .$$

● **PROBLEM 5-7**

Combine and simplify $1 + \dfrac{1}{1 + \dfrac{1}{1 - x}}$.

Solution: First combine the terms in the denominator. Recall $1 = (1-x)/(1-x)$.   Thus,

$$1 + \frac{1}{1 + \frac{1}{1 - x}} = 1 + \frac{1}{\frac{1 - x}{1 - x} + \frac{1}{1 - x}}$$

$$= 1 + \frac{1}{\frac{1 - x + 1}{1 - x}}$$

$$= 1 + \frac{1}{\frac{2 - x}{1 - x}}$$

Division by a fraction is equivalent to multiplica-tion by its reciprocal, thus

$$= 1 + 1 \cdot \frac{(1 - x)}{(2 - x)}$$

$$= 1 + \frac{1 - x}{2 - x}$$

Recall $1 = \frac{2 - x}{2 - x}$, therefore,

$$1 + \frac{1}{1 + \frac{1}{1 - x}} = \frac{2 - x}{2 - x} + \frac{1 - x}{2 - x}$$

$$= \frac{2 - x + 1 - x}{2 - x}$$

$$= \frac{3 - 2x}{2 - x} .$$

Simplify the complex fraction $\dfrac{\dfrac{1}{x} - \dfrac{1}{y}}{\dfrac{1}{x^2} - \dfrac{1}{y^2}}$.

Solution: Add both fractions of the numerator together

using the rule: $\frac{a}{b} + \frac{c}{d} = \frac{ad + bc}{bd}$; and obtain

$\frac{y - x}{xy}$. Similarly for the denominator, obtain:

$$\frac{y^2 - x^2}{x^2 y^2}$$

Now invert the fraction in the denominator and multiply by the numerator:

$$\frac{y - x}{xy} \cdot \frac{x^2 y^2}{y^2 - x^2} = \frac{(y - x)}{xy} \cdot \frac{(xy)(xy)}{(y - x)(y + x)}$$

$$= \frac{(y - x)(xy)(xy)}{xy(y - x)(y + x)}$$

$$= \frac{xy}{y + x} .$$

Simplify $\dfrac{\dfrac{2}{x} + \dfrac{3}{y}}{1 - \dfrac{1}{x}}$.

<u>Solution:</u> A first method is to just add the terms in the numerator and denominator, obtaining

$$\frac{\frac{2}{x} + \frac{3}{y}}{1 - \frac{1}{x}} = \frac{\frac{2y}{xy} + \frac{3x}{xy}}{\frac{x}{x} - \frac{1}{x}} = \frac{\frac{2y + 3x}{xy}}{\frac{x - 1}{x}}$$

Since dividing by fraction is equivalent to multiplying by its reciprocal,

$$= \frac{2y + 3x}{xy} \cdot \frac{x}{x - 1} = \frac{2y + 3x}{y(x - 1)}$$

A second method is to multiply both numerator and denominator by the least common denominator of the entire fraction, in this case xy:

$$\frac{\frac{2}{x} + \frac{3}{y}}{1 - \frac{1}{x}} = \frac{xy\left(\frac{2}{x} + \frac{3}{y}\right)}{xy\left(1 - \frac{1}{x}\right)}$$

Distributing,

$$= \frac{xy\left(\frac{2}{x}\right) + xy\left(\frac{3}{y}\right)}{xy(1) - xy\left(\frac{1}{x}\right)}$$

Cancelling like terms,

$$= \frac{2y + 3x}{xy - y}$$

Using distributive law,

$$= \frac{2y + 3x}{y(x - 1)} .$$

● PROBLEM 5-10

Combine $a + b - \dfrac{2ab}{a + b}$.

<u>Solution:</u> In order to combine fractions we must transform them into equivalent fractions with a common denominator. In our case we will use a + b as our least common denominator (LCD). Thus

$$a + b - \frac{2ab}{a+b} = \frac{a+b}{a+b}\left(\frac{a+b}{1}\right) - \frac{2ab}{a+b}$$

$$= \frac{(a+b)(a+b)}{a + b} - \frac{2ab}{a+b}$$

$$= \frac{a^2 + 2ab + b^2}{a + b} - \frac{2ab}{a+b}$$

$$= \frac{a^2 + 2ab + b^2 - 2ab}{a + b}$$

22

$$= \frac{a^2 + b^2}{a + b}$$

Add $\frac{2}{x - 3}$ and $\frac{5}{x + 2}$.

Solution: Change these fractions to fractions with a common denominator, then add fractions by adding numerators and placing over the common denominator. Neither of the denominators is factorable; therefore, the LCD is the product of the denominators. LCD = $(x - 3)(x + 2)$. To change $\frac{2}{x - 3}$ to an equivalent fraction with $(x - 3)(x + 2)$ as its denominator, multiply by the unit fraction $\frac{(x + 2)}{(x + 2)}$. To change $\frac{5}{x + 2}$ to an equivalent fraction with the LCD as its denominator, multiply by $\frac{x - 3}{x - 3}$. Then add the resulting fractions as follows:

$$\frac{2}{x - 3} + \frac{5}{x + 2} = \frac{2(x + 2)}{(x - 3)(x + 2)} + \frac{5(x - 3)}{(x - 3)(x + 2)}$$

$$= \frac{2(x + 2) + 5(x - 3)}{(x - 3)(x + 2)}$$

$$= \frac{2x + 4 + 5x - 15}{(x - 3)(x + 2)}$$

$$= \frac{7x - 11}{(x - 3)(x + 2)} \qquad \text{Combining Terms}$$

The numerator is not factorable, so the result can not be reduced.

Perform the indicated operations:

$$\frac{3a}{2xy} - \frac{2 - 5x}{y^3} + 6$$

Solution: The first step in adding or subtracting fractions is to convert them into equivalent fractions having like denominators. The simplest method is to find the least common denominator (LCD). The LCD is the product of the unique prime factors of all the original denominators, each factor having as its exponent the positive integer representing the largest number of times the factor appeared in an original denominator. In this example the first denominator is $2 \cdot x \cdot y$, and the second is y^3. Since the factor y appears to the third power in the second denominator, the LCD is $2xy^3$. Hence, we multiply the numerator and denominator of each term by the factor necessary to make the denominator equal to $2xy^3$.

$$\frac{3a}{2xy} - \frac{2-5x}{y^3} + \frac{6}{1} = \frac{3a(y^2)}{2xy(y^2)} - \frac{(2-5x)(2x)}{y^3 \quad (2x)} + \frac{6(2xy^3)}{1(2xy^3)}$$

$$= \frac{3ay^2}{2xy^3} - \frac{(4x-10x^2)}{2xy^3} + \frac{12xy^3}{2xy^3}$$

$$= \frac{3ay^2 - 4x + 10x^2 + 12xy^3}{2xy^3}$$

● **PROBLEM** 5-13

Simplify $\dfrac{\dfrac{x}{x+y} + \dfrac{y}{x-y}}{\dfrac{y}{x+y} - \dfrac{x}{x-y}}$.

<u>Solution:</u> To eliminate the fractions in this expression, we multiply numerator and denominator by the least common multiple (L.C.M.), the expression of lowest degree into which each of the original expressions can be divided without a remainder. The L.C.M. is the product obtained by taking each factor to the highest degree. In our case the L.C.M. is $(x + y)(x - y)$. Thus, multiplying numerator and denominator by $(x + y)(x - y)$,

$$\frac{\dfrac{x}{x+y} + \dfrac{y}{x-y}}{\dfrac{y}{x+y} - \dfrac{x}{x-y}} = \frac{\dfrac{x}{x+y} + \dfrac{y}{x-y}}{\dfrac{y}{x+y} - \dfrac{x}{x-y}} \cdot \frac{(x+y)(x-y)}{(x+y)(x-y)} .$$

Distributing, $\quad = \dfrac{\left(\dfrac{x}{x+y}\right)(x+y)(x-y) + \left(\dfrac{y}{x-y}\right)(x+y)(x-y)}{\left(\dfrac{y}{x+y}\right)(x+y)(x-y) - \left(\dfrac{x}{x-y}\right)(x+y)(x-y)}$

Cancelling like terms, $= \dfrac{x(x-y) + y(x+y)}{y(x-y) - x(x+y)}$

Distributing, $\quad = \dfrac{x^2 - xy + yx + y^2}{yx - y^2 - x^2 - xy}$

Using the commutative law, $= \dfrac{x^2 - xy + xy + y^2}{xy - y^2 - x^2 - xy}$

Combining terms, $\quad = \dfrac{x^2 + y^2}{-x^2 - y^2}$

Factoring (- 1) from the denominator $= \dfrac{x^2 + y^2}{(-1)(x^2 + y^2)}$

Cancelling $x^2 + y^2$,
$$= \frac{1}{-1}$$
$$= -1.$$

Thus,
$$\frac{\frac{x}{x+y} + \frac{y}{x-y}}{\frac{y}{x+y} - \frac{x}{x-y}} = -1.$$

A) If $x - \frac{c - ab}{a - b}$, find the value of the expression $a(x + b)$.

B) Also, if $x = \frac{c - ab}{a - b}$, find the value of the expression $bx + c$.

<u>Solution:</u> A) Substituting $x = \frac{c - ab}{a - b}$ for x in the expression $a(x + b)$,

$$a(x + b) = a\left(\frac{c - ab}{a - b} + b\right) \qquad (1)$$

Obtaining a common denominator of $a - b$ for the two terms in parenthesis; equation (1) becomes:

$$a(x + b) = a\left[\frac{c - ab}{a - b} + \frac{(a-b)b}{a - b}\right]$$

Distributing the numerator of the second term in brackets:

$$a(x + b) = a\left[\frac{c-ab}{a-b} + \frac{ab-b^2}{a-b}\right] = a\left[\frac{c-ab+ab-b^2}{a-b}\right]$$

$$= a\left[\frac{c-b^2}{a-b}\right]$$

$$a(x + b) = \frac{a\left(c-b^2\right)}{a-b}$$

B) Substituting $x = \frac{c-ab}{a-b}$ for x in the expression $bx + c$,

$$bx + c = b\left(\frac{c-ab}{a-b}\right) + c$$

$$= \frac{b(c-ab)}{a-b} + c \qquad (2)$$

Obtaining a common denominator of $a - b$ for the two terms on the right side of equation (2):

$$bx + c = \frac{b(c-ab)}{a-b} + \frac{(a-b)c}{a-b}$$

Distributing the numerator of each term on the right side:

$$bx + c = \frac{bc-ab^2}{a-b} + \frac{ac-bc}{a-b}$$

$$= \frac{bc-ab^2+ac-bc}{a - b} = \frac{-ab^2+ac}{a - b}$$

$$= \frac{ac-ab^2}{a-b}$$

Factoring out the common factor of a from the numerator of the right side:

$$bx + c = \frac{a(c-b^2)}{a-b}$$

When two resistances are installed in an electric circuit in parallel, the reciprocal of the resistance of the system is equal to the sum of the reciprocals of the parallel resistances. If r_1 and r_2 represent the resistances installed and R the resistance of the system, then

$$\frac{1}{R} = \frac{1}{r_1} + \frac{1}{r_2}$$

What single resistance is the equivalent of resistances of 10 ohms and 25 ohms wired in parallel?

Solution: Let r_1 = 10 ohms and r_2 = 25 ohms. We are looking for the single resistance R, which is equivalent to r_1 and r_2.

Here the reciprocal of R $= \frac{1}{R}$

Here the reciprocal of $r_1 = \frac{1}{r_1}$

and the reciprocal of $r_2 = \frac{1}{r_2}$

Now substitute the values for r_1 and r_2 respectively into the equation. Thus,

$$\frac{1}{R} = \frac{1}{10} + \frac{1}{25}$$

Add the fractions according to the rule

$$\frac{a}{b} + \frac{c}{d} = \frac{ad + bc}{bd}$$

$$\frac{1}{R} = \frac{25 + 10}{250} = \frac{35}{250}$$

$$R = \frac{250}{35} = \frac{50}{7} = 7.14 \text{ ohms.}$$

CHAPTER 6

BASE, EXPONENT, POWER

● PROBLEM 6-1

Simplify: (a) 3^{-2} (b) $\dfrac{1}{5^{-2}}$

<u>Solution:</u>   (a)   Since $x^{-a} = \dfrac{1}{x^a}$, $3^{-2} = \dfrac{1}{3^2} = \dfrac{1}{3 \cdot 3} = \dfrac{1}{9}$.

(b) Again, recall $\dfrac{1}{x^a} = x^{-a}$; hence,

$$\frac{1}{5^{-2}} = 5^{-(-2)} = 5^2 = 5 \cdot 5 = 25.$$

● PROBLEM 6-2

Perform the indicated operations:

$$(7 \cdot 10^5)^3 \cdot (3 \cdot 10^{-3})^4.$$

<u>Solution:</u> Since $(ab)^x = a^x b^x$,

$$(7 \cdot 10^5)^3 \cdot (3 \cdot 10^{-3})^4 = (7)^3 (10^5)^3 \cdot (3)^4 (10^{-3})^4.$$

Recall that $\left(a^x\right)^y = a^{xy}$. Thus,

$$= (7^3)(10^{5 \cdot 3}) \cdot (3^4)(10^{-3 \cdot 4})$$

$$= (7^3)(10^{15}) \cdot (3^4)(10^{-12})$$

$$= (7^3)(3^4)(10^{15})(10^{-12}).$$

27

Since $a^x \cdot a^y = a^{x+y}$,
$$= (7^3)(3^4)\left[10^{15+(-12)}\right]$$
$$= 7^3 3^4 10^3.$$

Simplify:

(a) $2^3 \cdot 2^2$ (b) $a^3 \cdot a^5$ (c) $x^6 \cdot x^4$

Solution: If a is any number and n is any positive integer, the product of the n factors a·a·a ... a is denoted by a^n. a is called the base and n is called the exponent. Also, for base a and exponents m and n, m and n being positive integers, we have the law:
$$a^m \cdot a^n = a^{m+n}.$$

Therefore,

(a) $2^3 \cdot 2^2 = (2 \cdot 2 \cdot 2)(2 \cdot 2) = 8 \cdot 4 = 32$

or $2^3 \cdot 2^2 = 2^{3+2} = 2^5 = 32$

(b) $a^3 \cdot a^5 = (a \cdot a \cdot a)(a \cdot a \cdot a \cdot a \cdot a)$

$= (a \cdot a \cdot a \cdot a \cdot a \cdot a \cdot a \cdot a) = a^8$

or $a^3 \cdot a^5 = a^{3+5} = a^8$

(c) $x^6 \cdot x^4 = x^{6+4} = x^{10}.$

Use the theorems on exponents to perform the indicated operations:

(a) $5x^5 \cdot 2x^2$ (b) $\left(x^4\right)^6$ (c) $\dfrac{8y^8}{2y^2}$ (d) $\dfrac{x^3}{x^6}\left(\dfrac{7}{x}\right)^2$.

Solution: Noting the following properties of exponents:

(1) $a^b \cdot a^c = a^{b+c}$ (2) $\left(a^b\right)^c = a^{b \cdot c}$ (3) $\dfrac{a^b}{a^c} = a^{b-c}$ (4) $\left(\dfrac{a}{b}\right)^c = \dfrac{a^c}{b^c}$

we proceed to evaluate these expressions.

(a) $5x^5 \cdot 2x^2 = 5 \cdot 2 \cdot x^5 \, x^2 = 10 \cdot x^5 \cdot x^2 = 10x^{5+2} = 10x^7$

(b) $\left(x^4\right)^6 \quad = x^{4 \cdot 6} \quad = x^{24}$

(c) $\dfrac{8y^8}{2y^2} \quad = \dfrac{8}{2} \cdot \dfrac{y^8}{y^2} \quad = 4 \cdot y^{8-2} \quad = 4y^6$

(d) $\left(\dfrac{x^3}{x^6}\right)\left(\dfrac{7}{x}\right)^2 = \left(\dfrac{x^3}{x^6}\right)\left(\dfrac{7^2}{x^2}\right) = \dfrac{x^3 \cdot 49}{x^6 \cdot x^2} = \dfrac{49x^3}{x^{6+2}} = \dfrac{49x^3}{x^8} = \dfrac{49x^3}{x^{5+3}}$

$$= \frac{49x^3}{x^5 \cdot x^3} \qquad = \frac{49}{x^5}$$

Simplify the quotient $\dfrac{2x^0}{(2x)^0}$.

Solution: The following two laws of exponents can be used to simplify the given quotient:

1) $a^0 = 1$ where a is any non-zero real number, and

2) $(ab)^n = a^n b^n$ where a and b are any two numbers.

In the given quotient, notice that the exponent in the numerator applies only to the letter x. However, the exponent in the denominator applies to both the number 2 and the letter x; that is, the exponent in the denominator applies to the entire term (2x). Using the first law, the numerator can be rewritten as:

$$2x^0 = 2(1) = 2$$

Using the second law with n = 0, the denominator can be rewritten as:

$$(2x)^0 = 2^0 x^0$$

Using the first law again to further simplify the denominator:

$$(2x)^0 = 2^0 x^0$$
$$= (1)(1)$$
$$= 1$$

Therefore,

$$\frac{2x^0}{(2x)^0} = \frac{2}{1} = 2$$

Write the expression $\left(x + y^{-1}\right)^{-1}$ without using negative exponents.

Solution: Since $x^{-a} = \dfrac{1}{x^a}$, $y^{-1} = \dfrac{1}{y^1} = \dfrac{1}{y}$,

$$\left(x + y^{-1}\right)^{-1} = \left(x + \frac{1}{y}\right)^{-1}$$

$$= \frac{1}{x + \frac{1}{y}}$$

Multiply numerator and denominator by y in order to eliminate the fraction in the denominator,

$$\frac{y(1)}{y\left(x + \frac{1}{y}\right)} = \frac{y}{yx + \frac{y}{y}} = \frac{y}{yx + 1}$$

Thus

$$\left(x + y^{-1}\right)^{-1} = \frac{y}{yx + 1}$$

● **PROBLEM 6-7**

Simplify the expression $xy\left(x^{-1} + y^{-1}\right)$.

<u>Solution:</u> The following two laws of exponents can be used to simplify the given expression:

1) $a^{-n} = \frac{1}{a^n}$ and

2) $a^m \cdot a^n = a^{m+n}$.

Using the first law,

$$xy\left(x^{-1} + y^{-1}\right) = xy\left(\frac{1}{x^1} + \frac{1}{y^1}\right)$$

$$= xy\left(\frac{1}{x} + \frac{1}{y}\right)$$

Using the distributive property, this last equation becomes:

$$= xy\left(\frac{1}{x}\right) + xy\left(\frac{1}{y}\right)$$

$$= x\left(\frac{1}{x}\right)y + xy\left(\frac{1}{y}\right)$$

$$= y + x$$

Using the second law, we can solve this problem in another way.

$$xy\left(x^{-1} + y^{-1}\right) = xyx^{-1} + xyy^{-1}$$

$$= x^{1+(-1)}y + xy^{1+(-1)}$$

$$= x^0 y + xy^0$$

$$= (1 \cdot y) + (x \cdot 1)$$

$$= y + x$$

● **PROBLEM 6-8**

Express $2c^{-2}d^{-1}/3x^{-1}y^3$ as an equal fraction involving only positive exponents.

<u>Solution</u>: Since $a^{-b} = \frac{1}{a^b}$ for all real b,

$$c^{-2} = \frac{1}{c^2}, \quad d^{-1} = \frac{1}{d}, \quad x^{-1} = \frac{1}{x}.$$

Hence $\dfrac{2c^{-2}d^{-1}}{3x^{-1}y^3} = \dfrac{2\left[\frac{1}{c^2}\right]\left[\frac{1}{d}\right]}{3\left[\frac{1}{x}\right](y^3)} = \dfrac{\frac{2}{c^2 d}}{\frac{3y^3}{x}}$. Division by a fraction is

equivalent to multiplication by its reciprocal, thus

$$\dfrac{\frac{2}{c^2 d}}{\frac{3y^3}{x}} = \left(\dfrac{2}{c^2 d}\right) \times \left(\dfrac{x}{3y^3}\right) = \dfrac{2x}{c^2 d 3y^3} = \dfrac{2x}{3y^3 c^2 d} .$$

● **PROBLEM 6-9**

Simplify the quotient $\dfrac{(x^{-2}y^4)^3}{(xy)^{-3}}$.

<u>Solution</u>: The following six laws of exponents will be used to simplify the given quotient:

(1) $\quad x^{-n} = \dfrac{1}{x^n}$, where n is any positive integer

(2) $\quad \left(\dfrac{x}{y}\right)^m = \dfrac{x^m}{y^m}$,

(3) $\quad (x^m)^n = x^{m \cdot n}$,

(4) $\quad (xy)^m = x^m y^m$,

(5) $\quad x^m \cdot x^n = x^{m+n}$,

(6) $\quad \dfrac{x^m}{x^n} = x^{m-n}$

Using the first law to simplify the quotient:

$$\dfrac{(x^{-2}y^4)^3}{(xy)^{-3}} = \dfrac{\left[\left(\frac{1}{x^2}\right)y^4\right]^3}{\frac{1}{(xy)^3}}$$

$$= \dfrac{\left(\frac{y^4}{x^2}\right)^3}{\frac{1}{(xy)^3}}$$

Using the second law to simplify the numerator,

$$\frac{(x^{-2}y^4)3}{(x-y)^{-3}} = \frac{\left(\dfrac{y^4}{x^2}\right)^3}{\dfrac{1}{(xy)^3}}$$

$$= \frac{\dfrac{(y^4)^3}{(x^2)^3}}{\dfrac{1}{(xy)^3}}$$

Using the third and fourth laws to simplify both the numerator and the denominator,

$$\frac{\left(x^{-2}y^4\right)^3}{(xy)^{-3}} = \frac{\dfrac{(y^4)^3}{(x^2)^3}}{\dfrac{1}{(xy)^3}}$$

$$= \frac{\dfrac{y^{4\cdot3}}{x^{2\cdot3}}}{\dfrac{1}{x^3y^3}}$$

$$= \frac{\dfrac{y^{12}}{x^6}}{\dfrac{1}{x^3y^3}}$$

Since multiplying the numerator by the reciprocal of the denominator is equivalent to division, the equation becomes:

$$\frac{\left(x^{-2}y^4\right)^3}{(xy)^{-3}} = \frac{y^{12}}{x^6} \ \frac{x^3y^3}{1}$$

$$= \frac{y^{12}x^3y^3}{x^6}$$

Using the fifth law to simplify the numerator:

$$\frac{\left(x^{-2}y^4\right)^3}{(xy)^{-3}} = \frac{y^{12+3}x^3}{x^6}$$

$$= \frac{y^{15}x^3}{x^6}$$

Using the sixth law to make the last simplification:

$$\frac{(x^{-2}y^4)^3}{(xy)^{-3}} = \frac{y^{15}x^3}{x^6} = y^{15}\left(\frac{x^3}{x^6}\right) = y^{15}x^{3-6} = y^{15}x^{-3}$$

Hence, $\dfrac{(x^{-2}y^4)^3}{(xy)^{-3}} = y^{15}x^{-3}$ or $\dfrac{y^{15}}{x^3}$.

● **PROBLEM 6-10**

Evaluate the following expression: $\dfrac{12x^7y}{3x^2y^3}$

Solution: Noting (1) $\dfrac{abc}{def} = \dfrac{a}{d} \cdot \dfrac{b}{e} \cdot \dfrac{c}{f}$, (2) $a^{-b} = \dfrac{1}{a^b}$ and

(3) $\dfrac{a^b}{a^c} = a^{b-c}$ for all non-zero real values of a,d,e,f, we

proceed to evaluate the expression:

$$\dfrac{12x^7y}{3x^2y^3} = \dfrac{12}{3} \cdot \dfrac{x^7}{x^2} \cdot \dfrac{y}{y^3} = 4 \cdot x^{7-2} \cdot y^{1-3} = 4x^5y^{-2} = \dfrac{4x^5}{y^2}.$$

● **PROBLEM 6-11**

Simplify the quotient $\dfrac{(x^{-2}y^4)^3}{(xy)^{-3}}$.

Solution: Since $(ab)^x = a^x b^x$, and $(a^x)^y = a^{xy}$:

$$\dfrac{(x^{-2}y^4)^3}{(xy)^{-3}} = \dfrac{(x^{-2})^3(y^4)^3}{x^{-3}y^{-3}} = \dfrac{x^{(-2)(3)}y^{4\cdot3}}{x^{-3}y^{-3}} = \dfrac{x^{-6}y^{12}}{x^{-3}y^{-3}} .$$

When dividing common bases with different exponents we subtract the exponent of the divisor from the exponent of the dividend

$$\left(\dfrac{a^x}{a^y} = a^{x-y}\right) ;$$

thus:

$$= x^{-6-(-3)}\, y^{12-(-3)}$$
$$= x^{-6+3}\, y^{12+3}$$
$$= x^{-3}\, y^{15} .$$

Find the following products.

    a. $(3x^2y)(2xy^2)$

    b. $(-xy^3)(4xyz)(2yz)$

<u>Solution:</u> Use the following law of exponents to find the indicated products:

$$a^m \cdot a^n \cdot a^x \cdot \ldots = a^{m+n+x+\ldots}$$

a) $(3x^2y)(2xy^2) = 6(x^2 \cdot x)(y \cdot y^2)$

$$= 6(x^{2+1})(y^{1+2})$$

$$= 6x^3y^3$$

b) $(-xy^3)(4xyz)(2yz) = -8(x \cdot x)(y^3 \cdot y \cdot y)(z \cdot z)$

$$= -8\left(x^{1+1}\right)\left(y^{3+1+1}\right)\left(z^{1+1}\right)$$

$$= -8(x^2)(y^5)(z^2)$$

$$= -8x^2y^5z^2$$

Perform the indicated operations, and simplify. (Write without negative or zero exponents.) Each letter represents a positive real number.

(a) $\left(7x^{-3}y^5\right)^{-2}$ (b) $\left(5x^2y^{-8}\right)^{-3}$.

<u>Solution:</u> Note that: (1) $(abc)^x = a^xb^xc^x$ (for all real a,b,c), (2) $a^{-x} = \dfrac{1}{a^x}$ (for all non-zero real a) and (3) $\left(a^b\right)^c = a^{bc}$ (for all real a,b,c). These will be useful in evaluating the given expressions.

(a) $\left(7x^{-3}y^5\right)^{-2} = 7^{-2}\left(x^{-3}\right)^{-2}\left(y^5\right)^{-2} = 7^{-2}(x)^{(-3)(-2)}(y)^{(5)(-2)}$

$$= 7^{-2}(x)^6(y)^{-10} \qquad = \frac{x^6}{(7^2)(y^{10})} = \frac{x^6}{49y^{10}}.$$

34

(b) $\left(5x^7y^{-8}\right)^{-3} = 5^{-3}\left(x^7\right)^{-3}\left(y^{-8}\right)^{-3} = 5^{-3}(x)^{(7)(-3)}(y)^{(-8)(-3)}$

$$= 5^{-3}(x)^{-21}(y)^{24} = \frac{y^{24}}{5^3x^{21}} = \frac{y^{24}}{125x^{21}}.$$

Evaluate the following expressions:

(a) $\dfrac{-12x^{10}y^9z^5}{3x^2y^3z^6}$ (b) $\dfrac{-16x^{16}y^6z^4}{-4x^4y^2z^7}.$

Solution: Noting (a) $\dfrac{abcd}{efgh} = \dfrac{a}{e}\cdot\dfrac{b}{f}\cdot\dfrac{c}{g}\cdot\dfrac{d}{h}$, (2) $a^{-b} = \dfrac{1}{a^b}$

and (3) $\dfrac{a^b}{a^c} = a^{b-c}$ for all non-zero real values of a,e,f,g,h,

we proceed to evaluate these expressions:

(a) $\dfrac{-12x^{10}y^9z^5}{3x^2y^3z^6} = \dfrac{-12}{3}\cdot\dfrac{x^{10}}{x^2}\cdot\dfrac{y^9}{y^3}\cdot\dfrac{z^5}{z^6} = -4\cdot x^{10-2}\cdot y^{9-3}\cdot z^{5-6}$

$$= -4x^8y^6z^{-1} = \dfrac{-4x^8y^6}{z^1}.$$

Thus $\dfrac{-12x^{10}y^9z^5}{3x^2y^3z^6} = \dfrac{-4x^8y^6}{z}.$

(b) $\dfrac{-16x^{16}y^6z^4}{-4x^4y^2z^7} = \dfrac{-16}{-4}\cdot\dfrac{x^{16}}{x^4}\cdot\dfrac{y^6}{y^2}\cdot\dfrac{z^4}{z^7}$

$$= 4x^{16-4}\cdot y^{6-2}\cdot z^{4-7} = 4x^{12}y^4z^{-3} = \dfrac{4x^{12}y^4}{z^3}.$$

Determine the value of $(0.0081)^{-3/4}$.

Solution: $(0.0081) = .3 \times .3 \times .3 \times .3 = (.3)^4$,

therefore, $(0.0081)^{-3/4} = (.3^4)^{-3/4}$

Recalling the property of exponents,
$$(a^x)^y = a^{x\cdot y}$$

we have,

$$\left(.3^4\right)^{-3/4} = .3^{(4)(-3/4)} = .3^{-3}.$$

Since $\quad a^{-x} = \dfrac{1}{a^x},\quad .3^{-3} = \dfrac{1}{.3^3} = \dfrac{1}{0.027} = \dfrac{\frac{1}{27}}{1000}$

Division by a fraction is equivalent to multiplication by its reciprocal, thus,

$$\dfrac{\frac{1}{27}}{1000} = \dfrac{1000}{27}.$$

Hence,

$$(0.0081)^{-3/4} = \dfrac{1000}{27}.$$

CHAPTER 7

ROOTS AND RADICALS

SIMPLIFICATION AND EVALUATION OF ROOTS

● **PROBLEM 7-1**

Evaluate $\sqrt{400}$.

Solution: $400 = 4 \times 100$

Thus, $\sqrt{400} = \sqrt{4 \times 100}$

Since $\sqrt{ab} = \sqrt{a} \ \sqrt{b}$,

$\sqrt{400} = \sqrt{4} \ \sqrt{100}$

$= 2 \cdot 10$

$= 20$

Check: If $\sqrt{400}$ is 20, then 20^2 must equal 400, which is true. Hence, 20 is the solution.

● **PROBLEM 7-2**

Evaluate $16^{-\frac{3}{4}}$.

Solution: $16^{-\frac{3}{4}} = \dfrac{1}{16^{\frac{3}{4}}}$

$= \dfrac{1}{\left(\sqrt[4]{16}\right)^3}$.

Note that $2^4 = 2 \cdot 2 \cdot 2 \cdot 2 = 16$, hence $\sqrt[4]{16} = 2$. Thus, $16^{-\frac{3}{4}}$

$$= \frac{1}{2^3} = \frac{1}{2 \cdot 2 \cdot 2} = \frac{1}{8} \, .$$

● **PROBLEM 7-3**

Find the indicated roots.

(a) $\sqrt[5]{32}$ (b) $\pm \sqrt[4]{625}$ (c) $\sqrt[3]{-125}$ (d) $\sqrt[4]{-16}$.

Solution: The following two laws of exponents can be used to solve these problems: 1) $\left(\sqrt[n]{a}\right)^n = \left(a^{1/n}\right)^n = a^1 = a$, and 2) $\left(\sqrt[n]{a}\right)^n = \sqrt[n]{a^n}$.

(a) $\sqrt[5]{32} = \sqrt[5]{2^5} = \left(\sqrt[5]{2}\right)^5 = 2$. This result is because $(2)^5 = 32$, that is, $2 \cdot 2 \cdot 2 \cdot 2 \cdot 2 = 32$.

(b) $\sqrt[4]{625} = \sqrt[4]{5^4} = \left(\sqrt[4]{5}\right)^4 = 5$. This result is true because $\left(5^4\right) = 625$, that is, $5 \cdot 5 \cdot 5 \cdot 5 = 625$.

$-\sqrt[4]{625} = -\left(\sqrt[4]{5^4}\right) = -\left[\left(\sqrt[4]{5}\right)^4\right] = -\left[5\right] = -5$. This result is true because $(-5)^4 = 625$, that is, $(-5) \cdot (-5) \cdot (-5) \cdot (-5) = 625$.

(c) $\sqrt[3]{-125} = \sqrt[3]{(-5)^3} = (\sqrt[3]{-5})^3 = -5$. This result is true because $(-5)^3 = -125$, that is, $(-5) \cdot (-5) \cdot (-5) = -125$.

(d) There is no solution to $\sqrt[4]{-16}$ because any number raised to the fourth power is a positive number, that is, $N^4 = (N) \cdot (N) \cdot (N) \cdot (N) =$ a positive number $\neq$ a negative number, -16.

● **PROBLEM 7-4**

Find the numerical value of each of the following.
(a) $8^{2/3}$ (b) $25^{3/2}$

Solution:

(a) Since $x^{a/b} = \left(x^{1/b}\right)^a$, $8^{2/3} = \left(8^{1/3}\right)^2 = \left(\sqrt[3]{8}\right)^2 = (2)^2 = 4$

(b) Similarly, $25^{3/2} = \left(25^{1/2}\right)^3 = 5^3 = 125$.

38

Simplify $\sqrt{12} - \sqrt{27}$.

Solution: Here we have two different radicals, yet when each is simplified, the distributive law gives a simpler form for the expression. Note that 12 and 27 both have a factor 3, hence

$$\sqrt{12} - \sqrt{27} = \sqrt{4 \cdot 3} - \sqrt{9 \cdot 3}$$

Because $\sqrt{ab} = \sqrt{a} \cdot \sqrt{b}$, $= \sqrt{4} \cdot \sqrt{3} - \sqrt{9} \cdot \sqrt{3}$

$$= 2\sqrt{3} - 3\sqrt{3}$$

Now, we use the distributive law, $= (2 - 3)\sqrt{3}$

$$= (-1)\sqrt{3}$$

$$= -\sqrt{3}$$

Simplify $5\sqrt{12} + 3\sqrt{75}$.

Solution: Express 12 and 75 as the product of perfect squares if possible. Thus, $12 = 4 \cdot 3$ and $75 = 25 \cdot 3$; and $5\sqrt{12} + 3\sqrt{75} = 5\sqrt{4 \cdot 3} + 3\sqrt{25 \cdot 3}$.

Since $\sqrt{a \cdot b} = \sqrt{a} \cdot \sqrt{b}$: $= [5 \cdot \sqrt{4} \cdot \sqrt{3}] + [3\sqrt{25} \cdot \sqrt{3}]$

$$= [(5 \cdot 2)\sqrt{3}] + [(3 \cdot 5)\sqrt{3}]$$

$$= 10\sqrt{3} + 15\sqrt{3}.$$

Using the distributive law:

$$= (10 + 15)\sqrt{3}$$

$$= 25\sqrt{3}.$$

Simplify the quotient $\sqrt{x}/\sqrt[4]{x}$. Write the result in exponential notation.

Solution: Since $\sqrt[b]{n^a} = n^{a/b}$, the numerator and the denominator can be rewritten as:

$$\sqrt{x} = x^{1/2} \quad \text{and}$$

$$\sqrt[4]{x} = x^{1/4}$$

Therefore,

$$\frac{\sqrt{x}}{\sqrt[4]{x}} = \frac{x^{1/2}}{x^{1/4}} \qquad\qquad (1)$$

According to the law of exponents which states that $\frac{n^a}{n^b} = n^{a-b}$, equation (1) becomes:

$$\frac{\sqrt{x}}{\sqrt[4]{x}} = \frac{x^{1/2}}{x^{1/4}}$$

$$= x^{\frac{1}{2}-\frac{1}{4}}$$

$$= x^{\frac{2}{4}-\frac{1}{4}}$$

$$= x^{\frac{1}{4}}$$

● **PROBLEM 7-8**

Simplify: (a) $\sqrt{8x^3y}$ (b) $\sqrt{\dfrac{2a}{4b^2}}$ (c) $\sqrt[4]{25x^2}$.

Solution: (a) $\sqrt{8x^3y}$ contains the perfect square $4x^2$. Factoring out $4x^2$ we obtain,

$$\sqrt{8x^3y} = \sqrt{4x^2 \cdot 2xy} \quad .$$

Recall that $\sqrt{ab} = \sqrt{a} \cdot \sqrt{b}$. Thus,

$$= \sqrt{4x^2} \cdot \sqrt{2xy}$$

$$= \sqrt{4}\sqrt{x^2}\sqrt{2xy} \quad .$$

Since $\sqrt{x^2} = |x|$,

$$\sqrt{8x^3y} = 2|x|\sqrt{2xy} \quad .$$

(b) $\sqrt{\dfrac{2a}{4b^2}}$ has a fraction for the radicand, but the denominator is a perfect square.

$$\sqrt{\frac{2a}{4b^2}} = \frac{\sqrt{2a}}{\sqrt{4b^2}} \quad , \text{ since } \sqrt{\frac{a}{b}} = \frac{\sqrt{a}}{\sqrt{b}} \; ; \; \frac{\sqrt{2a}}{\sqrt{4}\sqrt{b^2}} = \frac{\sqrt{2a}}{2|b|} \quad .$$

(c) $\sqrt[4]{25x^2}$ has a perfect square for the radicand.

$$\sqrt[4]{25x^2} = \sqrt[4]{(5x)^2} \quad .$$

Recall that $\sqrt[4]{x} = \sqrt[2]{\sqrt[2]{x}}$; hence $\sqrt[4]{(5x)^2} = \sqrt[2]{\sqrt[2]{(5x)^2}}$. Now, since

$$\sqrt[2]{(5x)^2} = |5x| , \qquad\qquad = \sqrt[2]{|5x|} . \text{ Since}$$

$$|ab| = |a||b| , = \sqrt[2]{|5||x|} = \sqrt[2]{5|x|} = \sqrt{5|x|} .$$

Radicals with the same index can be multiplied by finding the product of the radicands, the index of the product being the same as the factors.

RATIONALIZING THE DENOMINATOR

● **PROBLEM** 7-9

Write in fractional exponent form with no denominators.

(a) $\sqrt[3]{\dfrac{x}{y}}$ (b) $\sqrt[3]{3}$ (c) $\sqrt[4]{x^2}\ \sqrt[3]{xy^{-1}}$

<u>Solution:</u> Noting that $\sqrt[b]{a} = a^{1/b}$, $\left(\dfrac{a}{b}\right)^c = \dfrac{a^c}{b^c}$,

and $a^{-b} = \dfrac{1}{a^b}$, we proceed to evaluate these expressions.

(a) $\sqrt[3]{\dfrac{x}{y}} = \left(\dfrac{x}{y}\right)^{1/3} = \dfrac{x^{1/3}}{y^{1/3}} = x^{\frac{1}{3}} y^{-\frac{1}{3}}$

(b) $\sqrt[3]{3} = 3^{\frac{1}{3}}$

(c) $\sqrt[4]{x^2}\ \sqrt[3]{xy^{-1}} = (x^2)^{\frac{1}{4}} (xy^{-1})^{\frac{1}{3}}$

$= (x^{\frac{2}{4}})(x^{\frac{1}{3}})(y^{-\frac{1}{3}})$, since $(a^b)^c = a^{bc}$

and $(ab^c)^d = a^d b^{cd}$

$= (x^{\frac{1}{2}})(x^{\frac{1}{3}})(y^{-\frac{1}{3}})$

$= x^{\frac{1}{2}+\frac{1}{3}} y^{-\frac{1}{3}}$, since $(x^a)(x^b) = x^{a+b}$

$= x^{\frac{3}{6}+\frac{2}{6}} y^{-\frac{1}{3}}$

$= x^{\frac{5}{6}} y^{-\frac{1}{3}}$

● **PROBLEM** 7-10

Rationalize the denominator in the quotient $1\Big/\sqrt[5]{x^2}$.

<u>Solution:</u> $\sqrt[y]{a^x} = a^{\frac{x}{y}}$, thus $\dfrac{1}{\sqrt[5]{x^2}} = \dfrac{1}{x^{\frac{2}{5}}}$. Rationalizing a

denominator means eliminating the radical from the denominator, thus we want to eliminate the fractional exponent.
When multiplying numbers with the same base, exponents are
added, hence multiplying numerator and denominator by

$x^{\frac{3}{5}}$ will eliminate the fractional exponent in the denominator:

$$\frac{1}{\sqrt{x^2}} = \frac{1}{x^{\frac{2}{5}}} = \frac{1}{x^{\frac{2}{5}}} \frac{x^{\frac{3}{5}}}{x^{\frac{3}{5}}} = \frac{x^{\frac{3}{5}}}{x^{\frac{2}{5}+\frac{3}{5}}} = \frac{x^{\frac{3}{5}}}{x^1} = \frac{\sqrt[5]{x^3}}{x}.$$

● **PROBLEM 7-11**

Rationalize the denominator in the quotient:

$$\frac{1}{\sqrt{x} - \sqrt{y}}.$$

<u>Solution:</u> To rationalize a denominator we multiply numerator and de-
nominator by the complex conjugate of the denominator (recall $a + bi$
and $a - bi$ are complex conjugates). In our example the conjugate of
$\sqrt{x} - \sqrt{y}$ is $\sqrt{x} + \sqrt{y}$. Hence, multiplying numerator and denominator by
$\sqrt{x} + \sqrt{y}$:

$$\frac{1}{\sqrt{x} - \sqrt{y}} \cdot \frac{\sqrt{x} + \sqrt{y}}{\sqrt{x} + \sqrt{y}} = \frac{\sqrt{x} + \sqrt{y}}{\sqrt{x}\cdot\sqrt{x} + \sqrt{x}\sqrt{y} - \sqrt{x}\sqrt{y} - \sqrt{y}\sqrt{y}}.$$

Recall that $\sqrt{a}\cdot\sqrt{a} = \sqrt{a^2} = a$, thus $\sqrt{x}\sqrt{x} = x$ and $\sqrt{y}\sqrt{y} = y$; and we
obtain:

$$= \frac{\sqrt{x} + \sqrt{y}}{x - y}.$$

● **PROBLEM 7-12**

Rationalize $\dfrac{\sqrt{3xy}}{\sqrt{2x} - \sqrt{3y}}$.

<u>Solution:</u> To rationalize a fraction, we multiply
numerator and denominator by the conjugate of the denominator (where the conjugate of a + b is a - b). In
our example, we multiply numerator and denominator by
the conjugate of $\sqrt{2x} - \sqrt{3y}$, which is $\sqrt{2x} + \sqrt{3y}$. Thus,

$$\frac{\sqrt{3xy}}{\sqrt{2x} - \sqrt{3y}} = \frac{\sqrt{3xy}}{\sqrt{2x} - \sqrt{3y}} \cdot \frac{\sqrt{2x} + \sqrt{3y}}{\sqrt{2x} + \sqrt{3y}}$$

$$= \frac{\sqrt{3xy}\ (\sqrt{2x} + \sqrt{3y})}{(\sqrt{2x})^2 - (\sqrt{3y})^2}\ .$$

Since $(\sqrt{a})^2 = \sqrt{a} \cdot \sqrt{a} = \sqrt{a^2} = a$,

$$(\sqrt{2x})^2 = 2x$$

$$(\sqrt{3y})^2 = 3y.$$

Making these substitutions,

$$\frac{\sqrt{3xy}\ (\sqrt{2x} + \sqrt{3y})}{(\sqrt{2x})^2 - (\sqrt{3y})^2} = \frac{\sqrt{3xy}\ (\sqrt{2x} + \sqrt{3y})}{2x - 3y}$$

$$= \frac{\sqrt{3xy} \cdot \sqrt{2x} + \sqrt{3xy} \cdot \sqrt{3y}}{2x - 3y}$$

Since $\sqrt{a}\ \sqrt{b} = \sqrt{ab}$ and $\sqrt{a}\ \sqrt{b}\ \sqrt{c} = \sqrt{abc}$,

$$\frac{\sqrt{3xy} \cdot \sqrt{2x} + \sqrt{3xy} \cdot \sqrt{3y}}{2x - 3y} = \frac{\sqrt{6x^2y} + \sqrt{9xy^2}}{2x - 3y}$$

$$= \frac{\sqrt{x^2}\ \sqrt{6y} + \sqrt{9}\ \sqrt{y^2}\ \sqrt{x}}{2x - 3y}$$

$$= \frac{x\ \sqrt{6y} + 3y\ \sqrt{x}}{2x - 3y}\ .$$

OPERATIONS WITH RADICALS

● PROBLEM 7-13

Simplify $(\sqrt{3} + \sqrt{2}) \cdot (\sqrt{2} - \sqrt{6})$.

Solution: Using the distributive property the expression on the right can be multiplied by each term in the expression on the left or vice versa. Hence,

$$(\sqrt{3} + \sqrt{2})(\sqrt{2} - \sqrt{6}) = \sqrt{3}(\sqrt{2} - \sqrt{6}) + \sqrt{2}(\sqrt{2} - \sqrt{6})$$

The distributive property again enables us to multiply the terms on the left by their respective right hand members;

$$= (\sqrt{3} \cdot \sqrt{2}) - (\sqrt{3} \cdot \sqrt{6}) + (\sqrt{2} \cdot \sqrt{2})$$

$$- (\sqrt{2} \cdot \sqrt{6})$$

Then since,

$$\sqrt{a} \cdot \sqrt{b} = \sqrt{ab},$$

$$(\sqrt{3} + 2)(\sqrt{2} - \sqrt{6}) = (\sqrt{6}) - (\sqrt{18}) + (2) - (\sqrt{12})$$

43

$$= \sqrt{6} - 3\sqrt{2} + 2 - 2\sqrt{3}.$$

● **PROBLEM** 7-14

Multiply $(2\sqrt{3} + 3\sqrt{2})$ by $(3\sqrt{3} - 2\sqrt{2})$.

Solution: Using the following method (foil method) of polynomial multiplication:

$$(x + y)(a + b) = xa + xb + ya + yb,$$

we obtain

$$(2\sqrt{3} + 3\sqrt{2})(3\sqrt{3} - 2\sqrt{2}) = (2\sqrt{3})(3\sqrt{3}) + (2\sqrt{3})(-2\sqrt{2}) + (3\sqrt{2})(3\sqrt{3})$$
$$+ (3\sqrt{2})(-2\sqrt{2})$$
$$= (6)(\sqrt{3})^2 - 4(\sqrt{3}\sqrt{2}) + (9)(\sqrt{3}\sqrt{2}) - 6(\sqrt{2})^2 .$$

Since
$$(\sqrt{a})^2 = (a^{\frac{1}{2}})^2 = a^{2/2} = a^1 = a$$
$$(\sqrt{3})^2 = 3 \text{ and } (\sqrt{2})^2 = 2$$

Making these substitutions we obtain,

$$(2\sqrt{3} + 3\sqrt{2})(3\sqrt{3} - 2\sqrt{2}) = (6)(3) + 5(\sqrt{3})(\sqrt{2}) - 6(2)$$
$$= 18 + 5(\sqrt{3})(\sqrt{2}) - 12$$
$$= 6 + 5\sqrt{3}\sqrt{2}$$

Since $\sqrt{a} \cdot \sqrt{b} = \sqrt{ab}$
$$\sqrt{3} \cdot \sqrt{2} = \sqrt{3 \cdot 2} = \sqrt{6}$$

Therefore $(2\sqrt{3} + 3\sqrt{2})(3\sqrt{3} - 2\sqrt{2}) = 6 + 5\sqrt{6}$

● **PROBLEM** 7-15

Find the product by inspection: $\sqrt{3}(x - \sqrt{5})(x + \sqrt{5})$.

Solution: The formula for the difference of two squares can be used to obtain the product. This formula is: $(x^2 - y^2) = (x + y)(x - y)$. The product $(x - \sqrt{5})(x + \sqrt{5})$ corresponds to the right side of the formula where x is replaced by x and y is replaced by $\sqrt{5}$. Therefore,

$$3(x - \sqrt{5})(x + \sqrt{5}) = 3\left(x^2 - (\sqrt{5})^2\right)$$

Since $(\sqrt{a})^2 = \sqrt{a} \ \sqrt{a} = \sqrt{a^2} = a$, $(\sqrt{5})^2 = 5$. Thus

$$\sqrt{3}(x - \sqrt{5})(x + \sqrt{5}) = \sqrt{3}(x^2 - 5).$$

Distributing $\sqrt{3}$,

$$= \sqrt{3} \ x^2 - \sqrt{3}(5)$$

44

$$= \sqrt{3} \, x^2 - 5\sqrt{3}.$$

Thus $\sqrt{3}\,(x - \sqrt{5})\,(x + \sqrt{5}) = \sqrt{3} \, x^2 - 5\sqrt{3}.$

● PROBLEM 7-16

Find the following products:

    a. $\sqrt{x}\,(\sqrt{2x} - \sqrt{x})$

    b. $(\sqrt{x} - 2\,\sqrt{y})\,(2\sqrt{x} + \sqrt{y})$

Solution: The following two laws concerning radicals can be used to find the indicated products:

    1) $\sqrt{a}\,\sqrt{b} = \sqrt{ab}$

where a and b are any two numbers

    2) $\sqrt{a^2} = (\sqrt{a})^2 \left(a^{1/2}\right)^2 = a^{(1/2)\,2} = a^1 = a$

    or $\sqrt{a^2} = a$

a) Using the distributive property,

    $\sqrt{x}\,(\sqrt{2x} - \sqrt{x}) = \sqrt{x}\,(\sqrt{2x}) - \sqrt{x}\,(\sqrt{x})$

Using the first law concerning radicals to further simplify this equation,

    $\sqrt{x}\,(\sqrt{2x} - \sqrt{x}) = \sqrt{x \cdot 2x} - \sqrt{x \cdot x}$

$$= \sqrt{2x^2} - \sqrt{x^2}$$

$$= \sqrt{2}\,\sqrt{x^2} - \sqrt{x^2}$$

Using, the second law to simplify this equation,

    $\sqrt{x}\,(\sqrt{2x} - \sqrt{x}) = \sqrt{2}\,(x) - x$

$$= \sqrt{2}x - x$$

b) $(\sqrt{x} - 2\,\sqrt{y})\,(2\sqrt{x} + \sqrt{y}) = \sqrt{x}\,(2\sqrt{x}) - 2\sqrt{y}\left(2\sqrt{x}\right) + \sqrt{x}\,(\sqrt{y})$

    $- 2\sqrt{y}\,(\sqrt{y})$

Using the first law concerning radicals to simplify this equation,

$$(\sqrt{x} - 2\sqrt{y})(2\sqrt{x} + \sqrt{y}) = 2\sqrt{x \cdot x} - 4\sqrt{x \cdot y} + \sqrt{x \cdot y} - 2\sqrt{y \cdot y}$$

$$= 2\sqrt{x^2} - 4\sqrt{xy} + \sqrt{xy} - 2\sqrt{y^2}$$

$$= 2\sqrt{x^2} - 3\sqrt{xy} - 2\sqrt{y^2}$$

Using the second law to simplify this equation,

$$(\sqrt{x} - 2\sqrt{y})(2\sqrt{x} + \sqrt{y}) = 2(x) - 3\sqrt{xy} - 2(y)$$

$$= 2x - 3\sqrt{xy} - 2y$$

● **PROBLEM** 7-17

Find the value of $y^2 - 3y + 1$, for $y = 3 - \sqrt{2}$.

Solution: Substituting $3 - \sqrt{2}$ for y in the expression

$y^2 - 3y + 1$,

$$y^2 - 3y + 1 = (3 - \sqrt{2})^2 - 3(3 - \sqrt{2}) + 1$$

$$= (3 - \sqrt{2})(3 - \sqrt{2}) - 3(3 - \sqrt{2}) + 1$$

$$= (9 - 6\sqrt{2} + 2) - 3(3 - \sqrt{2}) + 1$$

$$= (11 - 6\sqrt{2}) - 9 + 3\sqrt{2} + 1$$

$$= 11 - 6\sqrt{2} - 9 + 3\sqrt{2} + 1$$

$$= 11 - 9 + 1 - 6\sqrt{2} + 3\sqrt{2}$$

$$= 3 - 3\sqrt{2}$$

● **PROBLEM** 7-18

Find the product by inspection:

$$\left(\sqrt[3]{2}a + \sqrt[3]{4}b\right)\left(\sqrt[3]{4}a^2 - 2ab + 2\sqrt[3]{2}b^2\right)$$

Solution: The formula for the sum of two cubes can be used to find the product. This formula is:

46

$$x^3 + y^3 = (x + y)(x^2 - xy + y^2).$$

The product $(\sqrt[3]{2}a + \sqrt[3]{4}b)(\sqrt[3]{4}a^2 - 2ab + 2\sqrt[3]{2}b^2)$ corresponds to the right side of the formula for the sum of two cubes where x is replaced by $\sqrt[3]{2}a$ and y is replaced by $\sqrt[3]{4}b$. Hence,

$$(\sqrt[3]{2}a + \sqrt[3]{4}b)(\sqrt[3]{4}a^2 - 2ab + 2\sqrt[3]{2}b^2) = (\sqrt[3]{2}a)^3 + (\sqrt[3]{4}b)^3$$

$$= (\sqrt[3]{2})^3 a^3 + (\sqrt[3]{4})^3 b^3$$

since $(ab)^x = a^x b^x$. Also,

$$(\sqrt[n]{x})^n = \left(x^{\frac{1}{n}}\right)^n = x^{\frac{n}{n}} = x^1 = x, \text{ hence}$$

$$(\sqrt[3]{2})^3 = 2 \text{ and } (\sqrt[3]{4})^3 = 4.$$

Therefore $(\sqrt[3]{2}a + \sqrt[3]{4}b)(\sqrt[3]{4}a^2 - 2ab + 2\sqrt[3]{2}b^2) = 2a^3 + 4b^3.$

● **PROBLEM** 7-19

Find the value of $3x^2 - 4x - 2$, for

$$x = \frac{2 - \sqrt{10}}{3}$$

Solution: Substituting $\frac{2 - \sqrt{10}}{3}$ for x in the expression

$3x^2 - 4x - 2$

$$3x^2 - 4x - 2 = 3 \left(\frac{2 - \sqrt{10}}{3}\right)^2 - 4 \left(\frac{2 - \sqrt{10}}{3}\right) - 2$$

$$= \frac{3(2 - \sqrt{10})^2}{(3)^2} - 4 \left(\frac{2 - \sqrt{10}}{3}\right) - 2$$

$$= \frac{3(2 - \sqrt{10})(2 - \sqrt{10})}{9} - 4 \left(\frac{2 - \sqrt{10}}{3}\right) - 2$$

$$= \frac{3(4 - 4\sqrt{10} + 10)}{9} - 4 \left(\frac{2 - \sqrt{10}}{3}\right) - 2$$

$$= \frac{\overset{1}{\cancel{3}}\, 14 - 4\sqrt{10}}{\underset{3}{\cancel{9}}} - 4 \left(\frac{2 - \sqrt{10}}{3}\right) - 2$$

$$= \frac{14 - 4\sqrt{10}}{3} - \frac{(8 - 4\sqrt{10})}{3} - 2$$

47

$$= \frac{14 - 4\sqrt{10}}{3} - \frac{(8 - 4\sqrt{10})}{3} - \frac{6}{3}$$

$$= \frac{14 - 4\sqrt{10} - 8 + 4\sqrt{10} - 6}{3}$$

$$= \frac{14 - 8 - 6 - 4\sqrt{10} + 4\sqrt{10}}{3}$$

$$= \frac{6 - 6}{3}$$

$$= \frac{0}{3}$$

$$= 0$$

CHAPTER 8

ALGEBRAIC ADDITION, SUBTRACTION, MULTIPLICATION, DIVISION

● **PROBLEM 8-1**

Find the value of the polynomial $3x^2y - 2xy^2 + 5xy$ when $x = 1$ and $y = -2$.

Solution: Replace x by 1 and y by - 2 in the given polynomial to obtain,

$$3x^2y - 2xy^2 + 5xy = \left[3(1)^2 - (-2)\right] - \left[2(1)(-2)^2\right]$$
$$+ \left[5(1)(-2)\right]$$
$$= \left[(3)(-2)\right] - \left[(2)(4)\right]$$
$$+ \left[(5)(-2)\right]$$
$$= -6 - 8 - 10$$
$$= -24.$$

Thus, when $x = 1$ and $y = -2$, the polynomial

$$3x^2y - 2xy^2 + 5xy = -24.$$

● **PROBLEM 8-2**

Add $(3xy^2 + 2xy + 5x^2y) + (2xy^2 - 4xy + 2x^2y)$.

Solution: Use the vertical form, align all like terms, and apply the distributive property.

49

$$3xy^2 + 2xy + 5x^2y$$
$$2xy^2 - 4xy + 2x^2y$$
$$(3 + 2)xy^2 + (2 - 4)xy + (5 + 2)x^2y$$

Thus, the sum is $5xy^2 - 2xy + 7x^2y$.

● **PROBLEM 8-3**

Subtract $4y^2 - 5y + 2$ from $7y^2 - 6$.

Solution: The problem is the following:

$$(7y^2-6) - (4y^2-5y + 2)$$

Whenever a minus sign (-) appears before an expression in parentheses, change the sign of every term in the parentheses.

In this problem, since a minus sign appears before the expression $(4y^2- 5y + 2)$, the sign of every term in this expression is changed.

$$(4y^2- 5y + 2) \text{ becomes } -4y^2 + 5y - 2.$$

After the signs have been changed, the new expression $-4y^2 + 5y - 2$ can be added to the expression $7y^2 - 6$ (changing the signs of the expression changes the original problem to an addition problem). Therefore

$$(7y^2- 6) - (4y^2- 5y + 2) = 7y^2 - 6 - 4y^2 + 5y - 2.$$

Place the terms with similar powers together. Therefore:

$$(7y^2- 6) - (4y^2- 5y + 2) \qquad 7y^2 - 6 - 4y^2 + 5y - 2$$

$$= 7y^2 - 4y^2 + 5y - 6 - 2. \qquad (1)$$

Since $7y^2 - 4y^2 = 3y^2$ and $-6- 2 = -8$, equation (1) becomes:

$$(7y^2 - 6) - (4y^2 - 5y + 2) = 3y^2 + 5y - 8,$$

which is the final answer.

● **PROBLEM 8-4**

Simplify $3ax(ax^2- 5bx + c)$.

Solution: Using the distributive property,

$$3ax(ax^2- 5bx + c) = 3ax(ax^2) + 3ax(-5bx) + 3ax(c)$$
$$=3a^2x^3 - 15abx^2 + 3acx.$$

Expand $(x + 5)(x - 4)$.

<u>Solution:</u> Distributing the second term:

$$(x + 5)(x - 4) = (x + 5)x + (x + 5)(-4) \qquad (1)$$

Distributing twice on the right side of equation (1):

$$\begin{aligned}(x + 5)(x - 4) &= (x + 5)x + (x + 5)(-4) \\ &= (x^2 + 5x) + (-4x - 20) \\ &= x^2 + 5x - 4x - 20 \\ &= x^2 + x - 20.\end{aligned}$$

Multiply $(4x - 5)(6x - 7)$.

<u>Solution:</u> We can apply the FOIL method. The letters indicate the order in which the terms are to be multiplied.

    F = first terms
    O = outer terms
    I = inner terms
    L = last terms

Thus,

$$(4x - 5)(6x - 7) = (4x)(6x) + (4x)(-7) + (-5)(6x) + (-5)(-7)$$
$$= 24x^2 - 28x - 30x + 35 = 24x^2 - 58x + 35.$$

Another way to multiply algebraic expressions is to apply the distributive law of multiplication with respect to addition. If a,b, and c are real numbers, then $a(b+c) = ab + ac$. In this case let $a = (4x-5)$ and $b + c = 6x - 7$.

$$(4x - 5)(6x - 7) = (4x - 5)(6x) + (4x - 5)(-7)$$

Then, apply the law again.

$$(4x - 5)(6x - 7) = (4x)(6x) - (5)(6x) + (4x)(-7) + (-5)(-7)$$
$$(4x - 5)(6x - 7) = 24x^2 - 30x - 28x + 35$$

Add like terms.

$$(4x - 5)(6x - 7) = 24x^2 - 58x + 35.$$

Show that $(3x - 2)(x + 5) + 15 = 3x^2 + 13x + 5$ is an identity.

<u>Solution:</u> An equation in x is an identity if it holds for all real values of x. Thus, the given equation is an identity since for each $x \in R$,

$$(3x - 2)(x + 5) + 15 = 3x^2 + 13x - 10 + 15$$

$$= 3x^2 + 13x + 5$$

● PROBLEM 8-8

Expand $(a + b - 2)^2$.

Solution: When we enclose $a + b$ in parentheses we may write
$$(a + b - 2)^2 = [(a + b) - 2]^2$$
$$= [(a + b) - 2][(a + b) - 2]$$

Employing our method of polynomial multiplication
$$(x + y)(u + v) = xu + xv + yu + yv$$
Substituting $(a + b)$ for x and u, and (-2) for y and v we obtain
$$[(a + b) - 2]^2 = (a + b)^2 - 4(a + b) + 4$$
Once again employ our method of polynomial multiplication on
$$(a + b)^2 = (a + b)(a + b).$$
Thus
$$(a + b - 2)^2 = a^2 + 2ab + b^2 - 4a - 4b + 4$$

● PROBLEM 8-9

Simplify $(x - y)(x^2 + xy + y^2)$.

Solution: By distributing,
$$\left(x - y\right)\left(x^2 + xy + y^2\right) = x\left(x^2 + xy + y^2\right) - y\left(x^2 + xy + y^2\right) \qquad (1)$$
Now, distribute the right side of equation (1):
$$\left(x - y\right)\left(x^2 + xy + y^2\right) = \left(x^3 + x^2y + xy^2\right) - \left(x^2y + xy^2 + y^3\right)$$
Combining terms:
$$\left(x - y\right)\left(x^2 + xy + y^2\right) = x^3 + \cancel{x^2y} + \cancel{xy^2} - \cancel{x^2y} - \cancel{xy^2} - y^3$$
$$= x^3 - y^3 .$$

● PROBLEM 8-10

Multiply $3x^2 - 5y^2 - 4xy$ by $2x - 7y$.

Solution: Write one algebraic expression under the other, and multiply the first expression by each term of the second expression, placing similar product terms in the same vertical column.

$3x^2 - 5y^2 - 4xy$

$\underline{2x \quad - 7y}$

$6x^3 - 10xy^2 - 8x^2y$ multiplying $3x^2 - 5y^2 - 4xy$ by $2x$

$\quad\quad 28xy^2 - 21x^2y + 35y^3$ multiplying $3x^2 - 5y^2 - 4xy$ by $-7y$

$\overline{6x^3 + 18xy^2 - 29x^2y + 35y^3}$ adding the partial products

Divide $(37 + 8x^3 - 4x)$ by $(2x + 3)$.

Solution: Arrange both polynomials in descending powers of the variable. The first polynomial becomes: $8x^3 - 4x + 37$. The second polynomial stays the same: $2x + 3$. The problem is: $2x + 3\sqrt{8x^3 - 4x + 37}$. In the dividend, $8x^3 - 4x + 37$, all powers of x must be included. The only missing power of x is x^2. To include this power of x, a coefficient of 0 is used; that is, $0x^2$. This term, $0x^2$, can be added to the dividendwithout changing the dividend because $0x^2 = 0$ (anything multiplied by 0 is 0).

Now to accomplish the division we proceed as follows: divide the first term of the divisor into the first term of the dividend. Multiply the quotient from this division by each term of the divisor and subtract the products of each term from the dividend. We then obtain a new dividend. Use this dividend, and again divide by the first term of the divisor, and repeat all steps again until we obtain a remainder which is of degree lower than that of the divisor or zero. Following this procedure we obtain :

$$
\begin{array}{r}
4x^2 - 6x + 7 \\
2x + 3\overline{)8x^3 + 0x^2 - 4x + 37} \\
\underline{8x^3 + 12x^2} \\
-12x^2 - 4x + 37 \\
\underline{-12x^2 - 18x} \\
14x + 37 \\
\underline{14x + 21} \\
16
\end{array}
$$

The degree of a polynomial is the highest power of the variable in the polynomial.

The degree of the divisor is 1. The number 16 can be written as $16x^0$ where $x^0 = 1$. Therefore, the number 16 has degree 0. When the degree of the divisor is greater than the degree of the dividend, we stop dividing.

Since the degree of the divisor in this problem is 1 and the degree of the dividend (16) is 0, the degree of the divisor is greater than the degree of the dividend. Therefore, dividing is stopped and the remainder is 16. Therefore, the quotient is $4x^2 - 6x + 7$ and the remainder is 16.

In order to verify this, multiply the quotient, $4x^2 - 6x + 7$, by the divisor, $2x + 3$, and then add 16. These two operations should total up to the dividend $8x^3 - 4x + 37$. Thus,

$$(4x^2 - 6x + 7)(2x + 3) + 16 =$$

$$8x^3 - 12x^2 + 14x + 12x^2 - 18x + 21 + 16 =$$
$$8x^3 - 4x + 37,$$

which is the desired result.

Find the quotient and remainder when $3x^7 - x^6 + 31x^4 + 21x + 5$ is divided by $x + 2$.

Solution: To divide a polynomial by another polynomial we set up the divisor and the dividend as shown below. Then we divide the first term of the divisor into the first term of the dividend. We multiply the quotient from this division by each term of the divisor, and subtract the products of each term from the dividend. We then obtain a new dividend. Use this dividend, and again divide by the first term of the divisor, and repeat all steps again until we obtain a remainder which is of degree lower than that of the divisor, or which is zero. Following this procedure we obtain:

$$
\begin{array}{r}
3x^6-7x^5+14x^4+3x^3-6x^2+12x-3 \\
x+2 \enclose{longdiv}{3x^7-x^6\quad+31x^4\qquad+21x+5} \\
\underline{3x^7+6x^6}\qquad\qquad\qquad\qquad\qquad \\
-7x^6\quad+31x^4\qquad+21x+5 \\
\underline{-7x^6-14x^5}\qquad\qquad\qquad\qquad \\
14x^5+31x^4\qquad+21x+5 \\
\underline{14x^5+28x^4}\qquad\qquad\qquad \\
3x^4\qquad+21x+5 \\
\underline{3x^4+6x^3}\qquad\qquad\qquad \\
-6x^3\quad+21x+5 \\
\underline{-6x^3-12x^2}\qquad\qquad \\
12x^2+21x+5 \\
\underline{12x^2+24x}\qquad\quad \\
-3x+5 \\
\underline{-3x-6} \\
11
\end{array}
$$

Thus the quotient is $3x^6 - 7x^5 + 14x^4 + 3x^3 - 6x^2 +12x - 3$, and the remainder is 11.

CHAPTER 9

FUNCTIONS AND RELATIONS

● PROBLEM 9-1

Find the image of each element in

$$A = \{1,2,3,4,5,6,7,8,9\}$$

under the following mapping:
$$f(x) = \begin{cases} 2x, & \text{if } x < 5 \\ 8, & \text{if } x \geq 5 \end{cases}$$

Solution: The image of each element in $A = \{1,2,3,4,5,6,7,8,9\}$ under the mapping $f(x)$, is $f(1),f(2),f(3),f(4),f(5),f(6),f(7),f(8),$ $f(9)$. $f(x)$ has two corresponding values, depending on the value of x. If $x < 5$, $f(x) = 2x$, thus for

$$x = 1, \ f(1) = 2(1) = 2$$
$$x = 2, \ f(2) = 2(2) = 4$$
$$x = 3, \ f(3) = 2(3) = 6$$
$$x = 4, \ f(4) = 2(4) = 8$$

and if
$$x \geq 5, \ f(x) = 8 , \quad \text{thus for}$$
$$x = 5, \ f(5) = 8$$
$$x = 6, \ f(6) = 8$$
$$x = 7, \ f(7) = 8$$
$$x = 8, \ f(8) = 8$$
$$x = 9, \ f(9) = 8$$

● PROBLEM 9-2

Find the relation Q over S × T if S = { 1,2,3}, T = { 4,5}, and the rule of correspondence is

$$r(x) = x + 2.$$

<u>Solution:</u> We first find the image of each element in S by substituting each element for x in the rule of correspondence r(x) = x + 2.

$$r(1) = 1 + 2 = 3 \qquad r(2) = 2 + 2 = 4$$

$$r(3) = 3 + 2 = 5.$$

Thus, the rule of correspondence determines the following set of ordered pairs:

$$\{(1,3), (2,4), (3,5)\}.$$

However, the relation Q must be a subset of S × T, which equals {(1,4), (1,5), (2,4), (2,5), (3,4), (3,5)}. Therefore the point (1,3) won't appear in Q because (1,3) doesn't appear in S × T. Therefore, the relation over S × T determined by r(x) = x + 2 is

$$Q = \{(2,4), (3,5)\}.$$

We can use set-builder notation to describe the relation discussed in the above example. In the example, a set of ordered pairs was determined by a rule of correspondence. The first component, x, was chosen from the domain, S. The second component, r(x), was the corresponding image from the range, T. Thus, we can describe the relation Q in the following manner:

$$Q = \{\left(x, r(x)\right): r(x) = x + 2\}.$$

This notation refers to all ordered pairs [x, r(x)], such that r(x) = x + 2.

● **PROBLEM 9-3**

Let the domain of $M = \{(x,y): y = x\}$ be the set of real numbers. Is M a function?

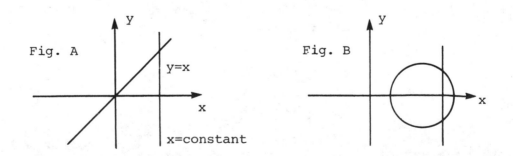

Fig. A

y=x

x=constant

Fig. B

<u>Solution:</u> The range is also the set of real numbers since y = {y| y = x}. The graph of y = x is the graph of a line (y = mx + b where m = 1 and b = 0). See fig. A. If for every value of x in the domain, there corresponds only one y value then y is said to be a function of x. Since each element in the domain

56

of M has exactly one element for its image, M is a function.
Also notice that a vertical line (x = constant) crosses the graph
y = x only once. Whenever this is true the graph defines a function.
Consult figure B.
The vertical line (x = constant) crosses the graph of the circle twice;
i.e., for each x,y is not unique, therefore the graph does not define a function.

● **PROBLEM 9-4**

If $g(x) = x^2 + 5x - 3$, find $g(-7)$.

<u>Solution:</u> Substitute -7 for x everywhere in the
equation:

$$g(-7) = (-7)^2 + 5(-7) - 3$$

$$= 49 - 35 - 3 = 11.$$

● **PROBLEM 9-5**

Let f be a mapping with the rule of correspondence
$$f(x) = 3x^2 - 2x + 1.$$
Find $f(1)$, $f(-3)$, $f(-b)$.

<u>Solution:</u> In order to find $f(1)$, $f(-3)$, $f(-b)$, we replace x by 1,
(-3), and (-b) respectively in our equation for $f(x)$, $f(x) = 3x^2 - 2x + 1$.
Thus

$$f(1) = 3(1)^2 - 2(1) + 1$$

$$= 3 - 2 + 1$$

$$= 1 + 1$$

$$= 2$$

$$f(-3) = 3(-3)^2 - 2(-3) + 1$$

$$= 3(9) + 6 + 1$$

$$= 27 + 7$$

$$= 34$$

$$f(-b) = 3(-b)^2 - 2(-b) + 1$$

$$= 3(b^2) + 2b + 1$$

$$= 3b^2 + 2b + 1$$

● **PROBLEM 9-6**

If $f(t) = 6t + 13$, find $f(5) - f(4)$.

Solution: To find $f(5)$ we substitute 5 for t everywhere in the equation, that is:

$$f(5) = 6(5) + 13 = 43$$

Similarly, $f(4) = 6(4) + 13 = 37$

and now subtract $f(4)$ from $f(5)$. Therefore,

$$f(5) - f(4) = 43 - 37 = 6.$$

If $f(x) = (x - 2)/(x + 1)$, find the function values $f(2)$, $f(\frac{1}{2})$, and $f(- 3/4)$.

Solution: To find $f(2)$, we replace x by 2 in the given formula for $f(x)$, $f(x) = x - 2/x + 1$; thus

$$f(2) = \frac{2 - 2}{2 + 1} = \frac{0}{3} = 0.$$

Similarly, $f(\frac{1}{2}) = \frac{\frac{1}{2} - 2}{\frac{1}{2} + 1}$.

Multiply numerator and denominator by 2,

$$= \frac{2(\frac{1}{2} - 2)}{2(\frac{1}{2} + 1)} .$$

Distribute, $\quad = \dfrac{2(\frac{1}{2}) - 2 \cdot 2}{2(\frac{1}{2}) + 2}$

$$= \frac{1 - 4}{1 + 2}$$

$$= - \frac{3}{3} = - 1.$$

$f(- 3/4) = \dfrac{- 3/4 - 2}{- 3/4 + 1}$.

Multiply numerator and denominator by 4,

$$= \frac{4(- 3/4 - 2)}{4(- 3/4 + 1)} .$$

Distribute, $\quad = \dfrac{4(- 3/4) - 4(2)}{4(- 3/4) + 4(1)}$

$$= \frac{- 3 - 8}{- 3 + 4}$$

$$= \frac{- 11}{1}$$

$$= - 11.$$

Let f be the function whose domain is the set of all real numbers, whose range is the set of all numbers greater than or equal to 2, and whose rule of correspondence is given by the equation $f(x) = x^2 + 2$. Find $3f(0) + f(-1)f(2)$.

Solution: The rule of correspondence in this example is expressed by the equation $f(x) = x^2 + 2$. To find the number in the range that is associated with any particular number in the domain, we merely replace the letter x wherever it appears in the equation $f(x) = x^2 + 2$ by the given number. Thus

$$f(0) = 0^2 + 2 = 2 , \quad f(-1) = (-1)^2 + 2 = 1 + 2 = 3 ,$$

$$f(2) = 2^2 + 2 = 4 + 2 = 6 , \quad \text{and}$$

$$3f(0) + f(-1)f(2) = 3(2) + (3)(6) = 6 + 18 = 24.$$

Show that $f(a) = f(-a)$ if $f(x) = x^2 + 3$.

Solution: If $f(a) = f(-a)$, one should obtain an identity when a and then -a are substituted into the equation. For the given equation we have:

$$f(-a) = (-a)^2 + 3 = a^2 + 3 = f(a).$$

Find the zeros of the function f if $f(x) = 3x - 5$.

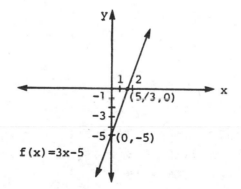

Solution: The zeros of the function $f(x) = 3x - 5$ are those values of x for which $3x - 5 = 0$:

$$3x - 5 = 0$$

$$3x = 5$$
$$x = \frac{5}{3}$$

Thus $x = 5/3$ is a zero of $f(x) = 3x - 5$, which means that the graph of $f(x)$ crosses the x axis at the point $(5/3, 0)$ (see figure).

For each of the following functions, with domain equal to the set of all whole numbers, find: (a) $f(0)$; (b) $f(1)$; (c) $f(-1)$; (d) $f(2)$; (e) $f(-2)$.

(1) $f(x) = 2x^3 - 3x + 4$

(2) $f(x) = x^2 + 1$.

<u>Solution:</u>   In order to find each $f(x)$ value, we replace x by the given value in each equation.   Thus:

(1) $f(x) = 2x^3 - 3x + 4$

(a) $f(0) = 2(0)^3 - 3(0) + 4$

$= 2(0) - 0 + 4$

$= 0 + 4$

$= 4$

(b) $f(1) = 2(1)^3 - 3(1) + 4$

$= 2(1) - 3 + 4$

$= 2 - 3 + 4$

$= 3$

(c) $f(-1) = 2(-1)^3 - 3(-1) + 4$

$= 2(-1) + 3 + 4$

$= -2 + 3 + 4$

$= 5$

(d) $f(2) = 2(2)^3 - 3(2) + 4$

$= 2(8) - 6 + 4$

$= 16 - 6 + 4$

$= 14$

(e) $f(-2) = 2(-2)^3 - 3(-2) + 4$

$= 2(-8) + 6 + 4$

$= -16 + 10$

$= -6$

(2) $f(x) = x^2 + 1$

(a) $\qquad$ $f(0) = (0)^2 + 1$

$\qquad\qquad\qquad = 0 + 1$

$\qquad\qquad\qquad = 1$

(b) $\qquad$ $f(1) = (1)^2 + 1$

$\qquad\qquad\qquad = 1 + 1$

$\qquad\qquad\qquad = 2$

(c) $\qquad$ $f(-1) = (-1)^2 + 1$

$\qquad\qquad\qquad = 1 + 1$

$\qquad\qquad\qquad = 2$

(d) $\qquad$ $f(2) = (2)^2 + 1$

$\qquad\qquad\qquad = 4 + 1$

$\qquad\qquad\qquad = 5$

(e) $\qquad$ $f(-2) = (-2)^2 + 1$

$\qquad\qquad\qquad = 4 + 1$

$\qquad\qquad\qquad = 5$

Notice that the range is contained in the set of whole numbers.

● **PROBLEM 9-12**

If $y = f(x) = (x^2 - 2)/(x^2 + 4)$ and $x = t + 1$, express y as a function of t.

Solution: y is given as a function of x, $y = f(x) = \dfrac{x^2 - 2}{x^2 + 4}$.

To express y as a function of t, replace x by t + 1 (since x - t + 1) in the formula for y. Thus,

$$y = f(x) = f(t + 1) = \frac{(t + 1)^2 - 2}{(t + 1)^2 + 4}$$

$$= \frac{(t^2 + 2t + 1) - 2}{(t^2 + 2t + 1) + 4}$$

$$= \frac{t^2 + 2t - 1}{t^2 + 2t + 5}$$

$$= g(t).$$

Hence, y = g(t); that is, y is now a function of t since y has been expressed in terms of t.

61

Let f be the linear function that is defined by the equation $f(x) = 3x + 2$. Find the equation that defines the inverse function f^{-1}.

<u>Solution:</u> To find the inverse function f^{-1}, the given equation must be solved for x in terms of y. Let $x = f^{-1}(y)$.

Solving the given equation for x:

$$y = 3x + 2, \text{ where } y = f(x).$$

Subtract 2 from both sides of this equation:

$$y - 2 = 3x + 2 - 2$$

$$y - 2 = 3x.$$

Divide both sides of this equation by 3:

$$\frac{y - 2}{3} = \frac{3x}{3}$$

$$\frac{y - 2}{3} = x$$

or

$$x = \frac{y}{3} - \frac{2}{3}$$

Hence, the inverse function f^{-1} is given by::

$$x = f^{-1}(y) = \frac{y}{3} - \frac{2}{3}$$

$$\text{or } x = f^{-1}(y) = \frac{1}{3}y - \frac{2}{3}.$$

Of course, the letter that we use to denote a number in the domain of the inverse function is of no importance whatsoever, so this last equation can be rewritten $f^{-1}(u) = \frac{1}{3}u - \frac{2}{3}$, or $f^{-1}(s) = \frac{1}{3}s - \frac{2}{3}$, and it will still define the same function f^{-1}.

Show that the inverse of the function $y = x^2 + 4x - 5$ is not a function.

<u>Solution:</u> Given the function f such that no two of its ordered pairs

have the same second element, the inverse function f^{-1} is the set of ordered pairs obtained from f by interchanging in each ordered pair the first and second elements. Thus, the inverse of the function

$y = x^2 + 4x - 5$ is $x = y^2 + 4y - 5$.

The given function has more than one first component corresponding to a given second component. For example, if $y = 0$, then $x = -5$ or 1. If the elements $(-5,0)$ and $(1,0)$ are reversed, we have $(0,-5)$ and $(0,1)$ as elements of the inverse. Since the first component 0 has more than one second component, the inverse is not a function (a function can have only one y value corresponding to each x value).

CHAPTER 10

SOLVING LINEAR EQUATIONS

UNKNOWN IN NUMERATOR

Solve 3x - 5 = 4 for x.

Solution: Since this equation is to be solved for x, place the term x on one side of the equation, 3x - 5 = 4. Add 5 to both sides of the equation.

$$3x - 5 + 5 = 4 + 5 \tag{1}$$

Since -5 + 5 = 0 and 4 + 5 = 9, Equation (1) reduces to:

$$3x = 9. \tag{2}$$

Since it is desired to get the term x on one side of the equation, divide both sides of Equation (2) by 3.

$$\frac{3x}{3} = \frac{9}{3}. \tag{3}$$

Since $\frac{3x}{3}$ reduces to 1x and since $\frac{9}{3}$ reduces to 3, Equation (3) becomes: 1x = 3. Since 1x = x, x = 3. Therefore, the equation has been solved for x.

Check: By substituting x = 3 into the original equation we have

$$3(3) - 5 \stackrel{?}{=} 4$$

$$9 - 5 \stackrel{?}{=} 4$$

$$4 = 4.$$

Note that, upon substitution of the solution into the original equation, the equation is reduced to the identity 4 = 4.

Solve the equation $6x - 3 = 7 + 5x$.

Solution: To solve for x in the equation $6x - 3 = 7 + 5x$, we wish to obtain an equivalent equation in which each term in one member involves x, and each term in the other member is a constant. If we add $(- 5x)$ to both members, then only one side of the equation will have an x term:

$$6x - 3 + (- 5x) = 7 + 5x + (- 5x)$$

$$6x + (- 5x) - 3 = 7 + 0$$

$$x - 3 = 7$$

Now, adding 3 to both sides of the equation we obtain,

$$x - 3 + 3 = 7 + 3$$

$$x + 0 = 10$$

$$x = 10$$

Thus, our solution is $x = 10$. Now we check this value.

Check: Substitute 10 for x in the original equation:

$$6x - 3 = 7 + 5x$$

$$6(10) - 3 = 7 + 5(10)$$

$$60 - 3 = 7 + 50$$

$$57 = 57.$$

Solve the equation $4x - 5 = x + 7$.

Solution: The problem here is to list the elements in the set

$$S = \{x \mid 4x - 5 = x + 7\}$$

To find these elements, use the additive principle and the multiplicative principle. By using these principles, convert the description of S to the form $S = \{x \mid x = \ldots\}$.

The computation can be arranged in the following manner:

$4x - 5 = x + 7$	Original equation
$4x - 5 + 5 = x + 7 + 5$	Adding 5 to both sides
$4x = x + 12$	
$4x + (-x) = x + 12 + (-x)$	Adding -x to both sides
$3x = 12$	

$$\tfrac{1}{3}(3x) = \tfrac{1}{3}(12) \qquad \text{Multiplying both sides by } \tfrac{1}{3}$$
$$x = 4$$

Hence the solution set is $S = \{x \mid x = 4\} = \{4\}$.

Solve, justifying each step. $3x - 8 = 7x + 8$.

<u>Solution:</u>

	$3x - 8 = 7x + 8$
Adding 8 to both members,	$3x - 8 + 8 = 7x + 8 + 8$
Additive inverse property,	$3x + 0 = 7x + 16$
Additive identity property,	$3x = 7x + 16$
Adding $(-7x)$ to both members,	$3x - 7x = 7x + 16 - 7x$
Commuting,	$-4x = 7x - 7x + 16$
Additive inverse property,	$-4x = 0 + 16$
Additive identity property,	$-4x = 16$
Dividing both sides by -4,	$x = \dfrac{16}{-4}$
	$x = -4$

Check: Replacing x by -4 in the original equation:

$$3x \quad - 8 \ = \ 7x \ + \ 8$$
$$3(-4) - 8 \ = \ 7(-4) + \ 8$$
$$- 12 - 8 \ = \ - 28 + \ 8$$
$$-20 \ = \ - 20$$

Solve for x: $7x - 3 = 2(x + 3)$.

<u>Solution:</u>

$$7x - 3 = 2(x + 3)$$

Distributing,

$$7x - 3 = 2x + 6$$

Adding $(-2x)$ to both sides,	$7x - 3 - 2x = 6$
Combining terms,	$5x - 3 = 6$
Adding 3 to both sides,	$5x = 6 + 3$
Combining terms,	$5x = 9$
Dividing both sides by 5,	$x = \dfrac{9}{5}$

Check: Replacing x by $\dfrac{9}{5}$ in the original equation,

$$7x - 3 = 2(x + 3)$$

$$7\left(\frac{9}{5}\right) - 3 = 2\left(\frac{9}{5} + 3\right)$$

$$\frac{63}{5} - \frac{15}{5} = \frac{18}{5} + 6$$

$$\frac{48}{5} = \frac{18}{5} + \frac{30}{5}$$

$$\frac{48}{5} = \frac{48}{5}$$

Solve the equation $\frac{3}{4} x + \frac{7}{8} + 1 = 0$.

<u>Solution:</u> There are several ways to proceed. First we observe that $\frac{3}{4} x + \frac{7}{8} + 1 = 0$ is equivalent to

$$\frac{3}{4} x + \frac{7}{8} + \frac{8}{8} = 0, \text{ where we have converted}$$

1 into $\frac{8}{8}$. Now, combining fractions we obtain:

$$\frac{3}{4} x + \frac{15}{8} = 0$$

Subtract $\frac{15}{8}$ from both sides:

$$\frac{3}{4} x = \frac{-15}{8}$$

Multiplying both sides by $\frac{4}{3}$:

$$\left(\frac{4}{3}\right) \frac{3}{4} x = \left(\frac{4}{3}\right)\left(\frac{-15}{8}\right)$$

Cancelling like terms in numerator and denominator:

$$x = \frac{-5}{2}$$

A second method is to multiply both sides of the equation by the least common denominator, 8:

$$8\left(\frac{3}{4} x + \frac{7}{8} + 1\right) = 8(0)$$

Distributing: $\quad 8\left(\frac{3}{4}\right)x + 8\left(\frac{7}{8}\right) + 8 \cdot 1 = 0$

$$(2 \cdot 3)x + 7 + 8 = 0$$

$$6x + 15 = 0$$

Subtract 15 from both sides: $\qquad$ $6x = -15$

Divide both sides by 6: $\qquad$ $x = \dfrac{-15}{6}$

Cancelling 3 from numerator and denominator: $x = \dfrac{-5}{2}$

Solve the equation

$$\tfrac{1}{2}x + \tfrac{2}{3} = \tfrac{1}{4}x - \tfrac{1}{6}$$

<u>Solution:</u> Since 2, 3, 4, and 6, the denominators of the fractions, are all factors of 12, and there is no smaller number which contains 2, 3, 4, and 6 as factors, 12 is the least common multiple (LCM). We may therefore multiply both sides of the given equation by 12 to eliminate the fractions.

$$\left(\tfrac{1}{2}x + \tfrac{2}{3}\right)12 = \left(\tfrac{1}{4}x - \tfrac{1}{6}\right)12$$

Distribute, $\left(\tfrac{1}{2}x\right)12 + \left(\tfrac{2}{3}\right)12 = \left(\tfrac{1}{4}x\right)12 - \left(\tfrac{1}{6}\right)(12)$

$$6x + 8 = 3x - 2$$

Add (- 3x) to both sides,

$$6x + 8 + (-3x) = 3x - 2 + (-3x)$$

$$6x + (-3x) + 8 = 3x + (-3x) - 2$$

$$3x + 8 = -2$$

Add (- 8) to both sides

$$3x + 8 + (-8) = -2 + (-8)$$

$$3x = -10$$

Divide both sides by 3, $\quad x = -\dfrac{10}{3}$

Thus, the solution is x = - 10/3, and we have

$$\left\{x \,\middle|\, \tfrac{1}{2}x + \tfrac{2}{3} = \tfrac{1}{4}x - \tfrac{1}{6}\right\} = \left\{\dfrac{-10}{3}\right\} \qquad \text{To verify this}$$

statement we perform the following check:

Check: Replace x by - 10/3 in the original equation,

$$\tfrac{1}{2}x + \tfrac{2}{3} = \tfrac{1}{4}x - \tfrac{1}{6}$$

$$\frac{1}{2}\left(-\frac{10}{3}\right) + \frac{2}{3} = \frac{1}{4}\left(-\frac{10}{3}\right) - \frac{1}{6}$$

$$\frac{-10}{6} + \frac{2}{3} = \frac{-10}{12} - \frac{1}{6}$$

Convert each fraction into a fraction whose denominator is 12. Here we are using the fact that 12 is the least common denominator (this is an alternative method to multiplying both members by the LCM 12). Thus

$$\frac{2}{2}\left(-\frac{10}{6}\right) + \frac{4}{4}\left(\frac{2}{3}\right) = \frac{-10}{12} - \frac{2}{2}\left(\frac{1}{6}\right)$$

$$\frac{-20}{12} + \frac{8}{12} = \frac{-10}{12} - \frac{2}{12}$$

$$\frac{-12}{12} = \frac{-12}{12}$$

$$-1 = -1$$

Since substitution of x by (- 10/3) results in this equivalent equation which is always true, - 10/3 is indeed a root of the equation.

● **PROBLEM 10-8**

> Solve for x:
>
> $$\frac{x}{2} + \frac{x}{3} = 12.$$

<u>Solution:</u> The Least Common Denominator is 6. Multiply both members of the equation by 6: $6\left(\frac{x}{2} + \frac{x}{3}\right) = 6(12).$

Use distributive law: $3x + 2x = 72.$

Collect terms: $5x = 72.$

Divide by 5:   Therefore, $x = 14\frac{2}{5}.$

Check: Substitute $14\frac{2}{5} = \frac{72}{5}$ for x in the given equation:

$$\frac{\frac{72}{5}}{2} + \frac{\frac{72}{5}}{3} = 12$$

$$\left(\frac{72}{5} \cdot \frac{1}{2}\right) + \left(\frac{72}{5} \cdot \frac{1}{3}\right) = 12$$

$$\frac{36}{5} + \frac{24}{5} = 12$$

$$\frac{60}{5} = 12$$

$$12 = 12$$

Solve $A = \frac{h}{2}(b + B)$ for h.

Solution: Since the given equation is to be solved for h, obtain h on one side of the equation. Multiply both sides of the equation $A = \frac{h}{2}(b + B)$ by 2. Then, we have:

$$2(A) = 2\left[\frac{h}{2}(b + B)\right].$$

Therefore:

$$2(A) = \frac{\cancel{2}h}{\cancel{2}}(b + B)$$

$$2A = h(b + B). \tag{1}$$

Since it is desired to obtain h on one side of the equation, divide both sides of equation (1) by (b + B).

$$\frac{2A}{(b + B)} = \frac{h\cancel{(b + B)}}{\cancel{(b + B)}}.$$

Therefore:

$$\frac{2A}{b + B} = h.$$

Thus, the given equation, $A = \frac{h}{2}(b + B)$, is solved for h.

This is the form of the formula used to determine values of h for a set of trapezoids, if the area and lengths of the bases are known.

UNKNOWN IN NUMERATOR AND/OR DENOMINATOR

Solve the equation

$$\frac{5}{x - 1} + \frac{1}{4 - 3x} = \frac{3}{6x - 8}.$$

Solution: By factoring out a common factor of −2 from the denominator of the term on the right side of the given equation, the given equation becomes:

$$\frac{5}{x - 1} + \frac{1}{4 - 3x} = \frac{3}{-2(-3x + 4)} = \frac{3}{-2(4 - 3x)} = \frac{3}{2(4 - 3x)}$$

Hence,

$$\frac{5}{x - 1} + \frac{1}{4 - 3x} = -\frac{3}{2(4 - 3x)}$$

Adding $\frac{3}{2(4 - 3x)}$ to both sides of this equation:

$$\frac{5}{x-1} + \frac{1}{4-3x} + \frac{3}{2(4-3x)} = 0. \qquad (1)$$

Now, in order to combine the fractions, the least common denominator (l.c.d.) must be found. The l.c.d. is found in the following way: list all the different factors of the denominators of the fractions. The exponent to be used for each factor in the l.c.d. is the greatest value of the exponent for each factor in any denominator. Therefore, the l.c.d. of the given fractions is:

$$2^1(x-1)^1(4-3x)^1 = 2(x-1)(4-3x)$$

Hence, equation (1) becomes:

$$\frac{(2)(4-3x)(5)}{(2)(4-3x)(x-1)} + \frac{(2)(x-1)(1)}{(2)(x-1)(4-3x)} + \frac{(x-1)(3)}{(x-1)(2)(4-3x)} = 0 \qquad (2)$$

Simplifying equation (2):

$$\frac{10(4-3x) + 2(x-1) + 3(x-1)}{2(x-1)(4-3x)} = 0$$

$$\frac{40 - 30x + 2x - 2 + 3x - 3}{2(x-1)(4-3x)} = 0$$

$$\frac{-25x + 35}{2(x-1)(4-3x)} = 0$$

Multiplying both sides of this equation by $2(x-1)(4-3x)$:

$$2(x-1)(4-3x)\frac{-25x+35}{2(x-1)(4-3x)} = 2(x-1)(4-3x)(0)$$

$$-25x + 35 = 0$$

Adding 25x to both sides of this equation:

$$-25x + 35 + 25x = 0 + 25x$$

$$35 = 25x$$

Dividing both sides of this equation by 25:

$$\frac{35}{25} = \frac{25x}{25}$$

$$\frac{7}{5} = x$$

Therefore, the solution set to the equation $\frac{5}{x-1} + \frac{1}{4-3x} =$
$= \frac{3}{6x-8}$ is: $\left\{\frac{7}{5}\right\}$.

Solve

$$\frac{3}{x - 1} + \frac{1}{x - 2} = \frac{5}{(x - 1)(x - 2)} .$$

<u>Solution</u>: First we will eliminate the fractions by finding the least common denominator, LCD. This is done by multiplying the denominators and taking the highest power of each factor which appears, only once.

$$(x - 1)(x - 2)(x - 1)(x - 2)$$

$$LCD = (x - 1)(x - 2)$$

Multiplying both sides of the equation by the LCD will remove the fractions and give:

$$(x - 1)(x - 2)\left(\frac{3}{x - 1} + \frac{1}{x - 2}\right)$$

$$= \left(\frac{5}{(x - 1)(x - 2)}\right)(x - 1)(x - 2)$$

$$3(x - 2) + (x - 1) = 5$$

$$3x - 6 + x - 1 = 5$$

$$4x - 7 = 5$$

$$4x = 12$$

$$x = 3$$

Substituting x = 3 into the original equation

$$\frac{3}{2} + 1 = \frac{5}{(2)(1)}$$

$$\frac{5}{2} = \frac{5}{2}$$

we find x = 3 satisfies the original equation.

Solve $\frac{3}{x - 1} + \frac{2}{x + 1} = \frac{6}{x^2 - 1} .$

<u>Solution:</u> First we obtain the Least Common Denominator, LCD, by multiplying the denominators,

$$(x - 1)(x = 1)(x^2 - 1), \text{or}$$

$(x - 1)(x + 1)[(x - 1)(x + 1)]$, and taking each factor's highest power once.

$$\text{LCD} = (x - 1)(x + 1) = (x^2 - 1) \qquad (1)$$

Then multiply both sides of the equation by the LCD to remove the fractions and obtain:

$$(x - 1)(x + 1)\left[\frac{3}{x - 1} + \frac{2}{x + 1}\right]$$

$$= \left[\frac{6}{x^2 - 1}\right](x - 1)(x + 1)$$

$$3(x + 1) + 2(x - 1) = 6 \qquad (2)$$

$$3x + 3 + 2x - 2 = 6$$

$$5x + 1 = 6$$

$$5x = 5$$

$$x = 1$$

Substituting x = 1 into Equation 2, we can readily see that it is a solution of that equation. However, x = 1 is not an admissible value of x for Equation 1, because division by 0 is undefined; therefore, x = 1 is not a solution of Equation 1. It is an extraneous root that was introduced by the multiplication by the LCD. The original equation does not have a solution.

UNKNOWN UNDER RADICAL SIGN

● **PROBLEM** 10-13

Solve $\sqrt{x - 3} = 4$.

<u>Solution:</u>   Square both sides of the given equation to obtain:

$$\left(\sqrt{x - 3}\right)^2 = 4^2$$

Note $\left(\sqrt{a}\right)^2 = \sqrt{a} \cdot \sqrt{a} = \sqrt{a \cdot a} = \sqrt{a^2} = a$; thus

$\left(\sqrt{x - 3}\right)^2 = x - 3$, and we obtain:

$$x - 3 = 16$$

$$x = 19$$

Check: Substitute 19 for x in the original equation,

$$\sqrt{x - 3} = 4$$

$$\sqrt{19 - 3} = 4$$

$$\sqrt{16} = 4$$

$$4 = 4$$

● **PROBLEM 10-14**

Solve the equation $\sqrt{3x + 1} = 5$.

Solution: Square both members:

$$3x + 1 = 25.$$

Solve for x: $\qquad x = 8.$

Check: $\sqrt{3(8) + 1} = \sqrt{25} = 5.$

It should be recalled that $\sqrt{25} = +5$, and does not equal ± 5; that is, when no sign precedes the radical the positive value of the root is to be taken. If both positive and negative roots are meant, we shall write both signs before the radical.

● **PROBLEM 10-15**

Solve the equation

$$\sqrt{x} = 7 + \sqrt{x - 7}$$

Solution: Squaring both sides of the given equation,

$$x = 49 + 14 \sqrt{x - 7} + x - 7$$

Simplifying

$$- 42 = 14 \sqrt{x - 7}$$

$$- 3 = \sqrt{x - 7} \qquad (1)$$

Squaring both sides of equation (1),

$$9 = x - 7$$

$$x = 16$$

Checking the root by substitution in the given equation:

$$\sqrt{16} \neq 7 + \sqrt{16 - 7}$$

$$4 \neq 7 + 3$$

Clearly x = 16 does not satisfy the given equation, and therefore the equation has no roots. The fact that the given equation has no roots could have been anticipated from equation (1), $- 3 = \sqrt{x - 7}$, since the positive root is indicated in the original equation.

● **PROBLEM** 10-16

Solve $\sqrt{2}x - 2 = 2x - \sqrt{2}$.

Solution: Add (−2x) to both sides of the given equation:

$$\sqrt{2}x - 2 - 2x = -\sqrt{2}$$

Now, add 2 to both sides:

$$\sqrt{2}x - 2x = 2 - \sqrt{2}$$

Use the distributive law:

$$x(\sqrt{2} - 2) = 2 - \sqrt{2}$$

$$x = \frac{2 - \sqrt{2}}{\sqrt{2} - 2}$$

Multiply both sides by (−1):

$$-x = \frac{-(2 - \sqrt{2})}{\sqrt{2} - 2}$$

$$-x = \frac{-2 + \sqrt{2}}{-2 + \sqrt{2}}$$

$$- x = 1$$

$$x = -1$$

CHAPTER 11

PROPERTIES OF STRAIGHT LINES

SLOPES, INTERCEPTS AND POINTS ON GIVEN LINES

Find the slope of $f(x) = 3x + 4$.

Solution: Two points on the line determined by $f(x) = 3x + 4$ are   A(0,4)   and   B(1,7).

$$\frac{\text{difference of ordinates}}{\text{difference of abscissas}} = \frac{7 - 4}{1 - 0} = 3$$

Note that the ordinates are the y-coordinates and the abscissas are the x-coordinates. The slope determined by points A and B is 3. Hence, the slope of $f(x) = 3x + 4$ is 3. In general, the slope of a linear function of the form $f(x) = mx + b$ is m.

Show that the slope of the segment joining (1,2) and (2,6) is equal to the slope of the segment joining (5,15) and (10,35).

Solution: The slope of the line segment, m, joining the points (x_1, y_1) and (x_2, y_2) is given by the formula

$$m = \frac{(y_2 - y_1)}{(x_2 - x_1)}$$

Therefore, the slope of the segment joining (1,2) and (2,6) is

$$\frac{6 - 2}{2 - 1} = \frac{4}{1} = 4.$$

The slope of the segment joining (5,15) and (10,35) is

$$\frac{35 - 15}{10 - 5} = \frac{20}{5} = 4.$$

Thus, the slopes of the two segments are equal.

● **PROBLEM 11-3**

Determine the constant A so that the lines $3x - 4y = 12$ and $Ax + 6y = -9$ are parallel.

Solution: If two non-vertical lines are parallel, their slopes are equal. Thus the lines $Ax + By + C = 0$ and $Ax + By + D = 0$ are parallel(since both have slope $= - A/B$). We are given two lines:

$$3x - 4y = 12 \qquad\qquad (1)$$

$$Ax + 6y = -9 \qquad\qquad (2)$$

We must make the coefficients of y the same for both equations in order to equate the coefficients of x. Multiply (1) by -3/2 to obtain

$$\frac{-3}{2}(3x - 4y) = -\frac{3}{2}(12)$$

$$-\frac{9}{2}x + 6y = -18 \qquad\qquad (3)$$

$$Ax + 6y \quad = -9 \qquad\qquad (2)$$

Transpose the constant terms of (3) and (2) to the other side.

Adding 18 to both sides , $\quad -\frac{9}{2}x + 6y + 18 = 0 \qquad (4)$

Adding 9 to both sides, $\quad Ax + 6y + 9 = 0 \qquad (5)$

(4) and (5) will now be parallel if the co-efficients of the x-terms are the same. Thus the constant A is $-9/2$. Then equation (5) becomes $-9/2x + 6y + 9 = 0$. We can also express (5) in its given form, $Ax + 6y = -9$ or $- 9/2\, x + 6y = -9$.
We also can write it in a form that has the same coefficient of x as (1), which clearly shows that they have equal slopes.

$$3x - 4y = 12 \qquad\qquad\qquad (1)$$

$$-\frac{9}{2}x + 6y = -9$$

Multiply the second equation by - 2/3 to obtain a coefficient of x equal to 3.

$$-\frac{2}{3}\left(-\frac{9}{2}x + 6y\right) = -\frac{2}{3}(-9)$$

$$3x - 4y = 6$$

Now equations (1), $3x - 4y = 12$, and the equation $3x - 4y = 6$ are parallel since the coefficients of x and y are identical.

● **PROBLEM 11-4**

Find the slope and Y-intercept of the following lines.

(a) $y = 3x - 1$ (b) $y = 1 - 4x$ (c) $2y = 4x + 7$

77

<u>Solution:</u> a) The equation of a line is: $y = mx + b$, where m is the slope of the line and b is the y-intercept of the line. Hence, the line $y = 3x - 1$ has slope = 3 and y-intercept = -1.

b) The line $y = 1 - 4x$ can be rewritten, using the commutative law, as $y = -4x + 1$. Hence, the slope of this line = -4 and the y-intercept = 1.

c) The line $2y = 4x + 7$, after dividing both sides by 2, can be rewritten as:

$$\frac{2y}{2} = \frac{4x + 7}{2}$$

$$y = 2x + \frac{7}{2}$$

Hence, the slope = 2 and the y-intercept = $\frac{7}{2}$.

● **PROBLEM 11-5**

Find the slope, the y-intercept, and the x-intercept of the equation $2x - 3y - 18 = 0$.

<u>Solution:</u> The equation $2x - 3y - 18 = 0$ can be written in the form of the general linear equation, $ax + by = c$.

$$2x - 3y - 18 = 0$$
$$2x - 3y = 18$$

To find the slope and y-intercept we derive them from the formula of the general linear equation $ax + by = c$. Dividing by b and solving for y we obtain:

$$\frac{a}{b}x + y = \frac{c}{b}$$

$$y = \frac{c}{b} - \frac{a}{b}x$$

where $-\frac{a}{b}$ = slope and $\frac{c}{b}$ = y-intercept.

To find the x-intercept, solve for x and let y = 0:

$$x = \frac{c}{b} - \frac{b}{a}y$$

$$x = \frac{c}{a}$$

In this form we have $a = 2$, $b = -3$, and $c = 18$. Thus,

$$\text{slope} = -\frac{a}{b} = -\frac{2}{-3} = \frac{2}{3}$$

$$\text{y-intercept} = \frac{c}{b} = \frac{18}{-3} = -6$$

$$\text{x-intercept} = \frac{c}{a} = \frac{18}{2} = 9$$

The equation $F = \frac{9}{5} C + 32$ relates the Fahrenheit and centigrade temperature scales. What do the numbers $\frac{9}{5}$ and 32 represent?

Solution: An equation in the form $y = mx + b$ is a linear equation with slope m and y-intercept b. Thus, with $F = 9/5\ C + 32$, 32 is the y-intercept and 9/5 is the slope. That is, the number 32 tells us that when the centigrade thermometer reads 0, the Fahrenheit thermometer reads 32. The number 9/5 is the slope of the line we would obtain if we graphed our equation in an axis system in which centigrade temperatures are measured on the horizontal axis and Fahrenheit temperatures are measured on the vertical axis; that is, the number 9/5 is the number of units of Fahrenheit temperature rise per unit of centigrade temperature rise. If a body's temperature increases 1^0C, then it increases $9/5^0$F. If a body's temperature increases -10^0 (decreases 10^0) C, then it increases $9/5(-10)^0 = -18^0$F.

FINDING EQUATIONS OF LINES

The two points $P_1(1,-2)$ and $P_2(4,1)$ determine a line. What is the equation of the line?

Solution: The slope of the line segment connecting the two points is

$$m = \frac{\Delta y}{\Delta x} = \frac{y_2 - y_1}{x_2 - x_1} = \frac{1 - (-2)}{4 - 1} = \frac{3}{3} = 1.$$

Now we know the slope and at least one point on the line. Therefore, let $P(x,y)$ be any point on the line. Then the slope between the points P and P_1 (or, alternatively, between P and P_2) must be 1. Therefore,

$$m = \frac{\Delta y}{\Delta x} = 1 = \frac{y - (-2)}{x - 1}$$

$$x - 1 = y + 2 \quad \text{by cross multiplying}$$

$$y = x - 3 \quad \text{by solving for y.}$$

The required equation is y = x - 3. Note that both of the given points satisfy this equation.

for $P_1(1,-2)$:   for $P_2(4,1)$:

y = x - 3   y = x - 3

$-2 \overset{?}{=} 1 - 3$ $1 \overset{?}{=} 4 - 3$

-2 = -2   1 = 1.

● **PROBLEM 11-8**

Write the equation of the lines that contain the following points:
(a) (1,2) and (3,4)   (b) (-2,1) and (2,3)

<u>Solution:</u> a) The equation of a line is: y = mx + b, where m = slope and b = y-intercept. The slope, m, of any line can be found by using the equation:

$$m = \frac{y_2 - y_1}{x_2 - x_1} \, ,$$

where (x_1, y_1) and (x_2, y_2) are two points. After the slope m is found, the y-intercept b can be found by substituting one point of the line and the value of the slope m into the equation of the line. Hence, for the line that contains the points (1,2) and (3,4) where $(x_1, y_1) =$ (1,2) and (3,4) = (x_2, y_2):

$$\text{slope:} \, m = \frac{4 - 2}{3 - 1}$$

$$= 2/2$$

$$= 1$$

Using m = 1 and the point (1,2) to find the y-intercept b we have:

$$y = mx + b$$
$$2 = 1(1) + b$$
$$2 = 1 + b$$
$$1 = b$$

Therefore, the equation of the line that contains the points (1,2) and (3,4) is:

$$y = 1x + 1$$

or

$$y = x + 1 \, .$$

b) For the line that contains the points (-2,1) and (2,3), where $(x_1, y_1) = (-2,1)$ and $(x_2, y_2) = (2,3)$:

$$\text{slope} = m = \frac{3 - 1}{2 - (-2)}$$

$$= \frac{2}{4} = \frac{1}{2}$$

Using m = 1/2 and the point (2,3) to find the y-intercept b we have:

$$y = mx + b$$

80

$$3 = \frac{1}{2}(2) + b$$

$$3 = \frac{2}{2} + b$$

$$3 = 1 + b$$

$$b = 2$$

Therefore, the equation of the line that contains the points (-2,1) and (2,3) is:

$$y = \frac{1}{2} x + 2 .$$

● **PROBLEM 11-9**

(a)   Find the equation of the line passing through (2,5) with slope 3.

(b)   Suppose a line passes through the y-axis at (0,b). How can we write the equation if the point-slope form is used?

Solution: (a)   In the point-slope form, let $x_1 = 2$, $y_1 = 5$, and $m = 3$. The point-slope form of a line is:

$$y - y_1 = m(x - x_1)$$
$$y - 5 = 3(x - 2)$$
$$y - 5 = 3x - 6 \qquad \text{Distributive property}$$
$$y = 3x - 1 \qquad \text{Transposition}$$

(b) $y - b = m(x - 0)$

$$y = mx + b .$$

● **PROBLEM 11-10**

What is the equation of the line through the point (3,5) whose slope is 2?

Solution: Let P(x,y) be any point on this line other than (3,5). Using the definition of slope we have

$$m = \frac{\Delta y}{\Delta x} \qquad 2 = \frac{y - 5}{x - 3}$$

$$2x - 6 = y - 5 \qquad \text{by cross-multiplying}$$

$$y = 2x - 1 \qquad \text{by solving for y.}$$

This equation is satisfied by the coordinates (3,5) and represents a line with a slope of 2.

GRAPHING TECHNIQUES

Construct the graph of the function defined by y = 3x - 9.

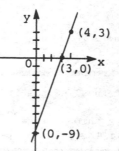

Solution: An equation of the form y = mx + b is a linear equation; that is, the equation of a line.

A line can be determined by two points. Let us choose the intercepts. The x-intercept lies on the x-axis and the y-intercept is on the y-axis.

We find the intercepts by assigning 0 to x and solving for y and by assigning 0 to y and solving for x. It is helpful to have a third point. We find a third point by assigning 4 to x and solving for y. Thus we get the following table of corresponding numbers:

x	y = 3x - 9	y
0	y = 3(0) - 9 = 0 - 9 =	-9
4	y = 3(4) - 9 = 12 - 9 =	3

Solving for x to get the x-intercept:

$$y = 3x - 9$$
$$y + 9 = 3x$$
$$x = \frac{y + 9}{3}$$

When y = 0, $x = \frac{9}{3} = 3$. The three points are (0,-9), (4,3), and (3,0). Draw a line through them (see sketch).

Graph the constant function 2y = 4.

Solution: First rewrite 2y = 4 in y-form. If 2y = 4, then y = 2. Hence, g = {(x,y): y = 2}.

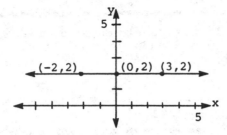

x	-2	0	3
y	2	2	2

For all values of x, y is equal to 2. The graph of g is a
straight line with slope 0 and y-intercept (0,2).

● **PROBLEM** 11-13

Graph the function defined by 3x - 4y = 12.

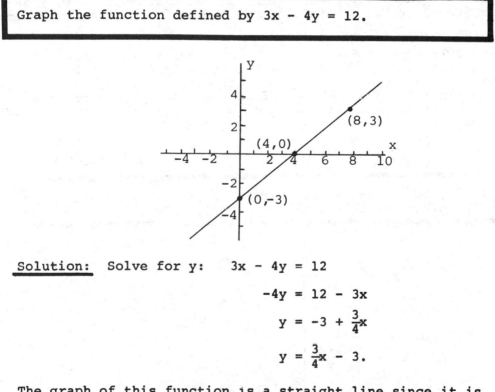

Solution: Solve for y: 3x - 4y = 12

$$-4y = 12 - 3x$$

$$y = -3 + \frac{3}{4}x$$

$$y = \frac{3}{4}x - 3.$$

The graph of this function is a straight line since it is
of the form y = mx + b. The y-intercept is the point
(0, -3) since for x = 0, y = b = -3. The x-intercept is
the point (4, 0) since for y = 0,

$x = (y + 3) \cdot \frac{4}{3} = (0 + 3) \cdot \frac{4}{3} = 4.$ These two points, (0,-3)

and (4,0) are sufficient to determine the graph (see the
figure). A third point, (8,3), satisfying the equation of
the function is plotted as a partial check of the inter-

cepts. Note that the slope of the line is $m = \frac{3}{4}$. This means that y increases 3 units as x increases 4 units anywhere along the line.

● **PROBLEM 11-14**

The following table was constructed by reading the coordinates of selected points on a graphed line. Determine the equation of the line.

x	-2	-1	0	1	2	3
y	5	3	1	-1	-3	-5

Solution: The equation of the line is of the form y = mx + b where m represents the slope and b represents the y-intercept. For each interval in the table, as x increases 1 unit, y decreases 2 units. Therefore, the slope of the line connecting these points is $m = \frac{\Delta y}{\Delta x} = \frac{-2}{1} = -2$. The y-intercept is given as (0,1) since for x = 0, y = 1 as given in the table. The required equation is one which represents a straight line with a slope of -2 and y-intercept of 1, that is, y = -2x + 1. It can be verified that each listed ordered pair will satisfy this equation.

● **PROBLEM 11-15**

a) Find the zeros of the function f if f(x) = 3x - 5.
b) Sketch the graph of the equation y = 3x - 5.

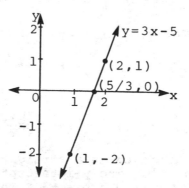

Solution: a) The zeros of a function are the numbers for which the value of the function is 0. Therefore, let f(x) = 3x - 5 = 0. Solving this equation:

$$3x - 5 = 0$$

Add 5 to both sides of this equation.

$$3x - 5 + 5 = 0 + 5$$
$$3x = 5$$

Divide both sides of this equation by 3.

$$\frac{3x}{3} = \frac{5}{3}$$

$$x = \frac{5}{3}$$

This number is the only zero of f (see the graph of f in the figure).

b) Note that the equation of a line is: $y = mx + b$ where m is the slope of the line and b is the y-intercept. Since the given equation is in this form, the graph is a line. It is only necessary to find two points of the graph in order to draw it. Let x = 1. Then $f(x) = f(1) = = 3(1) - 5 = 3 - 5 = -2$. Hence, one point is (1,-2). Let x = 2. Then $f(x) = f(2) = 3(2) - 5 = 6 - 5 = 1$. Therefore, (2,1) is the other point. These two points determine the straight line shown in the figure.

● **PROBLEM** 11-16

Discuss the graph of the function $y = -3x + 4$.

Solution: The graph is a straight line since it is of the form $y = mx + b$. The line intersects the y-axis at the point (0,4). That is, when x = 0 then y = 4. The y-intercept in this example corresponds to b = 4. The slope of the line is m = -3. This means that y decreases 3 units as x increases 1 unit, anywhere along the line.

● **PROBLEM** 11-17

Show that the graphs of $3x - y = 9$ and $6x - 2y + 9 = 0$ are parallel lines.

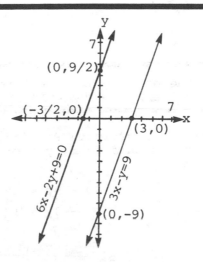

<u>Solution:</u> If the slopes of two lines are equal, the lines are parallel. Thus we must show that the two slopes are equal. In standard form the equation of a line is $y = mx + b$, where m is the slope.

Putting $3x - y = 9$ in standard form,

$$-y = 9 - 3x$$

$$y = -9 + 3x$$

$$y = 3x - 9.$$

Thus the slope of the first line is 3. Putting $6x - 2y + 9 = 0$ in standard form,

$$-2y + 9 = -6x$$

$$-2y = -6x - 9$$

$$y = 3x + \frac{9}{2}.$$

Thus the slope of this line is also 3. The slopes are equal. Hence, the lines are parallel.

To graph these equations pick values of x and substitute them into the equation to determine the corresponding values of y. Thus we obtain the following tables of values. Notice we need only <u>two</u> points to plot a line (2 points determine a line).

$6x - 2y + 9 = 0$ $3x - y = 9$

$\qquad y = 3x + \frac{9}{2}$ $\qquad y = 3x - 9$

x	0	$-\frac{3}{2}$
y	$\frac{9}{2}$	0

x	0	3
y	-9	0

(See accompanying figure)

● **PROBLEM 11-18**

Determine whether there is a point of intersection of the graphs of $2x - 3y = 5$ and $6x - 9y = 10$.

<u>Solution:</u> Geometric discussion. Rewriting the given linear equations in standard form, $y = mx + b$, the slope, m, can be read directly.

$2x - 3y = 5$ $6x - 9y = 10$

$\quad - 3y = 5 - 2x$ $\quad - 9y = 10 - 6x$

86

$$y = \frac{2}{3}x - \frac{5}{3} \qquad\qquad y = \frac{6}{9}x - \frac{10}{9}$$

$$m = \frac{2}{3} \qquad\qquad m = \frac{6}{9} = \frac{2}{3}$$

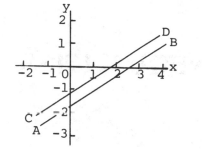

Recall that if the slope, m, of two lines are equal, the lines are parallel. This can be seen in the figure.

The graph of the first equation is the line AB through the point (1, -1) with slope $\frac{2}{3}$, and the graph of the second equation is the line CD through the point $\left(\frac{2}{3}, -\frac{2}{3}\right)$, with slope $\frac{2}{3}$. The lines are parallel, hence there is no point of intersection and the equations are inconsistent.

Algebraic discussion. If the members of the first equation are multiplied by 3, and if the members of the resulting equation are subtracted from the corresponding members of the second equation, we obtain

$$3(2x - 3y) = 3(5)$$
$$6x - 9y = 15$$

Then, $\quad 6x - 9y = 10$
$$-(6x - 9y = 15)$$
$$\overline{}$$
$$0 = -5, \text{ which is impossible.}$$

The steps that were taken were based on the assumption that the given equations had a solution. The fact that an impossible conclusion results proves that the assumption was false. In other words, the two equations have no common solution, and are therefore inconsistent.

CHAPTER 12

LINEAR INEQUALITIES

SOLVING INEQUALITIES AND GRAPHING

● **PROBLEM** 12-1

Solve the inequality $2x + 5 > 9$.

Solution:

$2x + 5 + (-5) > 9 + (-5)$.	Adding -5 to both sides.
$2x + 0 > 9 + (-5)$	Additive inverse property
$2x > 9 + (-5)$	Additive identity property
$2x > 4$	Combining terms
$\frac{1}{2}(2x) > \frac{1}{2} \cdot 4$	Multiplying both sides by $\frac{1}{2}$.
$x > 2$	

The solution set is

$$X = \{x \mid 2x + 5 > 9\}$$
$$= \{x \mid x > 2\}$$

(that is all x, such that x is greater than 2).

● **PROBLEM** 12-2

Determine the values of x for which $3x + 2 < 0$.

Solution: We may add $- 2$ to both members, to give $3x < - 2$. We may then multply both sides of the in-equality by 1/3; hence x < - 2/3, which is the solution. In other words, the solution consists of the set of all numbers which are less than - 2/3, and can be expressed

in solution set notation: {x : x < - 2/3} , (meaning the set of all x such that x is less than - 2/3).

Solve the inequality $2x - 5 > 3$.

Solution: $2x - 5 > 3$ Given

Add 5 to both sides of the given inequality.

$2x - 5 + 5 > 3 + 5$

Therefore: $2x > 8$ (1).

Divide both sides of inequality (1) by 2. Dividing both sides of an inequality by a positive number does not change the direction of the inequality.

$$\frac{2x}{2} > \frac{8}{2}$$

Therefore: $x > 4$, and x is any real number greater than 4.

Solve $4 - 5x < -3$.

Solution: $4 - 5x < -3$ (1)

Subtract 4 from both sides of inequality (1).

$4 - 5x - 4 < -3 - 4$

Therefore: $-5x < -7$ (2)

Divide both sides of inequality (2) by -5. Dividing both sides of an inequality by a negative number changes the direction of the inequality.

$$\frac{-5x}{-5} > \frac{-7}{-5}$$

Therefore: $x > \frac{7}{5}$.

Hence, x is any real number greater than $\frac{7}{5}$.

Find the solution set of inequality $5x - 9 > 2x + 3$.

<u>Solution:</u> To find the solution set of the inequality
5x - 9 > 2x + 3, we wish to obtain an equivalent inequality in which each term in one member involves x,
and each term in the other member is a constant. Thus,
if we add (- 2x) to both members, only one side of the
inequality will have an x term:

$$5x - 9 + (- 2x) > 2x + 3 + (- 2x)$$

$$5x + (-2x) - 9 > 2x + (- 2x) + 3$$

$$3x - 9 > 3$$

Now, adding 9 to both sides of the inequality we obtain,

$$3x - 9 + 9 > 3 + 9$$

$$3x > 12$$

Dividing both sides by 3, we arrive at x > 4.

Hence the solution set is {x│x > 4}, and is pictured
in the accompanying figure.

● **PROBLEM 12-6**

Solve   3(x + 2) < 5x.

-4 -3 -2 -1 0 1 2 3 4 5 6

<u>Solution:</u>   3(x + 2) < 5x   Given
          3x + 6 < 5x   Distributive property
          -2x < -6   Transposition (adding (-6)
                               and (-5x) to both sides of the
                               inequality and simplifying)
          x > 3   Multiplicative property (multi-
                               ply both members of the previous
                               inequality by $-\frac{1}{2}$). Note that
                               multiplying both sides of an
                               inequality by a negative number
                               changes the sense of the in-
                               equality.

The solution set is   {x: x > 3} (see figure).
The unshaded circle above 3 on the number line indicates that x = 3
is not included in the solution set.

● **PROBLEM 12-7**

Solve 2(x + 1) < 4.

90

Number line: -4 -3 -2 -1 0 1 2 3 4 5 6

Solution:

$2(x + 1) < 4$		Given
$2x + 2 < 4$		Distributive property
$2x < 2$		Additive property (with -2)
$x < 1$		Multiplicative property (with $\frac{1}{2}$)

The solution set of $2(x + 1) < 4$ is $\{x: x < 1\}$. The graph of the solution set can be seen in the accompanying figure.

The solution set of $x < 1$ is equal to the solution set of $2(x + 1) < 4$ because the inequalities are equivalent. We have solved an inequality when we know its solution set.

● **PROBLEM 12-8**

Solve $\quad \frac{1}{6}x - 3 < \frac{3}{4}x + \frac{1}{2}$.

Number line: -8 -7 -6 -5 -4 -3 -2 -1 0 1 2

Solution: We can eliminate the fractional coefficients by multiplying both members of the inequality by the least common denominator of the fractions. Multiplying by 12, we have

$$2x - 36 < 9x + 6.$$

Isolating the constant terms on the left side of the inequality sign and the x-terms on the right side by transposition, we have:

$$-36 - 6 < 9x - 2x .$$

Then simplifying:

$$-42 < 7x.$$

Dividing both members of this inequality by 7 yields:

$$-6 < x$$

Hence, the solution set is $\{x: x > -6\}$ and the graph is shown in the accompanying figure.

The unshaded circle above -6 on the number line indicates that $x = -6$ is not included in the solution set.

● **PROBLEM 12-9**

Solve the inequality

$$\frac{1}{x - 1} > \frac{1}{3} .$$

Solution: Since the fraction $\frac{1}{x - 1} > \frac{1}{3}$; that is, since the fraction $\frac{1}{x - 1}$ is greater than 0, $x - 1$ must be positive. Hence, $x - 1 > 0$. If both sides of the given equation are multiplied by $3(x - 1)$, then:

91

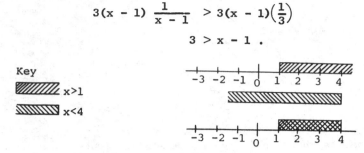

$$3(x - 1) \frac{1}{x - 1} > 3(x - 1)\left(\frac{1}{3}\right)$$

$$3 > x - 1 .$$

Key

x>1

x<4

Note that multiplying both sides of an inequality by a positive number (in this case, 3(x - 1)) does not change the sign of the inequality.

Now we have the double restrictions

$$x - 1 > 0 \quad \text{and} \quad 3 > x - 1$$

and the solution set is the intersection of the solution sets of these two inequalities. Solving each of the two inequalities, we find that

$$x > 1 \quad \text{and} \quad x < 4$$

The solution set is the intersection of the two inequalities, as can be seen on a number line (see diagrams). The intersection of these two inequalities is the set $1 < x < 4$. Hence, the solution set is:

$$X = \{x \mid 1 < x < 4\}$$

(The endpoints $X = 1$ and $X = 4$ are not included in the solution set).

● PROBLEM 12-10

What is the set $\{x < -2\} \cap \{x > 3\}$?

Solution: An element belongs to the intersection of two sets, if, and only if, it belongs to both of them. Thus, in order for a number to belong to our intersection, it would have to be both less than -2 and greater than 3. There is no such number, so the intersection is the empty set; that is,

$$\{x < -2\} \cap \{x > 3\} = \emptyset .$$

This can be seen from the accompanying number line representation, which illustrates that the two graphs have no points in common.

INEQUALITIES WITH TWO VARIABLES

● PROBLEM 12-11

Solve $2x - 3y \geq 6$

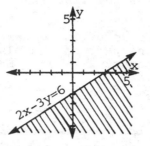

<u>Solution:</u> The statement $2x - 3y \geq 6$ means $2x - 3y$ is
greater than or equal to 6. Symbolically, we have
$2x - 3y > 6$ or $2x - 3y = 6$. Consider the corresponding
equality and graph $2x - 3y = 6$. To find the x-intercept,
set $y = 0$

$$2x - 3y = 6$$
$$2x - 3(0) = 6$$
$$2x = 6$$
$$x = 3$$

{3,0} is the x-intercept.

To find the y-intercept, set x=0

$$2x - 3y = 6$$
$$2(0) - 3y = 6$$
$$-3y = 6$$
$$y = -2$$

{0,-2} is the y-intercept.

A line is determined by two points. Therefore draw
a straight line through the two intercepts {3,0} and
{0,-2}. Since the inequality is mixed, a solid line is
drawn through the intercepts. This line represents the
part of the statement $2x - 3y = 6$.

We must now determine the region for which the
inequality $2x - 3y > 6$ holds.

Choose two points to decide on which side of the line
the region $x - 3y > 6$ lies. We shall try the points
(0,0) and (5,1).

For (0,0)	For (5,1)
$2x - 3y > 6$	$2x - 3y > 6$
$2(0) - 3(0) > 6$	$2(5) - 3(1) > 6$
$0 - 0 > 6$	$10 - 3 > 6$
$0 > 6$	$7 > 6$
False	True

The inequality, $2x - 3y > 6$, holds true for the point
(5,1). We shade this region of the xy-plane. That is,

the area lying below the line 2x - 3y = 6 and containing (5,1).

Therefore, the solution contains the solid line, 2x - 3y = 6, and the part of the plane below this line for which the statement 2x - 3y > 6 holds.

● **PROBLEM** 12-12

Solve the inequality x + 2y ≥ 6 for y in terms of x and draw its graph.

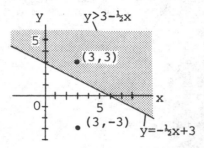

Solution: To solve for y in terms of x, obtain y alone on one side of the inequality and x and any constants on the other. Subtracting x from both sides of

x + 2y ≥ 6 gives 2y ≥ 6 - x
Divide the equation by 2

$y \geq 3 - \frac{1}{2} x$

The points in the x - y plane which will satisfy this equation are those satisfying

$y > 3 - \frac{1}{2} x$ and $y = 3 - \frac{1}{2} x$.

Consider the case,

$y = 3 - \frac{1}{2} x$

which is a graph of the solid straight line with y -intercept 3 and slope - ½. (See diagram.)

We must also find those points which satisfy

$y > 3 - \frac{1}{2} x$.

Choose two points which lie on either side of the line

$y = 3 - \frac{1}{2} x$ to find the region where

$y > 3 - \frac{1}{2} x$.

We shall choose (3, 3) and (3, - 3) (see diagram)

For (3, 3)

$$y > 3 - \frac{1}{2}x$$

$$3 > 3 - \frac{1}{2}(3)$$

$$3 > \frac{3}{2}$$

(3, 3) satisfies the inequality.

For (3, - 3)

$$y > 3 - \frac{1}{2}x$$

$$- 3 > 3 - \frac{1}{2}(3)$$

$$- 3 \not> \frac{3}{2}$$

(3, - 3) does not satisfy the inequality.

Thus, all the points in the region where (3, 3) lies satisfy $y > 3 - \frac{1}{2}x$. That is all those points above the line $y = 3 - \frac{1}{2}x$ satisfy $y > 3 - \frac{1}{2}x$ and lie in the shaded area.

Consequently, the graphical solution of $y \geq -\frac{1}{2}x + 3$ are those points which lie on the solid line $y = -\frac{1}{2} + 3$ and those points in the shaded area $y > -\frac{1}{2}x + 3$.

● PROBLEM 12-13

Solve the inequality 2x - y > 4 for y in terms of x, and draw its graph.

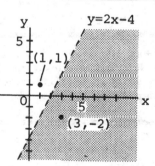

Solution: To solve for y in terms of x obtain y on one side of the inequality and x on the other. Given

$$2x - y > 4 \qquad (1)$$

Add - 2x to both sides of

$$2x - y > 4 \qquad (1)$$

We obtain   - y > 4 - 2x   (2)

Multiply (2) by - 1 and reverse the inequality

sign since we are multiplying by a negative number. We obtain y in terms of x

$$y < -4 + 2x \qquad (3)$$

Rewriting (3)

$$y < 2x - 4 \qquad (3)$$

Graphing (3) consider the equation first as an equality

$$y = 2x - 4 \qquad (4)$$

We draw the graph of (4) as a dotted line since the points of the given inequality $y < 2x - 4$ do not satisfy $y = 2x - 4$. To draw $y = 2x - 4$, we note the slope is 2 and the y-intercept is -4.

To determine what region of the x - y plane satisfies $y < 2x - 4$ choose a point on either side of the dotted line. Let us take the points (3, - 2) and (1, 1) (see diagram). Substitute these points into the given inequality and see which point will satisfy it.

For (3, - 2)

$$y < 2x - 4$$

$$-2 < 2(3) - 4$$

$$-2 < 2$$

For (1, 1)

$$y < 2x - 4$$

$$1 < 2 - 4$$

$$1 \not< -2$$

Now hatch in that portion of the plane containing (3, - 2). All the points to the right of the dotted line $y = 2x - 4$ will satisfy the given inequality.

● PROBLEM 12-14

A livestock farmer has 500 acres to devote to grazing. He estimates that cattle require 5 acres per head and sheep require 3 acres per head. He has winter shelter facilities for 40 head of cattle and for 125 sheep. What constraints are imposed on the number of cattle and sheep he can raise?

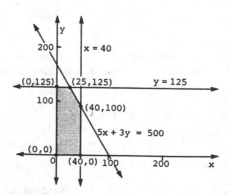

96

Solution: Let x represent the number of cattle raised and y the number of sheep. Since he cannot raise a negative number of either cattle or sheep, we have the constraints

$$x \geq 0 \qquad\qquad (1)$$
$$y \geq 0 \qquad\qquad (2)$$

Since 5x acres are required for the cattle and 3y acres for the sheep and there are only 500 acres available, we have

$$5x + 3y \leq 500 \qquad\qquad (3)$$

Since he can winter only 40 cattle,

$$x \leq 40 \qquad\qquad (4)$$

Since he can winter only 125 sheep,

$$y \leq 125 \qquad\qquad (5)$$

Relations (1) through (5) are the constraints.

The graph of the constraints in this example is a convex set of points. The corner points of the shaded polygon are (0,0), (40,0), (40,100),(25,125), and (0,125).

INEQUALITIES COMBINED WITH ABSOLUTE VALUES

● **PROBLEM 12-15**

Express the inequality $|x| < 3$ without using absolute value signs.

Solution: According to the law of absolute values which states that $|a| < b$ is equivalent to $-b < a < b$, where b is any positive number, $|x| < 3$ is equivalent to $-3 < x < 3$.

● **PROBLEM 12-16**

Solve the inequality $|5 - 2x| > 3$.

Solution: The property of absolute values states that $|a| = +a$ or $|a| = -a$. Therefore: $|5 - 2x| = 5 - 2x$ or $-(5 - 2x)$. Thus, the given inequality becomes two new inequalities:

$$5 - 2x > 3, \quad -(5 - 2x) > 3.$$

Now, we must solve for x in both inequalities. For the first, we subtract 5 from both sides of the inequality, and then divide by -2. We must keep in mind that division or multiplication by a negative number reverses the inequality sign. Thus, for $5 - 2x > 3$ we have:

$$5 - 5 - 2x > 3 - 5$$

$$-2x > -2$$

$$\frac{-2x}{-2} > \frac{-2}{-2}$$

$$x < 1.$$

For the second inequality, we first take the negative of all the terms inside the parentheses. Thus, for $-(5 - 2x) > 3$ we have:

$$-5 + 2x > 3.$$

Now, we add 5 to both sides of the inequality, and then divide by 2. Thus, we obtain:

$$-5 + 5 + 2x > 3 + 5$$

$$2x > 8$$

$$\frac{2x}{2} > \frac{8}{2}$$

$$x > 4.$$

Therefore, the above inequality holds when $x < 1$, and when $x > 4$.

● **PROBLEM** 12-17

Solve

$$\left| \frac{4x}{5} - 1 \right| > 3$$

Solution: We note the following about absolute values. If b is a nonnegative real number, then a is a real number for which $|a| > b$ if and only if $a > b$ or $a < -b$. See the figure.

In the given example, this inequality is satisfied if either

$$\frac{4x}{5} - 1 > 3 \quad \text{or} \quad \frac{4x}{5} - 1 < -3$$

is satisfied. By adding 1 to each member of these inequalities, we get

$$\frac{4x}{5} > 4 \qquad \text{and} \qquad \frac{4x}{5} < -2$$

Hence, by multiplying by 5/4 in each case, we note that the original inequality is satisfied by values of x that are greater than 5 and by values of x that are less than - 5/2, that is, by x > 5 and by x < - 5/2.

The solution set is therefore

$\{x|\ x > 5\}\ \cup\ \{x|x < -5/2\}$.

Solve $|3x - 1| \leq 8$.

Solution: Since $|a| = a$ if $a \geq 0$ and $|a| = -a$ if $a \leq 0$. We must solve two equations

$$3x - 1 \leq 8$$

$$-(3x - 1) \leq 8 \text{ or } 3x - 1 \geq -8.$$

(Note that multiplying an inequality by a negative number, i.e., -1, reverses the inequality.)
The solution set will be the conjunction of the solution sets of each equation; that is,

$$\{x:\ 3x - 1 \leq 8\} \text{ and } \{x:\ 3x - 1 \geq -8\}.$$

We must find

$$\{x:\ 3x - 1 \leq 8\} \cap \{x:\ 3x - 1 \geq -8\}$$

$$3x - 1 \leq 8 \text{ and } 3x - 1 \geq -8$$

$$3x \leq 9 \text{ and } \quad 3x \geq -7$$

$$x \leq 3 \text{ and } \quad x \geq -2\tfrac{1}{2}.$$

The solution set is $\left\{x:\ -2\tfrac{1}{2} \leq x \leq 3\right\}$. See the figure.

Replace the inequality 1 < x < 3 by a single inequality involving an absolute value.

Solution: Recall:

a - b < x < a + b

= - b < x - a < b ,   subtracting a

= |x - a| < b , definition of absolute value

Replacing a by 2 and b by 1 we obtain:

2 - 1 < x < 2 + 1

- 1 < x - 2 < 1

|x - 2| < 1.

CHAPTER 13

SYSTEMS OF LINEAR EQUATIONS AND INEQUALITIES

● **PROBLEM** 13-1

Solve the simultaneous equations $2x + 4y = 11$, $-5x + 3y = 5$ by the method of substitution and by the method of elimination by addition.

Solution: The method of substitution involves solving for one variable in terms of the other and then substituting the obtained value into the second equation. Thus, we solve the first equation for x and substitute in the second:

$$2x + 4y = 11$$
$$2x = 11 - 4y$$
$$x = \frac{11 - 4y}{2}$$

Replacing x by $\left(\frac{11 - 4y}{2}\right)$ in the second equation,

$$-5\left(\frac{11 - 4y}{2}\right) + 3y = 5$$

$$\frac{-55 + 20y}{2} + 3y = 5$$

$$\frac{-55}{2} + 10y + 3y = 5$$

Multiply both sides by 2,

$$-55 + 20y + 6y = 10$$
$$26y = 65$$

$$y = \frac{65}{26} = \frac{5}{2} .$$

Substituting this value for y into the first equation:

$$2x + 4\left(\frac{5}{2}\right) = 11$$

$$2x + 10 = 11$$
$$2x = 1$$
$$x = \frac{1}{2} .$$

We obtain the same result by the method of elimination by addition.

$$2x + 4y = 11 \qquad (1)$$
$$-5x + 3y = 5 \qquad (2)$$

Multiplying equation (1) by 5 and equation (2) by 2 and adding the result we obtain:

$$10x + 20y = 55$$
$$-\ \underline{10x + 6y = \ 10}$$
$$26y = 65$$
$$y = \frac{65}{26} = \frac{5}{2}$$

Once again, replacing y by $\frac{5}{2}$ in equation (1):

$$2x + 4\left(\frac{5}{2}\right) = 11$$
$$2x + 10 = 11$$
$$2x = 1$$
$$x = \frac{1}{2}$$

Thus $\left\{\left(\frac{1}{2}, \frac{5}{2}\right)\right\}$ is the solution to the given system of equations.

● **PROBLEM** 13-2

Solve the equations $3x + 2y = 1$ and $5x - 3y = 8$ simultaneously.

Solution: We have 2 equations in 2 unknowns,

$$3x + 2y = 1 \qquad (1)$$

and

$$5x - 3y = 8 \qquad (2)$$

There are several methods to solve this problem. We have chosen to multiply each equation by a different number so that when the two equations are added, one of the variables drops out. Thus

multiplying the first by 3: $9x + 6y = 3$

and the second by 2: $10x - 6y = 16$

and adding: $19x = 19$

$$x = 1$$

Substituting $x = 1$ in the first equation:

$$3(1) + 2y = 3 + 2y = 1$$
$$2y = -2$$
$$y = -1$$

102

(Alternatively, y might have been found by multiplying the first equation by 5, the second by -3, and adding.)

In this case, then, there is a unique solution: x = 1, y = -1. This may be checked by replacing x by 1 and y by (-1) in each equation. In equation (1):

$$3x + 2y = 1$$
$$3(1) + 2(-1) = 1$$
$$3 - 2 = 1$$
$$1 = 1$$

In equation (2):

$$5x - 3y = 8$$
$$5(1) - 3(-1) = 8$$
$$5 - (-3) = 8$$
$$5 + 3 = 8$$
$$8 = 8$$

In other words, the lines whose equations are 3x+2y=1 and 5x-3y=8 meet in one and only one point: (1,-1). This, again, may be checked graphically, as seen in the diagram.

● **PROBLEM 13-3**

Solve for x and y .

$$x + 2y = 8 \qquad (1)$$
$$3x + 4y = 20 \qquad (2)$$

<u>Solution:</u> Solve equation (1) for x in terms of y:

$$x = 8 - 2y \qquad (3)$$

Substitute (8 - 2y) for x in (2):

$$3(8 - 2y) + 4y = 20 \qquad (4)$$

Solve (4) for y as follows:

Distribute: $24 - 6y + 4y = 20$

Combine like terms and then subtract 24 from both sides:

$$24 - 2y = 20$$
$$24 - 24 - 2y = 20 - 24$$
$$-2y = -4 \qquad \text{Divide both sides by } -2: \quad y = 2$$

Substitute 2 for y in equation (1):

$$x + 2(2) = 8$$
$$x = 4$$

Thus, our solution is x = 4, y = 2.

Check: Substitute x = 4, y = 2 in equations (1) and (2):

$$4 + 2(2) = 8$$
$$8 = 8$$
$$3(4) + 4(2) = 20$$
$$20 = 20$$

● **PROBLEM** 13-4

Solve algebraically:
$$\begin{cases} 4x + 2y = -1 & \quad (1) \\ 5x - 3y = 7 & \quad (2) \end{cases}$$

<u>Solution:</u> We arbitrarily choose to eliminate x first.

Multiply (1) by 5: $\qquad 20x + 10y = -5 \qquad\qquad$ (3)

Multiply (2) by 4: $\qquad 20x - 12y = 28 \qquad\qquad$ (4)

Subtract, (3) - (4): $\qquad\quad 22y = -33 \qquad\qquad$ (5)

Divide (5) by 22: $\qquad\qquad y = -\dfrac{33}{22} = -\dfrac{3}{2}.$

To find x, substitute $y = -\dfrac{3}{2}$ in either of the original equations. If we use Eq. (1), we obtain $4x + 2(-3/2) = -1$, $4x - 3 = -1$, $4x = 2$, $x = \dfrac{1}{2}$.

The solution $\left(\dfrac{1}{2}, -\dfrac{3}{2}\right)$ should be checked in both equations of the given system.

Replacing $\left(\dfrac{1}{2}, -\dfrac{3}{2}\right)$ in Eq. (1):

$$4x + 2y = -1$$
$$4\left(\frac{1}{2}\right) + 2\left(-\frac{3}{2}\right) = -1$$
$$\frac{4}{2} - 3 = -1$$
$$2 - 3 = -1$$
$$-1 = -1$$

Replacing $\left(\dfrac{1}{2}, -\dfrac{3}{2}\right)$ in Eq. (2):

$$5x - 3y = 7$$
$$5\left(\frac{1}{2}\right) - 3\left(-\frac{3}{2}\right) = 7$$
$$\frac{5}{2} + \frac{9}{2} = 7$$
$$\frac{14}{2} = 7$$
$$7 = 7$$

(Instead of eliminating x from the two given equations, we could have eliminated y by multiplying Eq. (1) by 3, multiplying Eq. (2) by 2, and then adding the two derived equations.)

Solve one equation for one unknown and substitute in the other equation to find the solutions of the following systems.

$$xy = 1 \qquad\qquad (1)$$
$$x + 2y = 3 \qquad\qquad (2)$$

<u>Solution:</u> We can solve equation (2) for x by adding (-2y) to both sides:

$$x = 3 - 2y \qquad\qquad (3)$$

Substituting (3 - 2y) for x in equation (1):

$$(3-2y)y = 1$$

Distributing,

$$3y - 2y^2 = 1$$

$$3y - 2y^2 - 1 = 0$$

$$-2y^2 + 3y - 1 = 0$$

Factoring,

$$(-2y + 1)(y-1) = 0$$

Whenever the product of two numbers ab = 0, either a = 0 or b = 0. Thus, either

$$- 2y + 1 = 0 \quad \text{or} \quad y - 1 = 0$$
$$- 2y = -1$$

and

$$y = \frac{-1}{-2} = \frac{1}{2} \text{ or } y = 1$$

Replacing y by $\frac{1}{2}$ in equation (3), we obtain the corresponding x value:

$$x = 3 - 2\left(\frac{1}{2}\right)$$

$$x = 3 - 1$$

$$x = 2$$

Replacing y by 1 in equation (3), we obtain

$$x = 3 - 2(1)$$

$$x = 3 - 2$$

$$x = 1$$

Thus, the two solutions to this system appear to be $\left(2,\frac{1}{2}\right)$ and (1,1). These can be verified by the following check?
Replace (x,y) by (2,1/2) in equations (1) and (2):

$$xy = 1 \qquad\qquad (1)$$
$$(2)\left(\frac{1}{2}\right) = 1$$
$$\frac{2}{2} = 1$$
$$1 = 1$$

$$x + 2y = 3 \qquad\qquad (2)$$

$$2 + 2\left(\tfrac{1}{2}\right) = 3$$
$$2 + \frac{2}{2} = 3$$
$$2 + 1 = 3$$
$$3 = 3$$

Replace (x,y) by (1,1) in equations (1) and (2):

$$xy = 1 \qquad (1)$$
$$1 \cdot 1 = 1$$
$$1 = 1$$

$$x + 2y = 3 \qquad (2)$$
$$1 + 2(1) = 3$$
$$1 + 2 = 3$$
$$3 = 3$$

Thus, the solutions to this system are indeed $\left(2, \tfrac{1}{2}\right)$ and (1,1).

● **PROBLEM** 13-6

Determine the nature of the system of linear equations

$$x + 2y = 8$$
$$x - 2y = 2.$$

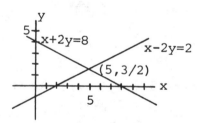

Solution: Add the two equations, eliminating the y-terms, to obtain a single equation in terms of x. Values of x satisfying this equation will yield solutions of the system.

$$x + 2y = 8 \qquad (1)$$
$$+ \ x - 2y = 2 \qquad (2)$$
$$\overline{2x \qquad = 10}$$
$$x \qquad = 5$$

Substituting $x = 5$ into Equation (1) yields
$y = (8 - x)/2 = (8 - 5)/2 = \frac{3}{2}$ or into Equation (2) yields

$y = (2 - x)/(-2) = (2 - 5)/(-2) = \frac{3}{2}$. Thus we have x = 5, $y = \frac{3}{2}$ as the only solution of the system. Alternately, the figure indicates that the lines intersect in the point $\left(5,\frac{3}{2}\right)$. The system is therefore consistent and independent. Substitution of x = 5 and $y = \frac{3}{2}$ in both equations yields

$$5 + 2\left(\frac{3}{2}\right) = 8, \text{ or } 8 = 8$$

$$5 - 2\left(\frac{3}{2}\right) = 2, \text{ or } 2 = 2$$

so that x = 5, y = 3/2, is a solution, and the only solution of the system.

● **PROBLEM** 13-7

Solve for x and y: $\begin{cases} 3x + 5y = 9, & (1) \\ 7x - 10y = 8 & (2) \end{cases}$

Solution: Multiply each member of the first equation by 2; thus 6x + 10y = 18. Now add each member of the resulting equation to the corresponding member of the second equation.

$$6x + 10y = 18$$
$$\underline{7x - 10y = 18}$$
$$13x = 26$$
$$x = 2$$

To solve for y, replace x by 2 in either equation. Using equation (1),

$$3x + 5y = 9$$
$$3(2) + 5y = 9$$
$$6 + 5y = 9$$
$$5y = 3$$
$$y = 3/5$$

Therefore our solution is x = 2, y = 3/5.

Check: To verify our solutions, we substitute the values 2 and 3/5 for x and y in equations (1) and (2):

$$3x + 5y = 9$$
$$3(2) + 5(3/5) = 9$$
$$6 + 3 = 9$$
$$9 = 9$$

$$7x - 10y = 8$$
$$7(2) - 10(3/5) = 8$$
$$14 - 6 = 8$$
$$8 = 8$$

Find the point of intersection of the graphs of the equations:
$$\begin{cases} x + y = 3, \\ 3x - 2y = 14. \end{cases}$$

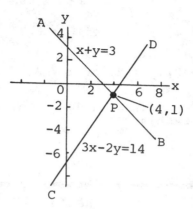

Solution: To solve these linear equations, solve for y in terms of x. The equations will be in the form $y = mx + b$, where m is the slope and b is the intercept on the y-axis.

$$x + y = 3$$
$$y = 3 - x \qquad \text{subtract } x \text{ from both sides}$$

$$3x - 2y = 14 \qquad \text{subtract } 3x \text{ from both sides}$$

$$-2y = 14 - 3x \qquad \text{divide by } -2.$$

$$y = -7 + \frac{3}{2} x$$

The graphs of the linear functions, $y = 3 - x$ and $y = -7 + \frac{3}{2} x$, can be determined by plotting only two points. For example, for $y = 3 - x$, let x = 0, then y = 3. Let x = 1, then y = 2. The two points on this first line are (0,3) and (1,2). For y = -7 + 3/2 x, let x = 0, then y = -7. Let x = 1, then $y = -5\frac{1}{2}$. The two points on this second line are (0,-7) and (1, $-5\frac{1}{2}$).

To find the point of intersection P of

$$x + y = 3$$

and

$$3x - 2y = 14,$$

solve them algebraically. Multiply the first equation by 2. Add these two equations to eliminate the variable y.

$$2x + 2y = 6$$
$$\underline{3x - 2y = 14}$$
$$5x \qquad = 20$$

Solve for x to obtain x = 4. Substitute this into $y = 3 - x$ to get y = 3 - 4 = -1. P is (4,1). AB is the graph of the first equation, and CD is the graph of the second equation. The point of intersection P of the two graphs is the only point on both lines. The coordinates of P satisfy both equations and represent the desired solution of the problem. From the graph, P seems to be the point (4,-1). These coordinates satisfy both equations, and hence are the exact coordinates of the point of intersection of the two lines.

To show that (4,-1) satisfies both equations, substitute this point into both equations.

$$x + y = 3$$
$$4 + (-1) = 3$$
$$4 - 1 = 3$$
$$3 = 3$$

$$3x - 2y = 14$$
$$3(4) - 2(-1) = 14$$
$$12 + 2 = 14$$
$$14 = 14$$

● **PROBLEM 13-9**

Find the solution set of the system

$$2x - 12y = 3 \qquad (1)$$

$$3x + 9y = 4 \qquad (2)$$

<u>Solution:</u> This system can be solved using the multiplication-addition method: The least common multiple of the x coefficients is 6. Multiply equation (1) by 3 and equation (2) by -2 to obtain

$$3(2x - 12y) = 3 \cdot 3$$

$$6x - 36y = 9 \qquad (3)$$

$$-2(3x + 9y) = 4 \cdot (-2)$$

$$-6x - 18y = -8 \qquad (4)$$

Adding equations (3) and (4),

$$6x - 36y = 9$$
$$\underline{-6x - 18y = -8}$$
$$-54y = 1$$
$$y = -\frac{1}{54}$$

To solve for x, we substitute this value of y in either of our given equations. Substituting $\left(\frac{-1}{54}\right)$ for y in (2):

$$3x + 9y = 4$$

$$3x + 9\left(-\frac{1}{54}\right) = 4$$

$$3x - \frac{1}{6} = 4$$

$$3x = 4 + \frac{1}{6}$$

$$3x = \frac{24}{6} + \frac{1}{6}$$

$$3x = \frac{25}{6}$$

$$x = \frac{25}{18}$$

Thus our solution set is $\left\{\left(\frac{25}{18}, -\frac{1}{54}\right)\right\}$, and we perform the following check to verify this result.

Check: Replace x and y by $\left(\frac{25}{18}, -\frac{1}{54}\right)$ respectively in (1) and (2):

(1)
$$2x - 12y = 3$$
$$2\left(\frac{25}{18}\right) - 12\left(\frac{-1}{54}\right) = 3$$
$$\frac{50}{18} + \frac{12}{54} = 3$$
$$\frac{50}{18} + \frac{4}{18} = 3$$
$$\frac{54}{18} = 3$$
$$3 = 3$$

(2)
$$3x + 9y = 4$$
$$3\left(\frac{25}{18}\right) + 9\left(\frac{-1}{54}\right) = 4$$
$$\frac{75}{18} - \frac{9}{54} = 4$$
$$\frac{75}{18} - \frac{3}{18} = 4$$
$$\frac{72}{18} = 4$$
$$4 = 4$$

CHAPTER 14

FACTORING EXPRESSIONS AND FUNCTIONS

NONFRACTIONAL

Factor $x(y + z) + u(y + z)$.

<u>Solution:</u> By the distributive law,

$$x(y + z) + u(y + z) = (x + u)(y + z) \qquad (1)$$

To check if this factoring is correct, distribute the two products on the left side of equation (1).

$$x(y + z) + u(y + z) = (xy + xz) + (uy + uz)$$

$$\text{or } x(y + z) + u(y + z) = xy + xz + uy + uz \qquad (2)$$

Calculating the product on the right side of equation (1):

$$(x + u)(y + z) = xy + uy + xz + uz$$

$$\text{or } (x + u)(y + z) = xy + xz + uy + uz \qquad (3)$$

Since the right side of equations (2) and (3) are equal, equation (1) is true.

Factor   A) $4a^2b - 2ab$

B) $9ab^2c^3 - 6a^2c + 12ac$

C) $ac + bc + ad + bd$

<u>Solution:</u> Find the highest common factor of each polynomial.

A)　$4a^2b = 2 \cdot 2 \cdot a \cdot a \circ b$

$2ab = 2 \cdot a \cdot b$

The highest common factor of the two terms is therefore　2ab.　Hence,

$4a^2b - 2ab = 2ab(2a - 1)$

B)　$9ab^2c^3 = 3 \cdot 3 \cdot a \cdot b \cdot b \cdot c \cdot c \cdot c$

$6a^2c = 3 \circ 2 \cdot a \cdot a \cdot c$

$12ac = 3 \circ 2 \cdot 2 \cdot a \cdot c$

The highest common factor of the three terms is　3ac.　Then,

$9ab^2c^3 - 6a^2c + 12ac = 3ac(3b^2c^2 - 2a + 4)$

C) An expression may sometimes be factored by grouping terms having a common factor and thus getting new terms containing a common factor. The type form for this case is ac+bc+ ad+bd, because the terms ac and bc have the common factor c, and ad and bd have the common factor d. Then,

$ac + bc + ad + bd = c(a + b) + d(a + b)$

Factoring out (a + b), we obtain:

$= (a + b)(c + d).$

● **PROBLEM 14-3**

Factor ax + by + ay + bx completely.

Solution:　Group the terms which have a common factor.　The first and last terms have the factor x in common, while the second and third terms have the factor y in common.　Hence we may rewrite the expression, and we have

$ax + bx + ay + by = x(a + b) + y(a + b)$

Now factor out (a + b)

$= (a + b)(x + y).$

● **PROBLEM 14-4**

Factor $x^2 + 7x + 12$.

Solution:　Since $7x = 4x + 3x$, $x^2 + 7x + 12 = x^2 + 4x + 3x + 12$.　Factor out the common factor of x from the first two terms.　Also, factor out the common factor of 3 from the last two terms.　Therefore,

$x^2 + 7x + 12 = x(x + 4) + 3(x + 4).$

Now factor out the common factor of (x + 4) from the right

side to obtain:

$$x^2 + 7x + 12 = (x + 4)(x + 3).$$

Factor $xy - 3y + y^2 - 3x$ completely.

Solution: Note that the first and last terms have a common factor of x. Also note that the second and third factors have a common factor of y. Hence, group the x and y terms together and factor out the x and y from their respective two terms. Therefore,

$$xy - 3y + y^2 - 3x = (xy - 3x) + \left(-3y + y^2\right)$$

Since $(-3y + y^2) = (y^2 - 3y)$,

$$xy - 3y + y^2 - 3x = (xy - 3x) + (y^2 - 3y)$$
$$= x(y - 3) + y(y - 3)$$

Now factor out the common factor $(y - 3)$ from both terms:

$$xy - 3y + y^2 - 3x = (x + y)(y - 3).$$

Factor $2ax - 3by - 2ay + 3bx$ completely.

Solution: Note that the first and the last terms have a common factor of x. Also note that the second and third factors have a common factor of y. Hence, group the x and y terms and factor out the x and y from their respective two terms. Therefore:

$$2ax - 3by - 2ay + 3bx = (2ax + 3bx) + (-3by - 2ay)$$
$$= x(2a + 3b) + y(-3b - 2a)$$

Since $-3b - 2a = -2a - 3b$,

$$2ax - 3by - 2ay + 3bx = x(2a + 3b) + y(-2a - 3b)$$

Factor out -1 from the term $(-2a - 3b)$:

$$(-2a - 3b) = -1(2a + 3b).$$

Therefore,

$$2ax - 3by - 2ay + 3bx = x(2a + 3b) + y\left[(-1)(2a + 3b)\right]$$
$$= x(2a + 3b) - y(2a + 3b)$$

Factoring out the common factor $(2a + 3b)$ from both terms:

$$2ax - 3by - 2ay + 3bx = (x - y)(2a + 3b).$$

113

Factor $x^2 + 7x + 10$.

Solution: We are given $x^2 + 7x + 10$. We may use the formula

$$x^2 + (b+c)x + bc = (x+b)(x+c) \qquad (1)$$

to factor this polynomial. That is, we set

$$x^2 + 7x + 10 = x^2 + (b+c)x + bc \ .$$

Thus the coefficient of the x term, $7 = b + c$ and $10 = bc$. We now must find the two numbers b and c whose sum is seven and whose product is 10. We first check all **pairs** of numbers whose product is ten:

    (a) $1 \times 10 = 10$; hence $b = 1$, $c = 10$.

We reject these values because $b + c$ must equal 7, but $1 + 10 = 11$.

    (b) $2 \times 5 = 10$; hence $b = 2$, $c = 5$.

We check the sum of these values, and note $b + c = 2 + 5 = 7$.

Thus $b = 2$ and $c = 5$ are the correct values. Now we go back to equation (1)

    $x^2 + (b+c)x + bc = (x+b)(x+c)$, and substituting our values of b and c we obtain:

$$x^2 + (2+5)x + (2 \cdot 5) = (x+2)(x+5)$$
$$x^2 + 7x + 10 = (x+2)(x+5) \ .$$

Factor $2x^2 - 3y^2$.

Solution: Since $a = (\sqrt{a})^2$, $2 = (\sqrt{2})^2$ and $3 = (\sqrt{3})^2$.

    Therefore, $2x^2 - 3y^2 = (\sqrt{2}x)^2 - (\sqrt{3}y)^2$

$(\sqrt{2}x)^2 - (\sqrt{3}y)^2$ is the difference of two squares, hence we apply the formula for the difference of two squares,

$u^2 - v^2 = (u + v)(u - v)$, letting $u = \sqrt{2}x$ and $v = \sqrt{3}y$.

    Thus, we obtain: $(\sqrt{2}x + \sqrt{3}y)(\sqrt{2}x - \sqrt{3}y)$

Factor the expression $16a^2 - 4(b - c)^2$.

<u>Solution:</u> $16 = 4^2$, thus $16a^2 = 4^2a^2$. Since $a^x b^x = (ab)^x$, $16a^2 = 4^2a^2 = (4a)^2$. Similarly $4 = 2^2$, thus $4(b-c)^2 = 2^2(b-c)^2 = [2(b-c)]^2$. Hence $16a^2 - 4(b-c)^2 = (4a)^2 - [2(b-c)]^2$. We are now dealing with the difference of two squares. Applying the formula for the difference of two squares, $x^2 - y^2 = (x+y)(x-y)$, and replacing x by 4a and y by 2(b-c) we obtain:

$$(4a)^2 - [2(b-c)]^2 = [4a + 2(b-c)][4a - 2(b-c)]$$

$$= (4a + 2b - 2c)(4a - 2b + 2c).$$

Therefore, $16a^2 - 4(b-c)^2 = (4a + 2b - 2c)(4a - 2b + 2c)$.

Factor $x^2 - y^2$.

<u>Solution:</u> Add and subtract xy from the given expression. Note that this procedure doesn't change the value of the expression because $x^2 - y^2 + xy - xy = x^2 - y^2 + (xy - xy) = x^2 - y^2 + 0 = x^2 - y^2$.

Therefore,
$$x^2 - y^2 = x^2 - y^2 + xy - xy.$$

Also, by the commutative law of addition:

$$x^2 - y^2 = x^2 - y^2 + xy - xy$$
$$= x^2 - y^2 + (xy - xy)$$
$$= x^2 + (xy - xy) - y^2$$

or $x^2 - y^2 = x^2 + xy - xy - y^2$ \qquad (1)

Again, applying the commutative law of addition to the second and third terms of equation (1):

$$x^2 - y^2 = x^2 - xy + xy - y^2 \qquad (2)$$

Factoring x from the first two terms of equation (2) and also factoring y from the last two terms of equation (2):

$$x^2 - y^2 = x(x - y) + y(x - y)$$

By the distributive property:

$$x^2 - y^2 = x(x - y) + y(x - y)$$
$$= (x + y)(x - y)$$

Factor $x^3 - 8$.

Solution: Since $8 = 2^3$, $x^3 - 8 = (x)^3 - (2)^3$. Therefore, $x^3 - 8$ is the difference of two cubes. The formula for the difference of two cubes is:

$$a^3 - b^3 = (a - b)\left(a^2 + ab + b^2\right)$$

Replacing a by x and b by 2;

$$x^3 - 8 = (x)^3 - (2)^3$$
$$= (x - 2)\left[x^2 + (x)(2) + (2)^2\right]$$
$$x^3 - 8 = (x - 2)\left(x^2 + 2x + 4\right)$$

Factor $8a^3 - 27$.

Solution: Note that $8 = (2)^3$, hence $8a^3 = \left(2^3\right)\left(a^3\right) = (2a)^3$
and $27 = (3)^3$

So, $8a^3 - 27 = (2a)^3 - (3)^3$.

Recall the formula for the difference of two cubes:

$$x^3 - y^3 = (x - y)(x^2 + xy + y^2)$$

Substituting 2a for x, and 3 for y:

$$(2a)^3 - (3)^3 = (2a - 3)\left[(2a)^2 + 3(2a) + 3^2\right]$$
$$= (2a - 3)(4a^2 + 6a + 9)$$

Hence, $8a^3 - 27 = (2a - 3)(4a^2 + 6a + 9)$.

Factor $125x^3 + 64y^3$.

Solution: Noting that $125x^3 = 5^3x^3 = (5x)^3$ and

$64y^3 = 4^3y^3 = (4y)^3$, we obtain

$$125x^3 + 64y^3 = (5x)^3 + (4y)^3.$$

Thus we have the sum of two cubes. Applying the formula for the sum of two cubes,

$$a^3 + b^3 = (a+b)\left(a^2 - ab + b^2\right),$$

and replacing a by (5x) and b by (4y) we obtain $(5x)^3 + (4y)^3$

$$= (5x + 4y)\left[(5x)^2 - (5x)(4y) + (4y)^2\right]$$

$$= (5x + 4y)(5^2x^2 - 20xy + 4^2y^2)$$

$$= (5x + 4y)(25x^2 - 20xy + 16y^2).$$

● **PROBLEM 14-14**

Factor: (a) $2x^2 + 2y^2$ (b) $a^3x + b^3x.$

Solution: (a) First we factor out a 2 from this expression. Thus $2x^2 + 2y^2 = 2\left(x^2 + y^2\right)$. $x^2 + y^2$, the sum of two like even powers, cannot be factored. Thus, it is a prime expression. Hence $2x^2 + 2y^2 = 2(x^2 + y^2)$.

(b) First we factor out an x from this expression. Thus, $a^3x + b^3x = (a^3 + b^3)x$. $(a^3 + b^3)$ is the sum of two cubes. Applying the formula for the sum of two cubes: $c^3 + d^3 = (c + d)\left(c^2 - cd + d^2\right)$, replacing c by a and d by b we obtain

$$a^3 + b^3 = (a + b)\left(a^2 - ab + b^2\right).$$

Hence, $a^3x + b^3x = (a + b)\left(a^2 - ab + b^2\right)x.$

● **PROBLEM 14-15**

Factor $a^4 - b^4.$

Solution: Note that $a^4 = (a^2)^2$ and $b^4 = (b^2)^2$; thus

$a^4 - b^4 = (a^2)^2 - (b^2)^2$, the difference of two squares. Thus we apply the formula for the difference of two squares, $x^2 - y^2 = (x + y)(x - y)$, replacing x by a^2 and y by b^2 to obtain:

$$a^4 - b^4 = (a^2)^2 - (b^2)^2 = (a^2 + b^2)(a^2 - b^2).$$

Since $a^2 - b^2$ is also the difference of two squares, we once again apply the above formula to obtain:

$$a^2 - b^2 = (a + b)(a - b).$$

Therefore, $a^4 - b^4 = (a^2 + b^2)(a + b)(a - b)$.

Factor $a^4 - a^2 - 12$ completely.

Solution: We factor a trinomial of degree two in this manner:

$$x^2 + (c + d)x + cd = (x + c)(x + d).$$

In this case $x = (a^2)$

$$a^4 - a^2 - 12 = (a^2)^2 - (a^2) - 12.$$

$$c + d = -1 \qquad c \cdot d = -12.$$

We must find two numbers whose sum is -1 and whose product is -12. The two numbers which satisfy these two conditions are -4 and 3. Thus,

$$a^4 - a^2 - 12 = (a^2)^2 - a^2 - 12$$

$$= (a^2)^2 + (-4 + 3)(a^2) + (-4)(3)$$

$$= a^4 - a^2 - 12.$$

Therefore,

$$a^4 - a^2 - 12 = (a^2 + 3)(a^2 - 4).$$

The first factor on the right does not factor further, but the second factor; $a^2 - 4$, is a difference of two squares. Completion of the factorization gives

$$a^4 - a^2 - 12 = (a^2 + 3)(a + 2)(a - 2).$$

Factor $x^6 - 64$ completely.

Solution: We observe that,

$$x^6 = x^{3 \cdot 2} = \left(x^3\right)^2 \quad \text{and} \quad 64 = 8^2.$$

Thus,

$$x^6 - 64 = \left(x^3\right)^2 - 8^2,$$

the difference of two squares. Applying the formula for the difference of two squares,

$$a^2 - b^2 = (a + b)(a - b)$$

and replacing a by x^3 and b by 8, we obtain,

$$x^6 - 64 = (x^3 + 8)(x^3 - 8).$$

Since ,

$$8 = 2^3, \; x^6 - 64 = (x^3 + 8)(x^3 - 8)$$

$$= (x^3 + 2^3)(x^3 - 2^3).$$

Thus each resulting factor, factors further, as a sum and as a difference of two cubes, respectively. Applying the formulas for the sum and difference of two cubes,

$$(a^3 + b^3) = (a + b)(a^2 - ab + b^2)$$

$$(a^3 - b^3) = (a - b)(a^2 + ab + b^2),$$

and replacing a by x and b by 2, we obtain,

$$x^6 - 64 = (x + 2)(x^2 - 2x + 4)(x - 2)(x^2 + 2x + 4).$$

It is of interest to see what results on factoring $x^6 - 64$ as a difference of two cubes. We get, in this case,

$$x^6 - 64 = (x^2)^3 - 4^3$$

$$= (x^2 - 4)(x^4 + 4x^2 + 16),$$

in which

$$x^2 - 4 = x^2 - 2^2$$

factors as $(x + 2)(x - 2)$. A comparison of the two results shows that $x^4 + 4x^2 + 16$ must be factorable as

$$x^4 + 4x^2 + 16 = (x^2 - 2x + 4)(x^2 + 2x + 4).$$

This may be verified by multiplication, but it is not easy to see directly. Treating

$$x^6 - 64$$

as the difference of two squares is much simpler than thinking of it as the difference of two cubes.

● **PROBLEM 14-18**

Find the LCM of: $x^2 + 2x + 1$, $x^2 - 1$, and $x^2 - 3x + 2$.

<u>Solution:</u> Factor each term.

$$x^2 + 2x + 1 = (x + 1)^2, \; x^2 - 1 = (x - 1)(x + 1),$$

$$x^2 - 3x + 2 = (x - 1)(x - 2)$$

As with integers, the LCM must contain all of the prime factors as a product, and each prime factor must contain the largest exponent it has in any of the factored forms. Each factor is used only once, regardless of the number of times it appears. Therefore,

$$\text{LCM} = (x + 1)^2 (x - 1)(x - 2)$$

● **PROBLEM** 14-19

Find the LCM of: $(x - 1)^2$, $(1 - x)^3$, $1 - x^3$.

<u>Solution:</u> Factor each polynomial completely. Notice in the factoring of the second and the third polynomials that -1 may be factored from the expressions first so that the terms of highest degree in the factors will have positive coefficients.

$$(x - 1)^2 = (x - 1)^2$$

$$(1 - x)^3 = [-1(x - 1)]^3 = (-1)^3(x - 1)^3 = -(x - 1)^3$$

$$1 - x^3 = (-1)\left(x^3 - 1\right) = -(x - 1)(x^2 + x + 1).$$

$(x^3 - 1$ is the difference of two cubes.)

Each of the factors of these expressions appears in the product known as the LCM. Each factor is raised to the highest power to which it appears in any one of the expressions. Therefore the

$$\text{LCM} = (x - 1)^3 \left(x^2 + x + 1\right).$$

FRACTIONAL

● **PROBLEM** 14-20

Simplify $\dfrac{x^2 - y^2}{x + y}$.

<u>Solution:</u> $x^2 - y^2$ is the difference of two squares. Applying the formula for the difference of two squares, $a^2 - b^2$

$= (a + b)(a - b)$, with $x = a$ and $y = b$,

$$\frac{x^2 - y^2}{x + y} = \frac{(x + y)(x - y)}{x + y} = x - y .$$

● **PROBLEM** 14-21

Perform the indicated operation

$$\frac{x^2 - y^2}{2x} \cdot \frac{4x^2}{x + y}$$

Solution: $x^2 - y^2$ is the difference of two squares. Applying the formula for the difference of two squares

$$a^2 - b^2 = (a+b)(a -b)$$
$$x^2 - y^2 = (x+y)(x-y)$$

Thus
$$\frac{x^2 - y^2}{2x} \cdot \frac{4x^2}{x + y} = \frac{(x + y)(x - y)}{2x} \cdot \frac{4x^2}{x + y}$$

$$= \frac{(x+y)(x-y)\left(4x^2\right)}{(2x)(x+y)}$$

Since $4x^2 = (2x)(2x)$,

$$= \frac{(2x)(2x)(x+y)(x-y)}{(2x)(x+y)}$$

$$= 2x(x - y)$$

● **PROBLEM** 14-22

Combine the following fractions $\dfrac{x}{x^2 - y^2} + \dfrac{2}{y - x} - 5$.

Solution: Note that the denominator $x^2 - y^2$ is the difference of two squares. Using the formula for the difference of two squares

$$a^2 - b^2 = (a + b)(a - b) ,$$

factor $x^2 - y^2$ into $(x + y)(x - y)$. Next observe that $-(y-x) = -y+x = x-y$. Then multiplying numerator and denominator of

$$\left(\frac{2}{y - x}\right) \text{ by } -1,$$

$$\frac{-1}{-1}\left(\frac{2}{y - x}\right) = \frac{-2}{x - y} .$$

Therefore,

$$\frac{x}{x^2 - y^2} + \frac{2}{y - x} - 5 = \frac{x}{(x+y)(x-y)} + \frac{-2}{x - y} - \frac{5}{1}$$

Thus the terms $(x+y),(x-y)$, and 1 appear in our denominators. In order to combine fractions, transform them into equivalent fractions with a common denominator. Using $(x+y)(x-y)$ as our least common denominator, LCD, multiply each term by the necessary factor to yield a denominator of $(x+y)(x-y)$:

$$\frac{x}{x^2 - y^2} + \frac{2}{y - x} - 5 = \frac{x}{(x+y)(x-y)} + \left(\frac{x+y}{x+y}\right)\left(\frac{-2}{x-y}\right) + \frac{(x+y)(x-y)}{(x+y)(x-y)}\left(\frac{-5}{1}\right)$$

$$= \frac{x}{(x+y)(x-y)} + \frac{-2x - 2y}{(x+y)(x-y)} + \frac{-5(x^2 - y^2)}{(x+y)(x-y)}$$

$$= \frac{x - 2x - 2y - 5x^2 + 5y^2}{(x+y)(x-y)}$$

$$= \frac{-x - 2y - 5x^2 + 5y^2}{(x+y)(x-y)}$$

$$= \frac{-x - 2y - 5x^2 + 5y^2}{x^2 - y^2}$$

● PROBLEM 14-23

Reduce $\dfrac{3x - 6}{x^2 - 4}$ to lowest terms.

Solution: Factor the expression in both the numerator and denominator. In the numerator we factor 3 from both terms, and observing that the denominator is the difference of two squares, $x^2 - 2^2$, we obtain:

$$\frac{3x - 6}{x^2 - 4} = \frac{3(x - 2)}{(x - 2)(x + 2)}$$

$$= \frac{3}{x + 2}$$

The numerator and denominator were divided by $x - 2$.

● PROBLEM 14-24

Simplify $\dfrac{4x + 10}{4x^2 + 20x + 25}$.

Solution: First we factor a 2 from the numerator, thus

$$\frac{4x + 10}{4x^2 + 20x + 25} \qquad \frac{2(2x + 5)}{4x^2 + 20x + 25}.$$

Factoring the denominator, $= \dfrac{2(2x + 5)}{(2x + 5)(2x + 5)} = \dfrac{2}{2x + 5}$.
Since the factor $(2x + 5)$ appears in the denominator it may not equal zero, as division by zero is not defined. Thus

$$2x + 5 \neq 0$$

$$2x \neq -5$$

$$x \neq \frac{-5}{2}.$$

Therefore, $\dfrac{4x + 10}{4x^2 + 20x + 25} = \dfrac{2}{2x + 5}$, $x \neq \dfrac{-5}{2}$.

● **PROBLEM 14-25**

Reduce $\dfrac{4x - 20}{50 - 2x^2}$ to lowest terms.

<u>Solution:</u> Factor the numerator and the denominator:

$$\frac{4x - 20}{50 - 2x^2} = \frac{4(x - 5)}{2(25 - x^2)} = \frac{4(x - 5)}{2(5 - x)(5 + x)}$$

Multiply the numerator and denominator by (-1) to reverse the sign of the factor $(5 - x)$ in the denominator. Then divide both the numerator and denominator by $2(x - 5)$.

$$\frac{(-1)[4(x - 5)]}{(-1)[2(5 - x)(5 + x)]} = \frac{-4(x - 5)}{2(x - 5)(5 + x)}$$

Dividing, we obtain:

$$-\frac{2}{x + 5} \quad .$$

● **PROBLEM 14-26**

Simplify $\dfrac{a^2 - 3ab + 2b^2}{2b^2 + ab - a^2}$.

<u>Solution:</u> Factoring the numerator and denominator of the given fraction we obtain:

$$\frac{a^2 - 3ab + 2b^2}{2b^2 + ab - a^2} = \frac{(a - 2b)(a - b)}{(2b - a)(b + a)}$$

If we negate both factors in the numerator, we do not change the fraction's value (because negating both factors gives us -1 multiplied by -1, which equals 1; and multiplication by 1 does not change the expression's value). Thus, we have:

$$\frac{[-(a - 2b)][-(a - b)]}{(2b - a)(b + a)} = \frac{(2b - a)(b - a)}{(2b - a)(b + a)} = \frac{b - a}{b + a},$$

since $\dfrac{2b - a}{2b - a} = 1$.

● **PROBLEM 14-27**

Reduce $\dfrac{x^2 - 5x + 4}{x^2 - 7x + 12}$ to lowest terms.

<u>Solution:</u> Factor the expressions in both the numerator and denominator and cancel like terms.

$$\frac{x^2 - 5x + 4}{x^2 - 7x + 12} = \frac{(x - 1)(x - 4)}{(x - 3)(x - 4)}$$

$$= \frac{x - 1}{x - 3}$$

The numerator and the denominator were both divided by x - 4.

● **PROBLEM 14-28**

Reduce to lowest form: $\dfrac{a^3 - 8b^3}{2a^2 - 8b^2}$.

<u>Solution:</u> Factor the numerator and denominator as completely as possible.
The numerator, $a^3 - 8b^3 = a^3 - (2b)^3$, is the difference of two cubes. Apply the following formula:

$$\left(x^3 - y^3\right) = (x - y)\left(x^2 + xy + y^3\right)$$

Replacing x by a and y by 2b, we obtain:

$$\left(a^3 - 8b^3\right) = \left[a^3 - (2b)^3\right] = \left(a - (2b)\right)\left(a^2 + 2ab + 4b^2\right)$$

For the denominator, factor out the highest common factor 2.

$$2a^2 - 8b^2 = 2\left(a^2 - 4b^2\right)$$

where $a^2 - 4b^2$ is the difference of two squares. Recall the formula for the difference of two squares: $x^2 - y^2 = (x - y)(x + y)$. Substitute a for x and 2b for y to obtain:

$$\left(2a^2 - 8b^2\right) = 2\left(a^2 - 4b^2\right) = 2(a - 2b)(a + 2b)$$

Then, writing the factored forms and cancelling:

$$\frac{a^3 - 8b^3}{2a^2 - 8b^2} = \frac{\cancel{(a - 2b)}\left(a^2 + 2ab + 4b^2\right)}{2(a + 2b)\cancel{(a - 2b)}} = \frac{a^2 + 2ab + 4b^2}{2(a + 2b)}$$

CHAPTER 15

SOLVING QUADRATIC
EQUATIONS BY FACTORING

EQUATIONS WITHOUT RADICALS

● PROBLEM 15-1

Show that $x^2 + 2x + 5 = 20$ is a conditional equation.

Solution: A conditional equation is an equation for which there exists at least one value which may be substituted for the variable that makes the equation false, but is true for other values. It is sufficient to exhibit one replacement for x that makes the equation true and one that makes it false.

Let x = 3:
$$(3)^2 + 2(3) + 5 \overset{?}{=} 20$$
$$9 + 6 + 5 \overset{?}{=} 20$$
$$20 = 20$$

Let x = -4:
$$(-4)^2 + (-4) + 5 \overset{?}{=} 20$$
$$16 - 8 + 5 \overset{?}{=} 20$$
$$13 \neq 20$$

When x = -4, this value of x makes the equation false. For x = 3, the equation is **true**. Therefore, $x^2 + 2x + 5 = 20$ is a conditional equation.

Notice that we have not solved the equation in this example. An equation is solved when it's solution set is completely known.

Solve the equation $(3x - 7)(x + 2) = 0$.

Solution: When a given product of two numbers that are equal to zero, $ab = 0$, either a must equal zero or b must equal zero (or both equal zero). So if $(3x - 7)(x + 2) = 0$, then $(3x - 7) = 0$ or $(x + 2) = 0$.

$3x - 7 = 0$ | $x + 2 = 0$

Add 7 to both sides: | Subtract 2 from both sides:

$3x = 7$ |

Divide both sides by 3: |

$x = \frac{7}{3}$ | $x = -2$

Hence $x = \frac{7}{3}$ or $x = -2$, and our solution set is $\left\{\frac{7}{3}, -2\right\}$.

Solve the equation $3x^2 + 5x = 0$.

Solution: Because division by zero is impossible, we must not divide by x, since x might be equal to zero. Instead of dividing by x we factor x from the left side of the equation to obtain:

$$x(3x + 5) = 0.$$

Whenever we have a situation where $ab = 0$ (the product of two or more numbers equal to zero) either $a = 0$ or $b = 0$. Therefore $x = 0$, or $3x + 5 = 0$. Subtract 5 from each side of the second equation to obtain:

$$3x = -5$$

Divide both sides by 3 to obtain $x = -\frac{5}{3}$. The two solutions of the given equation are $x = 0$ and $x = -\frac{5}{3}$.

To check the validity of the two solutions we substitute them into the given equation. Thus, when $x = 0$

$$3x^2 + 5x = 0$$

$$3(0)^2 + 5(0) = 0$$

$$0 = 0$$

when $x = -\dfrac{5}{3}$

$$3x^2 + 5x = 0$$

$$3\left(-\dfrac{5}{3}\right)^2 + 5\left(-\dfrac{5}{3}\right) = 0$$

$$3\left(\dfrac{25}{9}\right) + 5\left(-\dfrac{5}{3}\right) = 0$$

$$\dfrac{25}{3} - \dfrac{25}{3} = 0$$

$$0 = 0$$

● **PROBLEM 15-4**

Solve the equation $x^2 + 8x + 15 = 0$.

<u>Solution:</u> Since $(x + a)(x + b) = x^2 + bx + ax + ab$ $= x^2 + (a + b)x + ab$, we may factor the given equation, $0 = x^2 + 8x + 15$, replacing a + b by 8 and ab by 15. Thus,

$$a + b = 8, \quad \text{and}$$

$$ab = 15.$$

We want the two numbers a and b whose sum is 8 and whose product is 15. We check all pairs of numbers whose product is 15:

(a) $1 \cdot 15 = 15$; thus a = 1, b = 15 and ab = 15.

1 + 15 = 16, therefore we reject these values because a + b ≠ 8.

(b) $3 \cdot 5 = 15$; thus a = 3, b = 5, and ab = 15.

3 + 5 = 8. Therefore a + b = 8, and we accept these values.

Hence $x^2 + 8x + 15 = 0$ is equivalent to

$$0 = x^2 + (3 + 5)x + 3 \cdot 5 = (x + 3)(x + 5)$$

Hence,   x + 5 = 0   or x + 3 = 0

since the product of these two numbers is zero, one of the numbers must be zero. Hence, x = - 5, or x = - 3, and

127

the solution set is X = {- 5, - 3}.

The student should note that x = - 5 or x = - 3. We are certainly not making the statement, that x = - 5, and x = - 3. Also, the student should check that both these numbers do actually satisfy the given equations and hence are solutions.

Check: Replacing x by (- 5) in the original equation:

$$x^2 + 8x + 15 = 0$$

$$(- 5)^2 + 8(- 5) + 15 = 0$$

$$25 - 40 + 15 = 0$$

$$- 15 + 15 = 0$$

$$0 = 0$$

Replacing x by (- 3) in the original equation:

$$x^2 + 8x + 15 = 0$$

$$(- 3)^2 + 8(- 3) + 15 = 0$$

$$9 - 24 + 15 = 0$$

$$- 15 + 15 = 0$$

$$0 = 0.$$

● PROBLEM 15-5

Solve: $x^2 - 5x - 14 = 0$.

Solution: To find the roots of this quadratic, we factor it (put it in the form (x + a)(x + b) = 0).

Note that $(x + a)(x + b) = x^2 + (a + b)x + ab$

Thus, in our quadratic, $x^2 + (- 5)x + (- 14)$,

$$a + b = - 5 \qquad (1)$$

and
$$ab = - 14 \qquad (2)$$

That is, we want the two numbers, a and b, whose sum is (- 5), and whose product is (- 14).

To find these numbers, we can check the set of numbers whose product is (- 14):

(a) (- 14) × (1) = - 14, therefore equation (2) is satisfied, now check these values in equation (1):

(− 14) + (1) = − 13 ≠ − 5   therefore we reject these values.

(b) (− 7) × (2) = − 14, therefore equation (2) is satisfied, now check these values in equation (1):

(− 7) + 2 = − 5 hence both equations are satisfied and we conclude

$$a = − 7 \quad \text{and } b = 2.$$

Thus $x^2 − 5x − 14 = x^2 + (− 7 + 2)x + (− 7)(2)$

$$= \left[x + (− 7)\right]\left[x + 2\right]$$

$$= (x − 7)(x + 2) = 0$$

By the fundamental principle, if the product of two numbers $yz = 0$, then either $y = 0$ or $z = 0$; hence if

$$(x − 7)(x + 2) = 0$$

either x − 7 = 0   or   x + 2 = 0

add 7 to both sides | subtract 2 from both sides

x = 7   or   x = − 2

This proves that if the equation has roots, they must be either 7 or − 2. We check these values by substituting in the given equation:

If x = 7, then $x^2 − 5x − 14 = (7)^2 − 5(7) − 14$

$$= 49 − 35 − 14$$

$$= 49 − 49$$

$$= 0$$

If x = − 2, then $x^2 − 5x − 14 = (− 2)^2 − 5(− 2) − 14$

$$= 4 + 10 − 14$$

$$= 14 − 14$$

$$= 0$$

We may now conclude that the solution to our equation is x = 7 or x = − 2.

● **PROBLEM 15-6**

Solve and check the roots of the equation

$$2x^2 − 3x + 1 = 0$$

<u>Solution:</u> Factor the given equation into a product of two polynomials: therefore: $(2x - 1)(x - 1) = 0$.

When $ab = 0$, either $a = 0$ or $b = 0$ where a and b are real numbers. Therefore, either $2x - 1 = 0$ or $x - 1 = 0$.

Therefore, either $x = \frac{1}{2}$ or $x = 1$.

Hence, the roots to the given equation are:

$x = \frac{1}{2}$ and $x = 1$.

To check these roots, substitute $x = \frac{1}{2}$ in the given equation:

$$2\left(\frac{1}{2}\right)^2 - 3\left(\frac{1}{2}\right) + 1 = 0$$

$$2\left(\frac{1}{4}\right) - \frac{3}{2} + 1 = 0$$

$$\frac{1}{2} - \frac{3}{2} + 1 = 0$$

$$- 1 + 1 = 0$$

$$0 = 0$$

Now, substitute $x = 1$ in the given equation:

$$2(1)^2 - 3(1) + 1 = 0$$

$$2 - 3 + 1 = 0$$

$$- 1 + 1 = 0$$

$$0 = 0$$

● **PROBLEM 15-7**

Solve the following for x:

(a) $x^2 - 3x = 0$

(b) $6x^2 + 5x - 4 = 0$

<u>Solution:</u> (a) Factor the common factor x from the left side of the given equation:

$$x^2 - 3x = x(x - 3)$$

Since $x^2 - 3x = 0$,

$$x(x - 3) = 0. \qquad\qquad (1)$$

Whenever a product $ab = 0$, where a and b are any two numbers, either $a = 0$ or $b = 0$. Then, equation (1) becomes,

$$x = 0 \text{ or } x - 3 = 0$$

$$x = 3$$

Hence, the solution set is: $\{0, 3\}$.

      (b) Factor the left side of the given equation into a product of two polynomials:

$$6x^2 + 5x - 4 = (3x + 4)(2x - 1)$$

Since $6x^2 + 5x - 4 = 0$,

$$(3x + 4)(2x - 1) = 0$$

Thus,

$3x + 4 = 0$	or	$2x - 1 = 0$
$3x = -4$	or	$2x = 1$
$x = \dfrac{-4}{3}$	or	$x = \dfrac{1}{2}$

Hence, the solution set is: $\left\{-\dfrac{4}{3}, \dfrac{1}{2}\right\}$.

● PROBLEM 15-8

Solve the equation $5y^2 = 6y$ by the factoring method.

Solution: Add $(-6y)$ to both members of the given equation
$$5y^2 - 6y = 0$$

Factor y from the left member, $y(5y - 6) = 0$.

When the product of two numbers $ab = 0$ either $a = 0$, or $b = 0$. Thus, either $y = 0$ or $(5y - 6) = 0$.

Solving for y in the second equation, $5y - 6 = 0$:

add -6 to both sides, $\qquad\qquad\qquad\qquad\qquad 5y = 6$

divide by 5, $\qquad\qquad\qquad\qquad\qquad\qquad\qquad y = 6/5$.

Therefore, the solution set is $\{0, 6/5\}$.

Check: To check these values we replace y by 0 and

131

then by 6/5 in the original equation:

(a) when y = 0 $5y^2 = 6y$

$$5(0)^2 = 6(0)$$

$$0 = 0$$

(b) when $y = \frac{6}{5}$ $5\left(\frac{6}{5}\right)^2 = 6\left(\frac{6}{5}\right)$

$$5\left(\frac{36}{25}\right) = \frac{36}{5}$$

$$\frac{36}{5} = \frac{36}{5}$$

Thus, the solution set of the given equation is indeed {0, 6/5}.

● **PROBLEM** 15-9

Solve $4x^2 = 8x$.

<u>Solution:</u> The temptation to divide both sides by 4x to arrive at: x = 2, should be avoided, for if x = 0 we are performing an operation which is undefined. Although 2 actually is a root, there happens to be another root, which is lost in this process.

When solving equations, avoid multiplying or dividing by anything but nonzero numbers. In this case, there is no harm in dividing both sides by the number 4:

$$x^2 = 2x$$

We then add -2x to both sides, to arrive at:

$$x^2 - 2x = 0$$

Factoring: $x(x-2) = 0$

Whenever the product of two numbers ab = 0, either a = 0 or b = 0. Therefore,

$$x = 0 \text{ or } x - 2 = 0,$$

and

$$x = 0 \text{ or } x = 2.$$

Check: To verify that the roots of this equation are x = 0 and x = 2, we replace x by each value in the original equation. Replacing x by 0 in $4x^2 = 8x$:

$$4(0)^2 = 8(0)$$

$$0 = 0$$

Replacing x by 2:

$$4(2)^2 = 8(2)$$
$$4(4) = 16$$
$$16 = 16$$

Thus, the roots of the equation are 0 and 2, and the solution set is

$$\{0,2\} .$$

Solve the equation $6x^2 = 2 - x$.

Solution: Write the equation in standard quadratic form by adding $x - 2$ to both sides of the equation. Then we have $6x^2 + x - 2 = 0$. In factored form this becomes $(3x + 2)(2x - 1) = 0$. The values of x that make this product $= 0$ satisfy

$$3x + 2 = 0 \quad \text{or} \quad 2x - 1 = 0$$
$$3x = -2 \quad \text{or} \quad 2x = 1$$
$$x = -\tfrac{2}{3} \quad \text{or} \quad x = \tfrac{1}{2}$$

Check:

for $x = -\tfrac{2}{3}$

$$6\left(-\tfrac{2}{3}\right)^2 \overset{?}{=} 2 - \left(-\tfrac{2}{3}\right)$$

$$6\left(\tfrac{4}{9}\right) \overset{?}{=} \tfrac{18}{9} - \left(-\tfrac{6}{9}\right)$$

$$\tfrac{24}{9} = \tfrac{24}{9}$$

for $x = \tfrac{1}{2}$

$$6\left(\tfrac{1}{2}\right)^2 \overset{?}{=} 2 - \left(\tfrac{1}{2}\right)$$

$$6\left(\tfrac{1}{4}\right) \overset{?}{=} \tfrac{8}{4} - \left(\tfrac{2}{4}\right)$$

$$\tfrac{6}{4} = \tfrac{6}{4}$$

Therefore the solution set is $\left\{-\tfrac{2}{3}, \tfrac{1}{2}\right\}$.

Solve the equation $2x^2 = x + 6$ by the factoring method.

Solution:

$$2x^2 = x + 6 \quad \text{given equation}$$

$$2x^2 - x - 6 = 0 \quad \text{adding } -x - 6 \text{ to each member}$$

$$(2x + 3)(x - 2) = 0 \quad \text{factoring left member}$$

Whenever the product of 2 numbers $ab = 0$ either $a = 0$ or $b = 0$. Thus either $2x + 3 = 0$ or $x - 2 = 0$

$$2x + 3 = 0 \quad \text{setting the first factor equal to 0}$$

$$2x = -3$$

$$x = -\frac{3}{2} \quad \text{solving for } x$$

$$x - 2 = 0 \quad \text{setting second factor equal to 0}$$

$$x = 2 \quad \text{solving for } x$$

Consequently the solution set is $\left\{-\frac{3}{2}, 2\right\}$.

The solution set can be verified by replacing x in the given equation by each element in the set.

Check:

$$x = -\frac{3}{2} \qquad\qquad\qquad x = 2$$

$$2x^2 = x + 6 \qquad\qquad\qquad 2x^2 = x + 6$$

$$2\left(\frac{-3}{2}\right)^2 = \frac{-3}{2} + 6 \qquad\qquad 2(2)^2 = 2 + 6$$

$$2\left(\frac{9}{4}\right) = \frac{-3}{2} + \frac{12}{2} \qquad\qquad 2 \cdot 4 = 2 + 6$$

$$\frac{9}{2} = \frac{9}{2} \checkmark \qquad\qquad\qquad 8 = 8 \checkmark$$

● **PROBLEM** 15-12

Solve the equation $4x^2 = 100$.

<u>Solution:</u> To solve this equation we must find the values for x which satisfy the equation. To do this we proceed as follows: Subtract 100 from both sides of the given equation. Thus,

$$4x^2 - 100 = 100 - 100$$

$$4x^2 - 100 = 0. \qquad\qquad (1)$$

Now, factor 4 from the left side of Equation (1):

$$4(x^2 - 25) = 0.$$

Next, factor $x^2 - 25$ into a product of two polynomials. To do this, notice that $x^2 - 25$ is the difference between two squares, that is, $x^2 - 5^2$. Thus, the two factors are $(x - 5)(x + 5)$. Thus, we have:

$$4(x - 5)(x + 5) = 0.$$

Dividing both sides of this equation by 4, we obtain:

$$\frac{4(x - 5)(x + 5)}{4} = \frac{0}{4}.$$

Therefore, $(x - 5)(x + 5) = 0$.

When ab = 0, where a and b are any numbers, either a = 0 or b = 0. Therefore, either x - 5 = 0, or x + 5 = 0. To solve for x in the first equation add 5 to both sides of x - 5 = 0. Thus,

$$x - 5 + 5 = 0 + 5$$

$$x = 5.$$

To solve for x in the second equation subtract 5 from both sides of x + 5 = 0. Thus,

$$x + 5 - 5 = 0 - 5$$

$$x = -5.$$

Therefore, the solution of the given equation is x = 5, x = -5.

To check these two solutions, do the following:

Substituting x = 5 in the given equation, we find:

$$4(5)^2 = 100$$

$$100 = 100.$$

Substituting x = -5 in the given equation, we find:

$$4(-5)^2 = 100$$

$$100 = 100.$$

Thus, the obtained values of x are valid.

● **PROBLEM 15-13**

Solve $\dfrac{x}{x-2} + \dfrac{x-1}{2} = x + 1.$

<u>Solution:</u> First eliminate the fractions to facilitate solution. This is done by multiplying both sides of the equation by the Least Common Denominator, LCD. The LCD is obtained by multiplying the denominators of every fraction: LCD = 2(x - 2); and multiplying each side by this, the equation becomes:

$$2(x - 2)\left[\frac{x}{x-2} + \frac{x-1}{2}\right] = (x + 1)2(x - 2)$$

$$2x + (x - 1)(x - 2) = 2(x +1)(x - 2)$$

$$2x + x^2 - 3x + 2 = 2x^2 - 2x - 4$$

$$x^2 - x - 6 = 0$$

This can be solved by factoring and setting each factor equal to zero.

$$(x - 3)(x + 2) = 0$$

$$\begin{array}{c|c} x - 3 - 0 & x + 2 - 0 \\ x = 3 & x = -2 \end{array}$$

135

Since both of these solutions are admissible values of x, they both should satisfy the original equation.

Check for x = 3:

$$\frac{3}{1} + \frac{2}{2} = 3 + 1$$

$$3 + 1 = 3 + 1$$

Check for x = - 2:

$$\frac{-2}{-4} + \frac{-3}{2} = -2 + 1$$

$$\frac{1}{2} + \frac{-3}{2} = -1$$

$$-1 = -1$$

EQUATIONS WITH RADICALS

● **PROBLEM** 15-14

Solve the equation $\sqrt{2x^2 - 9} = x$.

Solution: Squaring both sides, we have

$$2x^2 - 9 = x^2$$

$$x^2 = 9$$

$$x = 3 \quad \text{or} \quad x = -3$$

Both 3 and -3 will satisfy the equation $2x^2 - 9 = x^2$ since $2(3)^2 - 9 = 9 = (3)^2$ and $2(-3)^2 - 9 = 9 = (-3)^2$. However, -3 does not satisfy the original equation since $\sqrt{2(-3)^2 - 9} = \sqrt{9} = 3 \neq -3$. An extraneous root was introduced by squaring. Thus the solution set is $\{3\}$.

● **PROBLEM** 15-15

Solve $3\sqrt{x} + 4 = x$.

Solution: Adding (-4) to both sides of the given equation,

$$3\sqrt{x} = x - 4.$$

Squaring both sides

$$(3\sqrt{x})^2 = (x - 4)^2$$

$$3^2(\sqrt{x})^2 = (x - 4)(x - 4)$$

Since $(\sqrt{a})^2 = \sqrt{a} \cdot \sqrt{a} = \sqrt{a \cdot a} = \sqrt{a^2} = a$, $(\sqrt{x})^2 = x$, and we obtain:

$$9x = (x - 4)(x - 4)$$

$$9x = x^2 - 8x + 16$$

Adding $(-9x)$ to both sides,

$$x^2 - 17x + 16 = 0$$

Factoring, $(x - 1)(x - 16) = 0$

Whenever the product of two numbers $ab = 0$, either $a = 0$ or $b = 0$. Thus

$$x - 1 = 0 \quad \text{or} \quad x - 16 = 0$$
$$x = 1 \quad \text{or} \quad x = 16$$

Hence, the possible roots are 1 and 16.

Check, replacing x by 1:

$$3\sqrt{1} + 4 = 1,$$

$$3(1) + 4 = 7 = 1, \text{ which is false.}$$

Hence 1 is an extraneous root.

Check, replacing x by 16:

$$3\sqrt{16} + 4 = 16,$$

$$3(4) + 4 = 12 + 4 = 16, \text{ which is true.}$$

Therefore, the only root of the given equation is 16.

● **PROBLEM 15-16**

Solve the equation $\sqrt{x^2 - 3x} = 2x - 6$.

Solution: Remove the radical by squaring both sides of the equation, and obtain:

$$\sqrt{x^2 - 3x})^2 = (2x - 6)^2 \quad \text{or}$$

$$x^2 - 3x = 4x^2 - 24x + 36$$

Writing in standard form, move every term to one side of the equation.

$$3x^2 - 21x + 36 = 0$$

Dividing all terms by 3, and factoring,

$$\frac{3x^2}{3} - \frac{21x}{3} + \frac{36}{3} = \frac{0}{3}$$

$$x^2 - 7x + 12 = 0$$

$$(x - 3)(x - 4) = 0$$

The roots are: $x = 3$, $x = 4$.

Check: Substituting x = 3 in the original equation

$$\sqrt{9 - 9} = 6 - 6$$

$$0 = 0$$

Substituting x = 4 in the original equation

$$\sqrt{4} = 8 - 6$$

$$2 = 2.$$

Observe that both x = 3 and x = 4 satisfy the original equation, and there are no extraneous roots.

● **PROBLEM** 15-17

Solve the equation $\sqrt{x + 7} + x = 13$.

Solution: Subtract x from both sides of the equation which gives $\sqrt{x + 7} = 13 - x$. Then square both sides, obtaining

$$x + 7 = (13 - x)^2 = 169 - 26x + x^2,$$

Since we have just shown $169 - 26x + x^2 = x + 7$, we may subtract x + 7 from both members to obtain:

$$169 - 7 - 26x - x + x^2 = (x + 7) - (x + 7)$$

Thus, $x^2 - 27x + 162 = 0$

Factor to obtain, $(x - 9)(x - 18) = 0$.

When we have a product, ab = 0, either a = 0 or b = 0; thus with $(x - 9)(x - 18) = 0$, either x - 9 = 0 or x - 18 = 0.

Thus, x = 9 or x = 18.

Checking the value x = 9 in the original equation, we find

$$\sqrt{9 + 7} + 9 = 13$$

$$\sqrt{16} + 9 = 13$$

$$4 + 9 = 13$$

$$13 = 13$$

and x = 9 is seen to be a root. However, if we try to check x = 18, we find

$$\sqrt{18 + 7} + 18 \neq 13$$

138

Since $\sqrt{25} + 18 \neq 13$

$5 + 18 \neq 13$

$23 \neq 13;$

so that x = 18 is not a root of the original equation. Hence, there is only one solution of the problem: x = 9.

● PROBLEM 15-18

Find the solution set of the equation $\sqrt{x + 7} = 2x - 1$.

__Solution:__ Assume that there is a number x such that $\sqrt{x + 7} = 2x - 1$. Squaring both sides, we have

$$(\sqrt{x + 7})^2 = (2x - 1)^2$$

Note $(\sqrt{a})^2 = (a^{\frac{1}{2}})^2 = a^{2/2} = a^1 = a$ thus $(\sqrt{x + 7})^2 = x + 7$.

Replacing $(\sqrt{x + 7})^2$ by x + 7 we obtain

$$x + 7 = (2x - 1)(2x - 1)$$

$$x + 7 = 4x^2 - 4x + 1$$

Adding $-(x + 7)$ to both members,

$$0 = 4x^2 - 4x + 1 - (x + 7)$$

$$4x^2 - 4x + 1 - x - 7 = 0$$

$$4x^2 - 5x - 6 = 0$$

Thus factoring

$$4x^2 - 5x - 6 = (4x + 3)(x - 2) = 0$$

Whenever a product of two numbers ab = 0 either a = 0 or b = 0, thus either 4x + 3 = 0 or x - 2 = 0 and

$$x = \frac{-3}{4} \quad \text{or} \quad x = 2$$

Note that at this point we have not proved that either x = 2 or x = $-\frac{3}{4}$ is a solution of our equation, but simply that if there is any solution it must be either 2 or $-\frac{3}{4}$. Thus we must check our values by substituting them into our original equation. Replacing x by 2 in $\sqrt{x + 7} = 2x - 1$ we obtain

$$\sqrt{2 + 7} = 2(2) - 1$$

$$\sqrt{9} = 4 - 1$$

$$3 = 3.$$

So 2 is indeed a solution of our equation. On the other hand, $-\frac{3}{4}$ is not a solution since

$$\sqrt{-\frac{3}{4} + 7} = 2(-\frac{3}{4}) - 1$$

$$\sqrt{6\frac{1}{4}} = \frac{-6}{4} - 1$$

$$\sqrt{\frac{25}{4}} = \frac{-6}{4} - \frac{4}{4}$$

$$\frac{\sqrt{25}}{\sqrt{4}} = \frac{-10}{4}$$

139

$$\frac{5}{2} \neq \frac{-10}{4}$$

Thus the solution set is $\{2\}$.

A number such as $-\frac{3}{4}$ obtained in this way is sometimes called an extraneous root — a term we prefer not to use since it implies that we do have a root of some kind or another.

Note also that if the equation had been given in the form

$$\sqrt{x + 7} + 1 = 2x$$

and had we **squared both sides, we would have obtained**

$$x + 7 + 2\sqrt{x + 7} + 1 = 4x^2$$

and would not have eliminated the radical. For this reason we always "isolate" a radical on one side of the equation before squaring.

● **PROBLEM** 15-19

Solve the equation

$$\sqrt{x^2 - 3x + 27} = 2x + 3 .$$

Solution: Squaring both members,

$$\left(\sqrt{x^2 - 3x + 27}\right)^2 = (2x + 3)^2 \qquad (1)$$

Since

$$\left(\sqrt{a}\right)^2 = \sqrt{a}\sqrt{a} = \sqrt{a \cdot a} = \sqrt{a^2} = a,$$

$$\left(\sqrt{x^2 - 3x + 27}\right)^2 = x^2 - 3x + 27.$$

Thus equation (1) becomes:

$$x^2 - 3x + 27 = (2x + 3)(2x + 3)$$

$$x^2 - 3x + 27 = 4x^2 + 12x + 9$$

Adding $-(x^2 - 3x + 27)$ to both members,

$$x^2 - 3x + 27 - (x^2 - 3x + 27) = 4x^2 + 12x + 9 - (x^2 - 3x + 27)$$

$$0 = 4x^2 + 12x + 9 - x^2 + 3x - 27$$

$$4x^2 - x^2 + 12x + 3x + 9 - 27 = 0$$

$$3x^2 + 15x - 18 = 0$$

Dividing both members by 3, $x^2 + 5x - 6 = 0$

$$(x + 6)(x - 1) = 0;$$

Whenever the product of two numbers $ab = 0$, either $a = 0$, or $b = 0$. Thus

$$x + 6 = 0 \quad \text{or} \quad x - 1 = 0$$

and

$$x = -6 \quad \text{or} \quad x = 1$$

Before we can conclude that the roots to this equation are -6 and 1 we must perform the following check: Replacing x by -6 in the original equation,

$$\sqrt{x^2 - 3x + 27} = 2x + 3$$

140

$$\sqrt{(-6)^2 - 3(-6) + 27} \overset{?}{=} 2(-6) + 3$$

$$\sqrt{36 + 18 + 27} \overset{?}{=} -12 + 3$$

$$\sqrt{81} \neq -9$$

Since substitution of (-6) for x results in a statement which isn't true, $\sqrt{81} = +9$ not -9 (unless the negative square root is indicated), (-6) is not part of our solution. (-6) is an extraneous root. Replacing x by 1 in the original equation,

$$\sqrt{x^2 - 3x + 27} = 2x + 3$$

$$\sqrt{1^2 - 3(1) + 27} = 2(1) + 3$$

$$\sqrt{1 - 3 + 27} = 2 + 3$$

$$\sqrt{25} = 5$$

$$5 = 5$$

Thus the solution set is $\{1\}$.

● **PROBLEM** 15-20

Solve $2\sqrt{\dfrac{x}{a}} + 3\sqrt{\dfrac{a}{x}} = \dfrac{b}{a} + \dfrac{6a}{b}$.

<u>Solution:</u> Let $\sqrt{\dfrac{x}{a}} = y$; then $\sqrt{\dfrac{a}{x}} = \dfrac{1}{y}$;

Hence, $2y + \dfrac{3}{y} = \dfrac{b}{a} + \dfrac{6a}{b}$;

$$yab\left(2y + \dfrac{3}{y}\right) = \left(\dfrac{b}{a} + \dfrac{6a}{b}\right)yab$$

$$2y^2ab + 3ab = b^2y + 6a^2y$$

$$2aby^2 - 6a^2y - b^2y + 3ab = 0,$$

$(2ay - b)(by - 3a) = 0;$ $by - 3a = 0$

$$2ay - b = 0$$

$$2ay = b \qquad\qquad\qquad by = 3a$$

$$y = \dfrac{b}{2a} , \quad \text{or} \qquad \dfrac{3a}{b} ;$$

Substitute these two values of y:

$$\sqrt{\dfrac{x}{a}} = y$$

$$\sqrt{\dfrac{x}{a}} = \dfrac{b}{2a} \qquad\qquad\qquad \sqrt{\dfrac{x}{a}} = \dfrac{3a}{b}$$

square both sides.   square both sides

$$\dfrac{x}{a} = \dfrac{b^2}{4a^2} \qquad\qquad\qquad \dfrac{x}{a} = \dfrac{9a^2}{b^2}$$

multiply both sides by a.   multiply both sides by a.

$$x = \dfrac{b^2a}{4a^2} = \dfrac{b^2}{4a} \qquad\qquad x = \dfrac{9a^2 \cdot a}{b^2} = \dfrac{9a^3}{b^2}$$

The solution is:

$$x = \left\{ \frac{b^2}{4a} , \frac{9a^3}{b^2} \right\}$$

Solve $2(x + 2)^{\frac{1}{2}} = (x + 1)^{\frac{1}{2}} - 2$.

<u>Solution:</u> Squaring gives

$$4(x + 2) = x + 1 - 4(x + 1)^{\frac{1}{2}} + 4$$

$$4x + 8 = x + 5 - 4(x + 1)^{\frac{1}{2}}.$$

Transposing $-4(x + 1)^{\frac{1}{2}} = 3x + 3.$

Squaring again $16(x + 1) = 9x^2 + 18x + 9.$

$$16x + 16 = 9x^2 + 18x + 9.$$

Transposing again $9x^2 + 2x - 7 = 0.$

Factoring $(9x - 7)(x + 1) = 0.$

Set each factor = 0 to find all values of x for which the product = 0

$$9x - 7 = 0 \qquad x + 1 = 0$$

$$x = \frac{7}{9} \qquad\qquad x = -1.$$

Check: for $x = \frac{7}{9}$

$$2\left(\frac{7}{9} + 2\right)^{\frac{1}{2}} \overset{?}{=} \left(\frac{7}{9} + 1\right)^{\frac{1}{2}} - 2$$

$$2\left(\frac{7}{9} + \frac{18}{9}\right)^{\frac{1}{2}} \overset{?}{=} \left(\frac{7}{9} + \frac{9}{9}\right)^{\frac{1}{2}} - 2$$

$$2\sqrt{\frac{25}{9}} \overset{?}{=} \sqrt{\frac{16}{9}} - 2$$

$$2\left(\frac{5}{3}\right) \overset{?}{=} \frac{4}{3} - 2$$

$$\frac{10}{3} \neq -\frac{2}{3}$$

for $x = -1$

$$2(-1 + 2)^{\frac{1}{2}} \overset{?}{=} (-1 + 1)^{\frac{1}{2}} - 2$$

142

$$2\sqrt{1} \overset{?}{=} \sqrt{0} - 2$$

$$2 \neq -2.$$

Neither of these values is a root of the given equation.
The above example illustrates that:

    1. Two expressions involving radicals may not be equal
for any value of the unknown.
    2. Extraneous roots may be introduced by squaring.
    3. Results must always be checked. There is no other
way to determine whether or not a result is a root of the
given equation.

SOLVING BY COMPLETING THE SQUARE

● **PROBLEM 15-22**

Complete the square in $x^2 + x - 1$.

Solution: We proceed adding the square of half the coefficient of x
and, also subtracting it. That is, we write

$$x^2 + x - 1 = x^2 + x - 1 + \tfrac{1}{4} - \tfrac{1}{4}$$

$$= x^2 + x - 1 + \left(\tfrac{1}{2}\right)^2 - \left(\tfrac{1}{2}\right)^2$$

Associating, $\quad = \left[x^2 + x + \left(\tfrac{1}{2}\right)^2\right] - 1 - \left(\tfrac{1}{2}\right)^2$

$$= [x + \tfrac{1}{2}]^2 - 1 - \tfrac{1}{4}$$

$$= (x + \tfrac{1}{2})^2 - \tfrac{4}{4} - \tfrac{1}{4}$$

$$= (x + \tfrac{1}{2})^2 - \tfrac{5}{4}$$

● **PROBLEM 15-23**

Solve $x^2 - 6x + 8 = 0$.

Solution: This problem may be solved by the method of
completing the square: Arrange the equation with the constant term in the right member

$$x^2 - 6x = -8.$$

Take $\frac{1}{2}$ of the coefficient of x, square this, and add the
result to both members. Thus, $\frac{1}{2}$ of -6 is -3, and $(-3)^2 = 9$.

Add 9 to both members:

$$x^2 - 6x + 9 = -8 + 9 = 1.$$

This procedure makes the left member a perfect square. Factor,

$$(x - 3)^2 = 1.$$

Extract the square root of both members,

$$x - 3 = \pm 1.$$

When $x - 3 = +1$, then $x = 4$ and when $x - 3 = -1$, then $x = 2$.

Check: for $x = 4$:   for $x = 2$:

$$4^2 - 6(4) + 8 = 0 \qquad 2^2 - 6(2) + 8 = 0$$

$$16 - 24 + 8 = 0 \qquad 4 - 12 + 8 = 0$$

$$0 = 0 \qquad 0 = 0.$$

Sol: $x = \{4, 2\}$.

● **PROBLEM** 15-24

Solve $2x^2 + 8x + 4 = 0$ by completing the square.

Solution: $2x^2 + 8x + 4 = 0$

Divide both members by 2, the coefficient of x^2.

$$x^2 + 4x + 2 = 0$$

Subtract the constant term, 2, from both members.

$$x^2 + 4x = -2$$

Add to each member the square of one-half the coefficient of the term in x.

$$x^2 + 4x + 4 = -2 + 4$$

Factor
$$(x + 2)^2 = 2$$

Set the square root of the left member (a perfect square) equal to $\pm$ the square root of the right member and solve for x.

$$x + 2 = \sqrt{2} \quad \text{or} \quad x + 2 = -\sqrt{2}$$

The roots are $\sqrt{2} - 2$ and $-\sqrt{2} - 2$. Check each solution.

$$2(\sqrt{2} - 2)^2 + 8(\sqrt{2} - 2) + 4 = 2(2 - 4\sqrt{2} + 4) + 8\sqrt{2} - 16 + 4$$

$$= 4 - 8\sqrt{2} + 8 + 8\sqrt{2} - 16 + 4$$

$$= 0$$

144

$$2\left(-\sqrt{2}-2\right)^2 + 8\left(-\sqrt{2}-2\right) + 4 = 2\left(2+4\sqrt{2}+4\right) - 8\sqrt{2} - 16 + 4$$

$$= 4 + 8\sqrt{2} + 8 - 8\sqrt{2} - 16 + 4$$

$$= 0$$

● **PROBLEM** 15-25

Solve the equation $3x^2 + 6x - 7 = 0$.

Solution: This quadratic equation cannot be solved by factoring, but may be solved by the method of completing the square. Adding 7 to both sides, we have $3x^2 + 6x = 7$. Multiplying both sides now by $\frac{1}{3}$, we have $x^2 + 2x = 7/3$. We are now in a position to complete the square. The computation can be arranged in the following manner: Add the square of $\frac{1}{2}$ the coefficient of x to both sides, i.e., 1. Then rewrite as the equality of two squares.

$$x^2 + 2x + 1 = \frac{7}{3} + 1$$
$$(x + 1)^2 = \left(\sqrt{\frac{7}{3} + 1}\right)^2$$
$$(x + 1)^2 = \left(\sqrt{\frac{10}{3}}\right)^2$$

Adding $-\left(\sqrt{\frac{10}{3}}\right)^2$ to both sides,

$$(x + 1)^2 - \left(\sqrt{\frac{10}{3}}\right)^2 = 0$$

Factoring:

$$\left[(x + 1) + \sqrt{\frac{10}{3}}\right]\left[(x + 1) - \sqrt{\frac{10}{3}}\right] = 0$$

Hence

$$x + 1 + \sqrt{\frac{10}{3}} = 0 \quad \text{or} \quad x + 1 - \sqrt{\frac{10}{3}} = 0$$

$$x = -1 - \sqrt{\frac{10}{3}} \quad \text{or} \quad x = -1 + \sqrt{\frac{10}{3}}$$

Therefore the solution set is
$$\left\{ -1 + \sqrt{\frac{10}{3}} , \; -1 - \sqrt{\frac{10}{3}} \right\} .$$

● **PROBLEM** 15-26

Complete the square in both x and y in $x^2 + 2x + y^2 - 3y$.

Solution: To complete the square in x, take half the coefficient of x and square it. Add and subtract this value from the given expression. Therefore:

$$\left[\frac{1}{2}(2)\right]^2 = [1]^2 = 1, \text{ and } x^2 + 2x + y^2 - 3y = x^2 + 2x + y^2 - 3y + 1 - 1.$$

Commuting, $x^2+2x+y^2-3y = x^2+2x+1+y^2-3y-1 = (x+1)^2+y^2-3y-1$. (1)

Now, take half the coefficient of y and square it. Add and subtract this value from equation (1).

$$\left[\frac{1}{2}(-3)\right]^2 = \left[-\frac{3}{2}\right]^2 = \frac{9}{4}, \text{ and}$$

$x^2 + 2x + y^2 - 3y = (x+1)^2 + y^2 - 3y - 1 + \frac{9}{4} - \frac{9}{4}$. Commuting,

$x^2 + 2x + y^2 - 3y = (x+1)^2 + y^2 - 3y + \frac{9}{4} - 1 - \frac{9}{4}$

$= (x+1)^2 + \left(y-\frac{3}{2}\right)^2 - 1 - \frac{9}{4} = (x+1)^2 + \left(y-\frac{3}{2}\right)^2 - \frac{4}{4} - \frac{9}{4}$. Hence, x^2+2x+y^2-3y

$= (x+1)^2 + \left(y-\frac{3}{2}\right)^2 - \frac{13}{4}$.

CHAPTER 16

SOLUTIONS BY QUADRATIC FORMULA

COEFFICIENTS WITH INTEGERS, FRACTIONS, RADICALS AND VARIABLES

● **PROBLEM 16-1**

Obtain the quadratic equation in standard form that is equivalent to $4x - 3 = 5x^2$.

<u>Solution:</u> The standard form of a quadratic equation is $ax^2 + bx + c = 0$. Starting with our given equation $4x - 3 = 5x^2$, we add $(-5x^2)$ to both members,

$$(4x - 3) + (-5x^2) = 5x^2 + -5x^2$$

$$(4x - 3) + (-5x^2) = 0$$

commuting we obtain $\qquad -5x^2 + 4x - 3 = 0$

This is the required equation with $a = -5$, $b = 4$, and $c = -3$.

● **PROBLEM 16-2**

Find the roots of the equation $x^2 + 12x - 85 = 0$.

<u>Solution:</u> The roots of this equation may be found using the quadratic formula

$$x = \frac{-B \pm \sqrt{B^2 - 4AC}}{2A}$$

In this equation $A = 1$, $B = 12$, and $C = -85$. Hence, by the quadratic formula,

$$x = \frac{-12 + \sqrt{144 + 340}}{2} \qquad \text{or} \qquad x = \frac{-12 - \sqrt{144 + 340}}{2}$$

$$x = \frac{-12 + 22}{2} \qquad \text{or} \qquad x = \frac{-12 - 22}{2}$$

Therefore $x = 5$ or $x = -17$. This is equivalent to the statement that the solution set is $\{-17,5\}$.

● **PROBLEM** 16-3

Use the quadratic formula to solve for x in the equation $x^2 - 5x + 6 = 0$.

<u>Solution:</u> The quadratic formula, $x = \frac{-b \pm \sqrt{b^2 - 4ac}}{2a}$, is used to solve equations in the form $ax^2 + bx + c = 0$. Here $a = 1$, $b = -5$, and $c = 6$. Hence

$$x = \frac{-(-5) \pm \sqrt{(-5)^2 - 4 \cdot 1 \cdot 6}}{2 \cdot 1} = \frac{5 \pm \sqrt{25 - 24}}{2}$$

$$= \frac{5 \pm \sqrt{1}}{2}$$

$$= \frac{5 \pm 1}{2}$$

$$= \frac{5 + 1}{2} \quad \text{or} \quad \frac{5 - 1}{2}$$

$$= \frac{6}{2} \quad \text{or} \quad \frac{4}{2}$$

$$= 3 \quad \text{or} \quad 2$$

Thus the roots of the equation $x^2 - 5x + 6 = 0$ are $x = 3$ and $x = 2$.

● **PROBLEM** 16-4

Solve $6x^2 - 7x - 20 = 0$.

<u>Solution:</u> $6x^2 - 7x - 20 = 0$ is not factorable. Therefore, find the roots of the quadratic equation $ax^2 + bx + c$ using:

$$x = \frac{-b \pm \sqrt{b^2 - 4ac}}{2a},$$

where $a = 6$, $b = -7$, $c = -20$.

$$x = \frac{7 \pm \sqrt{49 - 4(6)(-20)}}{12}$$

$$x = \frac{7 \pm \sqrt{529}}{12} = \frac{7 \pm 23}{12}.$$

Therefore,
$$x_1 = \frac{7 + 23}{12} = \frac{30}{12} = \frac{5}{2}$$

$$x_2 = \frac{7 - 23}{12} = -\frac{16}{12} = -\frac{4}{3}.$$

● **PROBLEM 16-5**

Solve the equation $2x^2 - 5x + 3 = 0$.

Solution:

(1) $\qquad 2x^2 - 5x + 3 = 0$

Equation (1) is a quadratic equation of the form $ax^2 + bx + c = 0$ in which $a = 2$, $b = -5$, and $c = 3$. Therefore, the quadratic formula $x = \dfrac{-b \pm \sqrt{b^2 - 4ac}}{2a}$ may be used to find the solutions of equation (1). Substituting the values for a, b, and c in the quadratic formula:

$$x = \frac{-(-5) \pm \sqrt{(-5)^2 - 4(2)(3)}}{2(2)}$$

$$x = \frac{5 \pm \sqrt{1}}{4}$$

$$x = \frac{5 + 1}{4} = \frac{3}{2}, \quad \text{and } x = \frac{5 - 1}{4} = 1$$

Check: Substituting $x = \dfrac{3}{2}$ in the given equation,

$$2\left(\frac{3}{2}\right)^2 - 5\left(\frac{3}{2}\right) + 3 = 0$$

$$0 = 0$$

Substituting $x = 1$ in the given equation,

$$2(1)^2 - 5(1) + 3 = 0$$

$$0 = 0$$

● **PROBLEM 16-6**

Solve the equation $3x^2 - 5x + 2 = 0$ by means of the quadratic formula.

<u>Solution:</u> The quadratic formula, $x = \dfrac{-b \pm \sqrt{b^2 - 4ac}}{2a}$, applies to

equations of the form $ax^2 + bx + c = 0$. The equation $3x^2 - 5x + 2 = 0$ is in this form with $a = 3$, $b = -5$, and $c = 2$. Substituting these values into our quadratic formula we obtain

$$x = \frac{-(-5) \pm \sqrt{(-5)^2 - 4(3)(2)}}{2(3)}$$

$$= \frac{5 \pm \sqrt{25 - 24}}{6} = \frac{5 \pm 1}{6}$$

$$= \frac{6}{6} \quad \text{and} \quad \frac{4}{6}$$

$$x = 1 \quad \text{and} \quad \frac{2}{3}$$

Hence the solution set is $\left\{1, \dfrac{2}{3}\right\}$ We can verify that the elements of $\left\{1, \dfrac{2}{3}\right\}$ are the roots of the given equation by means of the following check: We replace x by 1 in our original equation

$$3(1)^2 - 5(1) + 2 = 0$$
$$3 - 5 + 2 = 0$$
$$-2 + 2 = 0$$
$$0 = 0$$

Now we replace x by $\dfrac{2}{3}$ in the original equation

$$3\left(\frac{2}{3}\right)^2 - 5\left(\frac{2}{3}\right) + 2 = 0$$

$$3\left(\frac{4}{9}\right) - \frac{10}{3} + 2 = 0$$

$$\frac{12}{9} - \frac{10}{3} \cdot \frac{3}{3} + 2 = 0$$

$$\frac{12}{9} - \frac{30}{9} + 2 = 0$$

$$\frac{-18}{9} + 2 = 0$$

$$-2 + 2 = 0$$
$$0 = 0$$

Thus $\left\{1, \dfrac{2}{3}\right\}$ are indeed the roots of the given equation.

● PROBLEM 16-7

Solve $x^2 + 2x - 5 = 0$.

<u>Solution:</u> $x^2 + 2x - 5 = 0$ is a nonfactorable quadratic equation of the form $ax^2 + bx + c = 0$. Therefore, to find the roots of the equation use the formula:

$$x = \frac{-b \pm \sqrt{b^2 - 4ac}}{2a}$$

with a = 1, b = 2, c = -5.

$$x = \frac{-2 \pm \sqrt{4 - 4(1)(-5)}}{2}$$

$$x = \frac{-2 \pm \sqrt{24}}{2} = \frac{-2 \pm \sqrt{4 \cdot 6}}{2} = \frac{-2 \pm \sqrt{4} \cdot \sqrt{6}}{2} \; .$$

This may be simplified as follows:

$$x = \frac{-2 \pm 2\sqrt{6}}{2} = \frac{2(-1 \pm \sqrt{6})}{2} = -1 \pm \sqrt{6}.$$

● **PROBLEM 16-8**

Use the Quadratic Formula to solve the following equation:
$x^2 - 7x - 7 = 0$.

<u>Solution:</u> The quadratic formula, $x = \frac{-b \pm \sqrt{b^2 - 4ac}}{2a}$,
is used to solve equations in the form $ax^2 + bx + c = 0$.
$x^2 - 7x - 7 = 0$ is in this form, with a = 1, b = -7, and
c = -7. Thus,

$$x = \frac{-(-7) \pm \sqrt{(-7)^2 - 4(1)(-7)}}{2(1)}$$

$$x = \frac{7 \pm \sqrt{49 + 28}}{2}$$

$$x = \frac{7 \pm \sqrt{77}}{2}$$

Thus, the solution to the given equation is $x = \frac{7 + \sqrt{77}}{2}$,
$x = \frac{7 - \sqrt{77}}{2}$.

● **PROBLEM 16-9**

Solve the equation $3x^2 + 5x - 7 = 0$.

<u>Solution:</u> In order to solve a quadratic of the form $ax^2 + bx + c = 0$,
we employ the quadratic formula,

$$x = \frac{-b \pm \sqrt{b^2 - 4ac}}{2a} \; .$$

In our example a = 3, b = 5, c = -7. Substituting these values in our
formula we obtain,

151

$$x = \frac{-5 \pm \sqrt{5^2 - 4(-7)(3)}}{2(3)}$$

$$= \frac{-5 \pm \sqrt{25 + 84}}{6}$$

$$= \frac{-5 \pm \sqrt{109}}{6}$$

Thus the two solutions to the equation $3x^2 + 5x - 7 = 0$ are $\frac{-5 + \sqrt{109}}{6}$ and $\frac{-5 - \sqrt{109}}{6}$ which can be verified by direct substitution in the original equation.

● **PROBLEM** 16-10

Use the quadratic formula to solve the equation

$$8z(z + 1) = 1 \quad \text{for} \quad z .$$

Solution: Distributing, $\quad 8z(z) + 8z(1) = 1$

$$8z^2 + 8z = 1$$

Adding (-1) to both sides, $\quad 8z^2 + 8z - 1 = 0$

We use the quadratic formula,

$$x = \frac{-b \pm \sqrt{b^2 - 4ac}}{2a} ,$$

to solve equations in the form $ax^2 + bx + c = 0$. In our case $a = 8$, $b = 8$, and $c = -1$. Applying the quadratic formula to solve for z we obtain

$$z = \frac{-8 \pm \sqrt{8^2 - 4(8)(-1)}}{2(8)}$$

$$= \frac{-8 \pm \sqrt{64 + 32}}{16}$$

$$= \frac{-8 \pm \sqrt{96}}{16}$$

$$= \frac{-8 \pm \sqrt{16 \cdot 6}}{16}$$

$$= \frac{-8 \pm \sqrt{16}\sqrt{6}}{16}$$

$$= \frac{-8 \pm 4\sqrt{6}}{16}$$

$$= \frac{4(-2 \pm 1\sqrt{6})}{4(4)}$$

$$= \frac{-2 \pm \sqrt{6}}{4}$$

$$= \frac{-2}{4} \pm \frac{\sqrt{6}}{4}$$

$$= -\frac{1}{2} \pm \frac{\sqrt{6}}{4}$$

Hence, $z = -\frac{1}{2} + \frac{\sqrt{6}}{4}, \ -\frac{1}{2} - \frac{\sqrt{6}}{4}$.

● **PROBLEM 16-11**

Solve $\frac{1}{x} + \frac{1}{x + 2} = 2$.

Solution: In order to eliminate the fractions in this equation, we multiply both sides of the equation by the lowest common multiple (L.C.M), the expression of lowest degree into which each of the original expressions can be divided without a remainder. The L.C.M. is the product obtained by taking each factor to the highest degree. Thus in our case the L.C.M. is $(x')(x + 2)'$ and we multiply each member by $x(x + 2)$.

$$x(x + 2)\left[\frac{1}{x} + \frac{1}{x + 2}\right] = 2\left[x(x + 2)\right]$$

Distributing, $\quad x(x + 2)\left(\frac{1}{x}\right) + x(x + 2)\left(\frac{1}{x + 2}\right) = 2x \cdot (x + 2)$

Cancelling, $\quad x + 2 + x = 2x^2 + 4x$

Combining, $\quad 2x + 2 = 2x^2 + 4x$

Dividing both sides by 2, $x + 1 = x^2 + 2x$

Adding $-(x + 1)$ to both sides, $\quad 0 = x^2 + 2x - (x + 1)$

$$x^2 + 2x - x - 1 = 0$$
$$x^2 + x - 1 = 0$$

Since this is an expression in the form $ax^2 + bx + c = 0$ we may use the quadratic formula,

$$x = \frac{-b \pm \sqrt{b^2 - 4ac}}{2a}$$

to find its roots. In our case $a = 1$, $b = 1$, and $c = -1$. Hence

$$x = \frac{-1 \pm \sqrt{(1)^2 - 4(1)(-1)}}{2(1)}$$

$$= \frac{-1 \pm \sqrt{1 + 4}}{2}$$

$$= \frac{-1 \pm \sqrt{5}}{2}$$

Thus, $\quad x = \frac{-1 + \sqrt{5}}{2}$ or $\frac{-1 - \sqrt{5}}{2}$.

Check: In order to verify these solutions, we substitute them for x in our original equation.

153

(a) Replace x by $\dfrac{-1 + \sqrt{5}}{2}$:

$$\frac{1}{x} + \frac{1}{x+2} = 2$$

$$\frac{1}{\dfrac{-1+\sqrt{5}}{2}} + \frac{1}{\dfrac{-1+\sqrt{5}}{2}+2} = 2$$

Since $\sqrt{5} \approx 2.24$ replace $\sqrt{5}$ by 2.24

$$\frac{1}{\dfrac{-1+2.24}{2}} + \frac{1}{\dfrac{-1+2.24}{2}+2} \approx 2$$

$$\frac{1}{\dfrac{1.24}{2}} + \frac{1}{\dfrac{1.24}{2}+2} \approx 2$$

$$\frac{1}{.62} + \frac{1}{.62+2} \approx 2$$

$$\frac{1}{.62} + \frac{1}{2.62} \approx 2$$

$$1.61 + .38 \approx 2$$

$$1.99 \approx 2$$

(b) Replace x by $\dfrac{-1 - \sqrt{5}}{2}$

$$\frac{1}{x} + \frac{1}{x+2} = 2$$

$$\frac{1}{\dfrac{-1-\sqrt{5}}{2}} + \frac{1}{\dfrac{-1-\sqrt{5}}{2}+2} = 2$$

Again replace $\sqrt{5}$ by 2.24

$$\frac{1}{\dfrac{-1-2.24}{2}} + \frac{1}{\dfrac{-1-2.24}{2}+2} \approx 2$$

$$\frac{1}{\dfrac{-3.24}{2}} + \frac{1}{\dfrac{-3.24}{2}+2} \approx 2$$

$$\frac{1}{-1.62} + \frac{1}{-1.62+2} \approx 2$$

$$\frac{1}{-1.62} + \frac{1}{.38} \approx 2$$

$$-.62 + 2.63 \approx 2$$

$$2.01 \approx 2$$

Therefore $x = \dfrac{-1 \overset{-}{+} \sqrt{5}}{2}$ are indeed solutions to our equation, and our

154

solution set is $\left\{ \dfrac{-1 + \sqrt{5}}{2}, \dfrac{-1 - \sqrt{5}}{2} \right\}$.

● **PROBLEM 16-12**

Solve the equation $x^2 - x + 1 = 0$.

<u>Solution:</u>　　(1)　$x^2 - x + 1 = 0$

Equation (1) is a quadratic equation of the form $ax^2 + bx + c = 0$ in which $a = 1$, $b = -1$, and $c = 1$. Therefore, the quadratic formula $x = \dfrac{-b \pm \sqrt{b^2 - 4ac}}{2a}$

may be used to find solutions of equation (1). Substituting the values for a, b, and c in the quadratic formula:

(2)　$x = \dfrac{-(-1) \pm \sqrt{(-1)^2 - (4)(1)(1)}}{2(1)}$

(3)　$x = \dfrac{1 \pm \sqrt{-3}}{2}$

(4)　$x = \dfrac{1 + \sqrt{-3}}{2}$　and $x = \dfrac{1 - \sqrt{-3}}{2}$

Substitution of each of these roots in the original Equation 1 will show that they satisfy the equation.

INTERRELATIONSHIPS OF ROOTS: SUMS: PRODUCTS

● **PROBLEM 16-13**

Show that the roots of the quadratic equation $x^2 - x - 3 = 0$ are

$x_1 = \dfrac{1 + \sqrt{13}}{2}$　and　$x_2 = \dfrac{1 - \sqrt{13}}{2}$

<u>Solution:</u>　We use the quadratic formula derived from the quadratic equation, $ax^2 + bc + c = 0$:

$$x = \dfrac{-b \pm \sqrt{b^2 - 4ac}}{2a}$$

For $x^2 - x - 3 = 0$, $a = 1$, $b = -1$, and $c = -3$. Replacing these values

155

in the quadratic formula,

$$x = \frac{-(-1) \pm \sqrt{(-1)^2 - 4(1)(-3)}}{2(1)}$$

$$x = \frac{1 \pm \sqrt{13}}{2}$$

$$x_1 = \frac{1 + \sqrt{13}}{2} \qquad\qquad x_2 = \frac{1 - \sqrt{13}}{2}$$

According to the Factor Theorem: If r is a root of the equation $f(x) = 0$, i.e., if $f(r) = 0$, then $(x - r)$ is a factor of $f(x)$.

x_1 and x_2 are roots of $x^2 - x - 3 = 0$. Thus,

$$\left(x - \frac{1 + \sqrt{13}}{2}\right)\left(x - \frac{1 - \sqrt{13}}{2}\right)$$

are factors, and

$$x^2 - x - 3 = \left(x - \frac{1 - \sqrt{13}}{2}\right)\left(x - \frac{1 - \sqrt{13}}{2}\right)$$

● **PROBLEM** 16-14

Determine the quadratic equation whose roots are $x = 2 + \sqrt{3}$ and $x = 2 - \sqrt{3}$.

Solution: We can determine the quadratic equation from the sum and the product of the roots. A quadratic equation whose roots are x_1 and x_2 may be written in the form

$$x^2 - \left(x_1 + x_2\right)x + x_1 \cdot x_2 = 0$$

where the sum of the roots is $x_1 + x_2 = -\frac{b}{a}$ and the product of the roots is $x_1 \cdot x_2 = \frac{c}{a}$. Here,

$$x_1 = 2 + \sqrt{3} \text{ and } x_2 = 2 - \sqrt{3}.$$

Then, $x_1 + x_2 = 2 + \sqrt{3} + 2 - \sqrt{3} = 4$ and

and $x_1 \cdot x_2 = (2 + \sqrt{3})(2 - \sqrt{3}) = 4 - 3 = 1.$

Hence, the equation is:

$$x^2 - 4x + 1 = 0.$$

● **PROBLEM** 16-15

Find the equation whose roots are $3 + \sqrt{2}$ and $3 - \sqrt{2}$.

<u>Solution</u>: The roots of a quadratic equation $ax^2 + bx + c$ can be characterized by the following:

the sum of the roots

$$r_1 + r_2 = \frac{-b}{a} \text{ and}$$

the product of the roots

$$r_1 \cdot r_2 = \frac{c}{a}.$$

The sum of the roots is $(3 + \sqrt{2}) + (3 - \sqrt{2}) = 6$. Hence,

$$-\frac{b}{a} = 6 \text{ or } \frac{b}{a} = -6.$$

The product of the roots is

$$(3 + \sqrt{2})(3 - \sqrt{2}) = 3^2 - (\sqrt{2})^2 = 9 - 2 = 7.$$

This is the constant term of the required equation. We obtain this from the quadratic function $ax^2 + bx + c = 0$. Divide by a.

$$x^2 + \frac{b}{a}x + \frac{c}{a} = 0.$$

Then $\frac{b}{a}$ is the coefficient of x and $\frac{c}{a}$ is the constant term. Thus, here $\frac{b}{a} = -6$ and $\frac{c}{a} = 7$. Hence, the equation is

$$x^2 - 6x + 7 = 0.$$

Check: $x^2 - 6x + 7 = 0$ with $a = 1$, $b = -6$, $c = 7$.

$$X = \frac{-b \pm \sqrt{b^2 - 4ac}}{2a} = \frac{-(-6) \pm \sqrt{(-6)^2 - 4(1)(7)}}{2(1)} = \frac{6 \pm \sqrt{3b - 28}}{2}$$

$$= \frac{6 \pm \sqrt{8}}{2} = \frac{6 \quad 2\sqrt{2}}{2} = 3 + \sqrt{2} \text{ and } 3 - \sqrt{2}.$$

● **PROBLEM 16-16**

Find a quadratic equation whose roots are $3 + 2\sqrt{3}$ and $3 - 2\sqrt{3}$.

<u>Solution:</u> A quadratic equation is an equation of the form $ax^2 + bx + c = 0$, where a, b, and c are constants and $a \neq 0$. If both sides of this quadratic equation are divided by a, then:

$$\frac{ax^2 + bx + c}{a} = \frac{0}{a}$$

$$x^2 + \frac{b}{a}x + \frac{c}{a} = 0 \qquad\qquad (1)$$

Note that this last result is valid since $a \neq 0$. If r_1 and r_2 are the roots of a quadratic equation, then the sum of these roots, S, is,

$$S = r_1 + r_2 = \frac{-b}{a} \text{ and the product of these roots, P,}$$

is: $P = r_1 \cdot r_2 = c/a$.

Note that the coefficient of the x-term in equation (1) is $\frac{b}{a}$. In relation to the sum of the roots, S, this coefficient $= \frac{b}{a} = -\left(-\frac{b}{a}\right) = -(S) = -S$. Hence, equation (1) can be rewritten as,

$$x^2 + (-S)x + \frac{c}{a} = 0$$

or

$$x^2 - Sx + \frac{c}{a} = 0 \qquad\qquad (2)$$

Also, note that the constant term on the left side of equation (1), or $\frac{c}{a}$, is also the product, P, of the roots. Hence, equation (2) can be rewritten as:

$$x^2 - Sx + P = 0 \qquad\qquad (3)$$

The sum of the roots is:

$$S = r_1 + r_2, \text{ and here } r_1 \text{ and } r_2 \text{ are } 3 + 2\sqrt{3},\ 3 - 2\sqrt{3}$$

Thus,

$$S = (3 + 2\sqrt{3}) + (3 - 2\sqrt{3})$$

$$= 3 + 2\sqrt{3} + 3 - 2\sqrt{3}$$

$$= 3 + 3$$

$$= 6$$

The product of the roots is:

$$P = r_1 \cdot r_2$$

$$= (3 + 2\sqrt{3})(3 - 2\sqrt{3})$$

$$= 9 + 6\sqrt{3} - 6\sqrt{3} - 4(3)$$

$$= 9 - 12$$

$$= -3$$

Then, replacing S and P by 6 and -3 respectively in equation (3):

$$x^2 - Sx + P = x^2 - 6x + (-3) = 0$$

or

$$x^2 - 6x - 3 = 0,$$

which is in the form $ax^2 + bx + c = 0$ of a quadratic equation.

● **PROBLEM 16-17**

Form the equation whose roots are $2 + \sqrt{3}$ and $2 - \sqrt{3}$.

<u>Solution:</u> The roots are $2 + \sqrt{3}$ and $2 - \sqrt{3}$. Hence, $x = 2 + \sqrt{3}$ and $x = 2 - \sqrt{3}$. Subtract $(2 + \sqrt{3})$ from the first equation:

$$x - (2 + \sqrt{3}) = (2 + \sqrt{3}) - (2 + \sqrt{3}) = 0 ,$$

or

$$x - (2 + \sqrt{3}) = 0.$$

Subtract $(2 - \sqrt{3})$ from the second equation:

$$x - (2 - \sqrt{3}) = (2 - \sqrt{3}) - (2 - \sqrt{3}) = 0 ,$$

or

$$x - (2 - \sqrt{3}) = 0 .$$

Therefore,

$$[x - (2 + \sqrt{3})][x - (2 - \sqrt{3})] = (0)(0) = 0 ,$$

or

$$[x - (2 + \sqrt{3})][x - (2 - \sqrt{3})] = 0 . \qquad (1)$$

Equation (1) is in the form $(x - a)(x - b) = 0$ where a corresponds to $(2 + \sqrt{3})$ and b corresponds to $(2 - \sqrt{3})$. Also:

$$(x - a)(x - b) = x^2 - ax - bx + ab$$

$$= x^2 - (a + b)x + ab . \qquad (2)$$

Notice that a and b are the roots; that is, $2 + \sqrt{3}$ and $2 - \sqrt{3}$. The sum of the roots is:

$$a + b = (2 + \sqrt{3}) + (2 - \sqrt{3}) = 2 + \sqrt{3} + 2 - \sqrt{3}$$

$$= 4 .$$

The product of the roots is:

$$a \cdot b = (2 + \sqrt{3})(2 - \sqrt{3}) = 4 + 2\sqrt{3} - 2\sqrt{3} - 3$$

$$= 4 - 3$$

$$= 1 .$$

Hence, using the form of equation (2):

$$[x - (2 + \sqrt{3})][x - (2 - \sqrt{3})] = x^2 - (4)x + 1 = 0$$

or

$$x^2 - 4x + 1 = 0,$$

which is the equation whose roots are

$$2 + \sqrt{3} \quad \text{and} \quad 2 - \sqrt{3}.$$

DETERMINING THE CHARACTER OF ROOTS

Determine the character of the roots of the equation $x^2 - 5x + 6 = 0$.

<u>Solution:</u> The given equation is a quadratic equation where a = 1, b = - 5, and c = 6. The discriminant of this equation, $b^2 - 4ac$, is 25 - 24 = 1.

By the quadratic formula, $x = \dfrac{-\ b\ \pm\ \sqrt{b^2 - 4ac}}{2a}$,

the roots of the given equation are:

$$x = \frac{-\ (-\ 5)\ \pm\ \sqrt{1}}{2(1)} = \frac{5 \pm 1}{2}.$$

Therefore, $x = \dfrac{5 + 1}{2} = 3$ and $x = \dfrac{5 - 1}{2} = 2.$

Hence, the roots of the given equation are real, unequal, and rational. [Note: The roots are rational since $x = 3 = \dfrac{3}{1}$ and $x = 2 = \dfrac{2}{1}$].

Can the expression $16x^2 - 76x + 21$ be factored into rational factors?

<u>Solution:</u> To determine if this quadratic polynomial has rational factors we look at its discriminant, $b^2 - 4ac$ (this is the term that appears under the radical in the quadratic formula: $x = \dfrac{-\ b \pm \sqrt{b^2 - 4ac}}{2a}$, used for equations in the form of $ax^2 + bx + c = 0$).

In our example, a = 16, b = - 76, c = 21 and our discriminant $b^2 - 4ac = (-\ 76)^2 - 4 \cdot 16 \cdot 21 =$
5776 - 1344 = 4432.

Now, recall what the discriminant tells us about the nature of the roots:

If the discriminant (b^2-4ac) is positive or zero,
roots are real

If the discriminant (b^2-4ac) is negative
roots are complex
If the discriminant (b^2-4ac) is a perfect square
roots are rational
If the discriminant (b^2-4ac) is zero
roots are equal and rational.

Hence, roots are rational only if the discriminant is zero or a perfect square.

Looking at the column of perfect squares in a table of square roots, we note that 4,432 is not a perfect square, hence the expression $16x^2 - 76x + 21$ cannot be factored into rational factors.

CHAPTER 17

SOLVING QUADRATIC INEQUALITIES

Solve the inequality $(2x - 1)(x + 2) < 0$.

<u>Solution:</u> Since the two factors must be of opposite sign for their product to be negative, we have the two tentative possibilities:

$2x - 1 < 0$, $x + 2 > 0$,

or $2x - 1 > 0$, $x + 2 < 0$.

Solving the first pair of inequalities:

$2x - 1 < 0$ and $x + 2 > 0$

add 1 to both sides: | subtract 2 from both sides:

$2x < 1$ |

divide both sides by 2: |

$x < \frac{1}{2}$ and $x > -2$

Thus, the first pair implies that $x < \frac{1}{2}$ and $x > -2$,
or $-2 < x < \frac{1}{2}$; the graph is as follows:

Solving the second pair of inequalities:

$2x - 1 > 0$ and $x + 2 < 0$

162

Adding 1 to both sides: |

    2x > 1 | Subtracting 2 from
                                both sides:
Dividing both sides by 2:|

    x > ½   and   x < - 2

    Thus, the second pair implies that x > ½ and
x < - 2; the graph is as follows:

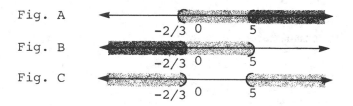

    Since there is no x such that x > ½ and x < - 2 we
reject this solution.

    The complete solution is thus the solution to the
first pair of inequalities, {x : - 2 < x < ½}.

● PROBLEM 17-2

Solve the quadratic inequality $3x^2 - 13x - 10 > 0$.

Fig. A

    -2/3 0   5

Fig. B

    -2/3 0   5

Fig. C

    -2/3 0   5

__Solution:__ This statement may be written in factored form as

            $(3x + 2)(x - 5) > 0$

Hence we know that either both factors are positive or both are negative, since the product of a positive factor and a negative factor
would be less than zero. This leads us to the following cases:

    Case (1) $3x + 2 > 0$ and $x - 5 > 0$

                    $3x > -2$ and $x > 5$

                    $x > -\frac{2}{3}$ and $x > 5$

    On the number line this part of the solution set may be represented
as the intersection of the intervals $(-\frac{2}{3}, \infty)$ and $(5, \infty)$, as pictured in
Fig. A.   Hence $(-\frac{2}{3}, \infty) \cap (5, \infty) = (5, \infty)$, which is represented by the
double-shaded region in diagram A.

    Case (2) $3x + 2 < 0$ and $x - 5 < 0$

                    $x < -\frac{2}{3}$ and $x < 5$

From Fig. B it can be seen that this appears as

            $(-\infty, -\frac{2}{3}) \cap (-\infty, 5) = (-\infty, -\frac{2}{3})$

Finally, since Case 1 and Case 2 represent the disjunction of two propositions, we conclude that the solution set of our inequality is the union of the sets identified in these two cases. That is,

$$\left(5,\infty\right) \cup \left(-\infty,-\tfrac{2}{3}\right)$$

is the solution set of the inequality, as pictured in Fig. C.

Obtain the solution set of $2x^2 > x + 6$.

Solution:

$$2x^2 > x + 6 \quad \text{given}$$

$$2x^2 - x - 6 > 0 \quad \text{adding } -x -6 \text{ to each member}$$

$$(2x + 3)(x - 2) > 0 \quad \text{factoring the left member}$$

Now the product of the two factors on the left is greater than zero, or positive, if both factors are positive or if both are negative. Hence we seek the simultaneous solution set of the two inequalities

$$2x + 3 > 0$$

and

$$x - 2 > 0$$

and also the simultaneous set of

$$2x + 3 < 0$$

and

$$x - 2 < 0$$

The first two inequalities form Case I.

$$2x + 3 > 0 \qquad\qquad x - 2 > 0$$
$$2x > -3$$
$$x > \frac{-3}{2} \qquad \text{and} \qquad x > 2$$

Therefore, in order for x > -3/2 and x > 2, x must be greater than two. That is, $x > -3/2 \cap x > 2 = x > 2$.

Case I $\quad x > -\dfrac{3}{2}$

Case II concerns the second pair of inequalities.

$$2x + 3 < 0 \quad \text{and} \quad x - 2 < 0$$
$$2x < -3$$
$$x < -\frac{3}{2} \qquad\qquad x < 2$$

164

The total solution for Case II is $x < -\frac{3}{2} \cap x < 2 = x < -\frac{3}{2}$

Case II $\quad x < -\frac{3}{2}$

$x < 2$

The solution set for $2x^2 > x + 6$ is the union of Case I and Case II; that is; $\{x \mid x > 2\} \cup \left\{x \mid x < -\frac{3}{2}\right\}$

● **PROBLEM 17-4**

Find the set $S = \left\{x \mid x^2 + 2x - 8 < 0\right\}$.

<u>Solution:</u> To get the required set, we find the solution set of

$$x^2 + 2x - 8 < 0$$

by the following procedure:

$\quad (x +4)(x - 2) < 0 \quad$ factoring left member of given inequality

In order for a product to be negative (less than zero), one factor must be positive and the other must be negative. Thus there are two cases to be considered here:

Case I $\qquad\qquad\qquad\qquad$ $x + 4 > 0$

$\qquad\qquad\qquad\qquad\qquad\quad$ $x - 2 < 0$

$\qquad\qquad\qquad\qquad\qquad$ or

Case II $\qquad\qquad\qquad\qquad$ $x + 4 < 0$

$\qquad\qquad\qquad\qquad\qquad\quad$ $x - 2 > 0$

The solution to Case I is $x > -4$ and $x < 2$. We can see this from diagram (A). Note that the solution includes all those numbers between -4 and 2, but not the endpoints themselves.

$\qquad\qquad\qquad\qquad\qquad$ $-4 < x < 2$

(A)

For the second case, the solutions are $x < -4$ and $x > 2$. See the accompanying number line ((B)).

165

$$x < -4 \qquad\qquad\qquad x > 2$$

```
     -5 -4 -3 -2 -1  0  1  2  3  4  5
```

However, we can see from diagram (B) that x cannot at the
same time be less than -4 and greater than 2. Hence, there
is no solution for this case. That is $x < -4 \cap x > 2 = \emptyset$

Therefore, the solution set is $S = \{x \mid -4 < x < 2\}$.

● **PROBLEM** 17-5

Find the solution set of $(x + 1)/(x - 2) > 0$.

$$x > 2$$

(A)
```
     -5 -4 -3 -2 -1  0  1  2  3  4  5
```
$$x > -1$$

$$x < 2$$

(B)
```
     -5 -4 -3 -2 -1  0  1  2  3  4  5
```
$$x < -1$$

(C)
```
   -6 -5 -4 -3 -2 -1  0  1  2  3  4  5  6
```

<u>Solution:</u> The fraction $(x + 1)/(x - 2)$ is positive, i.e.,
greater than zero, if the numerator and denominator are
both positive or both negative. Hence, we seek the set of
numbers that satisfies the **two** inequalities

$$x + 1 > 0 \qquad\qquad\qquad (1)$$
$$x - 2 > 0 \qquad\qquad\qquad (2)$$

simultaneously, and also those which satisfy

$$x + 1 < 0 \qquad\qquad\qquad (3)$$
$$x - 2 < 0 \qquad\qquad\qquad (4)$$

simultaneously.

Thus, we have two cases to consider in order to find
the solution set of $(x + 1)/(x - 2) > 0$.

Case I

$$x + 1 > 0 \qquad \text{and} \qquad x - 2 > 0$$

166

x > -1   and   x > 2

We can see the solution from diagram (A).
Hence, for Case I the solution set is the solution
of x > -1 ∩ x > 2, {x > 2}.

Case II

x + 1 < 0   and   x - 2 < 0

x < -1   and   x < 2

Thus the solution is the solution to x < -1 ∩ x < 2 or

{x | x < -1}. See (B).

Note that none of these solutions include the endpoints.

The solution set of (x + 1)/(x - 2) > 0 is thus the
union of Case I and Case II; that is {x | x > 2} U {x|< -1}
(see diagram (C)).

● PROBLEM 17-6

Solve $x^2 - 5x + 4 \leq 0$.

Solution: We factor $x^2 - 5x + 4$ and have

$$(x - 1)(x - 4) \leq 0$$

Since the product is negative, one of the factors is positive and the
other is negative. Therefore, either

x - 1 ≥ 0 and x - 4 ≤ 0   Case 1

or   x - 1 ≤ 0 and x - 4 ≥ 0   Case 2

Solving for x in each inequality, we obtain

x ≥ 1   and x ≤ 4   Case 1

or   x ≤ 1   and x ≥ 4   Case 2

The solution to the equation is the set of all x, such that x ≥ 1
and x ≤ 4, or

x ≤ 1   and x ≥ 4.

● PROBLEM 17-7

Find the solution set of $2x^2 - 3x - 5 > 0$.

Solution: Factoring, we have

$$(2x - 5)(x + 1) > 0.$$

If the product of two factors is positive, both factors

must be positive or both factors must be negative. We must
consider two cases.

    Case 1   Case 2

$(2x - 5 > 0$ and $x + 1 > 0)$ or $(2x - 5 < 0$ and $x + 1 < 0)$

$\left(x > \dfrac{5}{2}$ and $x > -1\right)$ or $\left(x < \dfrac{5}{2}$ and $x < -1\right)$

$\{x:\ x > \dfrac{5}{2}\}$ U $\{x:\ x < -1\}$

Since $\dfrac{5}{2} > -1$, then $x > \dfrac{5}{2}$ implies $x > -1$. Therefore the
solution set of Case 1 is $\left\{x:\ x > \dfrac{5}{2}\right\}$. Similarly,
$-1 < \dfrac{5}{2}$ so that $x < -1$ implies $x < \dfrac{5}{2}$. The solution set of
Case 2 is $\{x: x < -1\}$. The solution set is the union of
the solution sets of Case 1 and Case 2.

● **PROBLEM 17-8**

Solve the inequality $x^2 - x - 2 \le 0$.

<u>Solution:</u> Factoring the left side of the given inequality,

$$(x - 2)(x + 1) \le 0.$$

If the product of two numbers is negative, one of the
numbers is positive and the other is negative. Hence,
there are two cases:

Case 1: $x - 2 \ge 0, x + 1 \le 0$

Solving these two inequalities,

    $x \ge 2, \quad x \le -1$

Graph these new inequalities on number line (A).

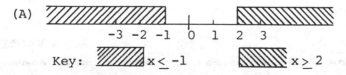

        Key: $x \le -1$ $x \ge 2$

Note that there is no value of x which satisfies both
inequalities at the same time since these two inequalities
do not intersect anywhere on the number line (A).

Thus $x \le -1 \cap x \ge 2 = \emptyset$

Case 2: $x - 2 \le 0, x + 1 \ge 0$.

Solving these two inequalities,

$$x \leq 2, \quad x \geq -1$$

Graph these inequalities on number line (B).

(B)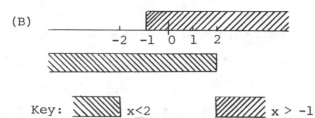

Key: $x \leq 2$ $x \geq -1$

The interval of x which satisfies both inequalities at the same time is $-1 \leq x \leq 2$. Note that the two inequalities intersect in this interval on number line (B), that is

$$x \geq -1 \cap x \leq 2 = -1 \leq x \leq 2.$$

Hence, the solution to the inequality $x^2 - x - 2 \leq 0$ is the set:

$$\{x \mid -1 \leq x \leq 2\}$$

● **PROBLEM 17-9**

Find the solution set of $x^2 - 5x + 4 \leq 0$.

Solution: First we find the solution for the equality.

$$x^2 - 5x + 4 = 0$$

$$(x - 4)(x - 1) = 0$$

$$x = 4 \text{ or } x = 1$$

For the product $(x - 4)(x - 1)$ to be less than zero, either of the two expressions must be less than zero, but not both simultaneously. $(x - 4)(x - 1)$ will equal zero only when $x = 4$ or $x = 1$ so that the endpoints 1 and 4 must be included in the solution set. $(x - 4)(x - 1)$ is less than zero when x is greater than one but less than four. The solution set is the union of the set whose elements are the included endpoints and the set whose elements are values of x between 1 and 4. Therefore the solution is the closed interval $\{x: 1 \leq x \leq 4\}$.

● **PROBLEM 17-10**

Solve the inequality $x^2 > 4$.

<u>Solution:</u> The given relation may be replaced by an equivalent one, by subtracting 4 from both sides of the inequality. Thus,

$$x^2 - 4 > 0 \qquad (1)$$

Now $x^2 - 4$ may be factored into two linear expressions, and we have

$$(x + 2)(x - 2) > 0 \qquad (2)$$

This expression is not true, when either of the two factors is zero; that is, when

$$(x + 2) = 0 \quad \text{or} \quad (x - 2) = 0,$$

or when

$$x = -2 \qquad \text{or} \quad x = 2.$$

Hence we have the product of two factors, one of which vanishes for $x = -2$ and the other for $x = 2$. These are therefore the critical values: as x increases from values less than -2 to values greater than -2, the expression $x + 2$ changes sign, from negative to positive; likewise, $x - 2$ changes from negative to positive as x passes through the critical value 2.

We now make use of the fact that the product of two quantities of like sign (both positive or both negative) is positive, whereas the product of two quantities of unlike sign is negative. Hence x must be such that either both factors in (2) are positive or both are negative. This yields the desired ranges

$$x > 2 \quad \text{or} \quad x < -2 \qquad (3)$$

It will often be found helpful to plot the critical values on a line representation of the real numbers, and then to consider in turn those values of x less than the left most critical point, those between each adjacent pair of critical points, and finally those greater than the rightmost critical point. It is possible also to plot the function $y = f(x)$ and thus determine the values of x for which $f(x) > 0$. Thus, if we plot $y = x^2 - 4$, we find that the graph lies above the X-axis when either of the inequalities (3) is obeyed.

● **PROBLEM 17-11**

Solve the inequality $2x^2 + 3x + 2 < 0$.

<u>Solution:</u> Divide the left side of the given inequality by 2:

$$\frac{2x^2 + 3x + 2}{2} < \frac{0}{2}$$

$$x^2 + \frac{3}{2}x + 1 < 0 \qquad (1)$$

To factor the left side of inequality (1), complete the square in x. This is done by taking half the coefficient of the x term and squaring this value. The result is then added to and subtracted from both sides of the inequality. Then,

$$\left[\frac{1}{2}\left(\frac{3}{2}\right)\right]^2 = \left[\frac{3}{4}\right]^2 = \frac{3}{4} \cdot \frac{3}{4} = \frac{9}{16}$$

$$x^2 + \frac{3}{2}x + 1 + \frac{9}{16} - \frac{9}{16} < 0 + \frac{9}{16} - \frac{9}{16}$$

or $\quad \left(x^2 + \frac{3}{2}x + \frac{9}{16}\right) + 1 - \frac{9}{16} < 0 + \frac{9}{16} - \frac{9}{16}$

$$\left(x + \frac{3}{4}\right)^2 + 1 - \frac{9}{16} < 0 + \frac{9}{16} - \frac{9}{16}$$

$$\left(x + \frac{3}{4}\right)^2 + \frac{7}{16} < 0 + \frac{9}{16} - \frac{9}{16}.$$

Subtract $\frac{7}{16}$ from both sides of this inequality:

$$\left(x + \frac{3}{4}\right)^2 + \frac{\cancel{7}}{\cancel{16}} - \frac{\cancel{7}}{\cancel{16}} < 0 + \frac{\cancel{9}}{\cancel{16}} - \frac{\cancel{9}}{\cancel{16}} - \frac{7}{16}$$

$$\left(x + \frac{3}{4}\right)^2 < -\frac{7}{16} \qquad\qquad (2)$$

(Note that the constant term in the squared polynomial, namely $\frac{3}{4}$, is just half the coefficient of the x-term in inequality (1)).

In reference to inequality (2), the square of any real number is always greater than or equal to zero; that is, the square of any real number cannot be negative. Therefore, there is no solution to inequality (2) and hence there is no solution to the given inequality.

● **PROBLEM 17-12**

Solve the inequalities

$x^2 - 6x + 4 > 0 \quad$ and $\quad x^2 - 6x + 4 < 0$.

Solution: The function which we are considering here is $x^2 - 6x + 4$; that is, $f(x) = x^2 - 6x + 4$. We must find where this function is positive or greater than zero and where it is negative or less than zero. We set $f(x) = 0$ and find the roots of this equation, $x^2 - 6x + 4 = 0$. Apply the quadratic formula. In this case $a = 1$, $b = -6$, and $c = 4$.

$$x = \frac{-(-6) \pm \sqrt{(-6)^2 - 4(1)(4)}}{2(1)} = \frac{6 \pm \sqrt{36 - 16}}{2} = \frac{6 \pm \sqrt{20}}{2}$$

$$= \frac{6 \pm \sqrt{4\sqrt{5}}}{2} = \frac{6 \pm 2\sqrt{5}}{2} = 3 \pm \sqrt{5}$$

Thus, the roots are:

$$x_1 = 3 + \sqrt{5} \approx 3 + 2.2 = 5.2$$
$$x_2 = 3 - \sqrt{5} \approx 3 - 2.2 = 0.8$$

171

Mark the roots on the x-axis and consider the regions into which the roots divide the x-axis (see Figure). They are $x < 0.8$, $0.8 < x < 5.2$, $x > 5.2$. For each of these regions choose a value of x and see if $f(x) < 0$ or if $f(x) > 0$ holds. For the first region, we select $x = 0$. Substitute this value into $f(x)$:

$$0^2 - 6(0) + 4 = 0 - 0 + 4 = 4 > 0$$

Therefore

$$f(x) > 0 \text{ for } x < 0.8$$

or more precisely

$$x < 3 - \sqrt{5} .$$

For the second region, $0.8 < x < 5.2$, we choose $x = 3$.

$$(3)^2 - 6(3) + 4 = 9 - 18 + 4 = -9 + 4 = -5 < 0$$

Therefore

$$f(x) < 0 \text{ for } 0.8 < x < 5.2 \text{ or more exactly}$$

$$3 - \sqrt{5} < x < 3 + \sqrt{5} .$$

For the third region $x > 5.2$, we try $x = 6$.

$$6^2 - 6(6) + 4 = 36 - 36 + 4 = 0 + 4 = 4 > 0$$

Therefore

$$f(x) > 0 \text{ when } x > 5.2;$$

that is,

$$f(x) > 0 \text{ when } x > 3 + \sqrt{5} .$$

In conclusion, recalling that $f(x) = x^2 - 6x + 4$, we have found that $x^2 - 6x + 4 > 0$ for $x < 3 - \sqrt{5}$ and for $x > 3 + \sqrt{5}$. Furthermore, $x^2 - 6x + 4 < 0$ for $3 - \sqrt{5} < x < 3 + \sqrt{5}$. Note that the function is zero at the points $3 - \sqrt{5}$ and $3 + \sqrt{5}$.

● **PROBLEM** 17-13

Solve the inequality $x^2 + 9x - 7 \leq 0$.

Fig A

$$\frac{-9-\sqrt{109}}{2} \qquad -9 \qquad \frac{-9+\sqrt{109}}{2} \quad 0$$

Fig. B

$$\frac{-9-\sqrt{109}}{2} \qquad -9 \qquad \frac{-9+\sqrt{109}}{2}$$

Solution: We solve the given inequality by the method of completing the square. To complete the square, take one half of the coefficient of x and square it. Add this quantity to both sides of the inequality. Here it is $\frac{1}{2}(9) = 9/2$ and $(9/2)^2 = 81/4$

$$x^2 + 9x + \frac{81}{4} \leq 7 + \frac{81}{4} \qquad (1)$$

Write this quadratic expression as a binomial squared.

$$\left(x + \frac{9}{2}\right)^2 \leq \frac{109}{4} \qquad (2)$$

Subtracting $\frac{109}{4}$ from both sides and expressing it as $\left(\sqrt{\frac{109}{4}}\right)^2$ on the

172

left side of equation (2)

$$\left(x + \frac{9}{2}\right)^2 - \left(\sqrt{\frac{109}{4}}\right)^2 \le 0$$

The expression $a^2 - b^2$ can be factored into $(a - b)(a + b)$. Similarly, for this example:

$$\left[\left(x + \frac{9}{2}\right) - \frac{\sqrt{109}}{2}\right]\left[\left(x + \frac{9}{2}\right) + \frac{\sqrt{109}}{2}\right] \le 0$$

Hence we know that, since the product here is nonpositive, either

Case (1) $\left(x + \frac{9}{2}\right) - \frac{\sqrt{109}}{2} \ge 0$ and $\left(x + \frac{9}{2}\right) + \frac{\sqrt{109}}{2} \le 0$

or

Case (2) $\left(x + \frac{9}{2}\right) - \frac{\sqrt{109}}{2} \le 0$ and $\left(x + \frac{9}{2}\right) + \frac{\sqrt{109}}{2} \ge 0$

Case (1) $\quad x + \frac{9}{2} - \frac{\sqrt{109}}{2} \ge 0$ and $x + \frac{9}{2} + \frac{\sqrt{109}}{2} \le 0$

$$x \ge \frac{-9 + \sqrt{109}}{2} \quad \text{and} \quad x \le \frac{-9 - \sqrt{109}}{2}$$

But this conjunction is logically false since no number can be larger than or equal to

$$\frac{-9 + \sqrt{109}}{2}$$

and at the same time be less than or equal to the smaller number

$$\frac{-9 - \sqrt{109}}{2}$$

(See Figure A). Thus, x cannot be a value in both sets at the same time. Therefore this case leads to the null or empty set.

Case (2) $\quad x + \frac{9}{2} - \frac{\sqrt{109}}{2} \le 0$ and $x + \frac{9}{2} + \frac{\sqrt{109}}{2} \ge 0$

$$x \le \frac{-9 + \sqrt{109}}{2} \quad \text{and} \quad x \ge \frac{-9 - \sqrt{109}}{2}$$

Diagrammatically, the solution set is given in Figure B. Thus, the solution set for this inequality is

$$\left\{x \mid \frac{-9 - \sqrt{109}}{2} \le x \le \frac{-9 + \sqrt{109}}{2}\right\} = \left[\frac{-9 - \sqrt{109}}{2}, \frac{-9 + \sqrt{109}}{2}\right]$$

CHAPTER 18

GRAPHING QUADRATIC EQUATIONS/ CONICS AND INEQUALITIES

PARABOLAS

● PROBLEM 18-1

Draw the graphs of $f(x) = x^2$, $g(x) = 3x^2$, and also $h(x) = \frac{1}{2}x^2$ on one set of coordinate axes.

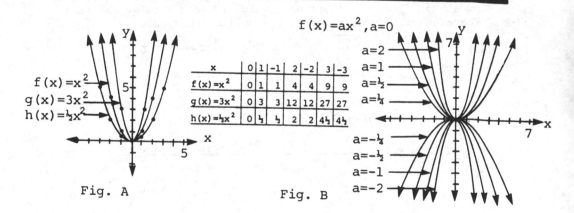

x	0	1	-1	2	-2	3	-3
$f(x)=x^2$	0	1	1	4	4	9	9
$g(x)=3x^2$	0	3	3	12	12	27	27
$h(x)=\frac{1}{2}x^2$	0	$\frac{1}{2}$	$\frac{1}{2}$	2	2	$4\frac{1}{2}$	$4\frac{1}{2}$

Fig. A   Fig. B

Solution: We construct a composite table showing the values of each function corresponding to selected values for x.

In the example, we graphed three instances of the function $f(x) = ax^2$, $a > 0$. For different values of a, how do the graphs compare? (Fig. A). Assigning a given value to a has very little effect upon the main characteristics of the graph. The coefficient a serves as a "stretching factor" relative to the y-axis. As a increases, the two branches of the curve approach the y-axis. The curve becomes "thinner". As a decreases, the curve becomes "flatter" and approaches the x-axis.

The graph of $f(x)^2 = ax$, $a \neq 0$, is called a parabola. (Fig. B). The point $(0,0)$ is the vertex, or turning point, of the curve; the y-axis is the axis of symmetry. The value of a determines the shape of the curve. For a > 0 the parabola opens upward and for a < 0 the parabola opens downward.

● PROBLEM 18-2

Graph the function $3x^2 + 5x - 7$.

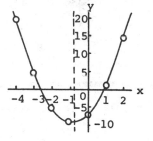

<u>Solution:</u> Let $y = 3x^2 + 5x - 7$. Substitute values for x and then find the corresponding values of y. This is done in the following table.

x	$y = 3x^2 + 5x - 7$
-4	21
-3	5
-2	-5
-1	-9
0	-7
1	1
2	15

These points are plotted and joined by a smooth curve in the figure.

● PROBLEM 18-3

Graph $y = 2x^2 - 5$.

<u>Solution:</u> Graphs of the form $y = kx^2 + c$ are parabolas that stretch upward from a minimum point on the y-axis. From the table

x	- 2	- 1	0	1	2
y	3	- 3	- 5	- 3	3

we obtain the graph shown in the accompanying figure.

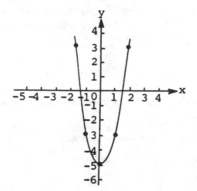

Draw a graph of the set of ordered pairs which satisfy the function $f(x) = x^2 - 7$.

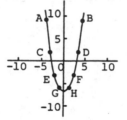

Solution: The following table lists a sufficient sequence of ordered pairs to determine the general nature of the curve:

x	0	1	2	3	4	-1	-2	-3	-4
y = f(x)	-7	-6	-3	2	9	-6	-3	2	9

Plotting these points, we obtain the curve illustrated in the figure. Note also that the function is given by a quadratic equation with the coefficient of the x^2-term positive. This implies that the graph will be a parabola opening upward. Since for this function, $f(x) = f(-x)$, the graph will be symmetric with respect to the y-axis. The point with x-coordinate 0 will be the vertex and minimum point of the parabola. The graph should confirm what the table suggests; the minimum point is (0,7). The range of the function is then limited to real numbers equal to or greater than -7. The domain of the parabola is the set of real numbers. The points A(-4,9) and B(4,9) in the figure are said to be symmetric with respect to the y-axis. Similarly, C and D, E and F, and G and H are symmetric with respect to the y-axis.

Graph $x^2 + y - 2x = 0$.

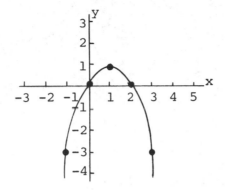

Solution: First we solve for y. Subtract x^2 from both sides of the given equation.

$$\cancel{x^2} + y - 2x - \cancel{x^2} = 0 - x^2$$
$$y - 2x = -x^2$$

Add 2x to both sides of this equation.

$$y - \cancel{2x + 2x} = -x^2 + 2x$$
$$y = -x^2 + 2x$$

Then we construct the table by substituting values of x into this derived equation to find corresponding values of y,

x	-2	-1	0	1	2	3	4
y	-8	-3	0	1	0	-3	-8

from which we obtain the Figure.

● **PROBLEM** 18-6

Find the equation of the tangent to the parabola
$y = x^2 - 6x + 9$, if the slope of the tangent equals 2.

Solution: The equation of a straight line is $y = mx + k$ where m is the slope and k is the y-intercept. The equation

$$y = 2x + k \qquad (1)$$

represents a family of parallel lines with slope 2, some of which intersect the parabola in two points, others which have no point of intersection with the parabola, and just one which intersects the parabola in only one point. The problem is to find the value of k so that the graph of Equation 1 intersects the parabola in just one point. If we solve the system

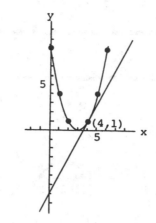

$$y = 2x + k \qquad (1)$$

$$y = x^2 - 6x + 9 \qquad (2)$$

by substitution, we get for the first step

$$2x + k = x^2 - 6x + 9 \qquad \text{or}$$

$$x^2 - 8x + 9 - k = 0 \qquad (3)$$

This is a quadratic equation of the form $ax^2 + bx + c = 0$. The discriminant determines the nature of the roots when $ax^2 + bx + c = 0$. The condition that Equation 3 has but one solution is that the discriminant, $b^2 - 4ac$ equals 0. Therefore, if $a = 1$, $b = -8$, $c = 9 - k$, then $b^2 - 4ac = 64 - 4(9 - k) = 0$ or $k = -7$.

Substituting this value of k in equation 1, we have $y = 2x - 7$ which is the equation of the tangent to the given parabola when the slope of the tangent is equal to 2. The figure is the graph of the parabola and the tangent. The student may verify that the point of contact is (4, 1). This is shown by substituting (4, 1) into

$$y = 2x - 7 = x^2 - 6x + 9$$

$$1 = 2(4) - 7 = 4^2 - 6(4) + 9$$

$$1 = \qquad 1 = 1$$

● **PROBLEM** 18-7

The surface S of a cube is given by the formula $S = 6x^2$, where x represents the length of an edge. Graph S as a function of x.

<u>Solution:</u> In the formula $S = 6x^2$, negative values of x may be used as well as positive ones. The points determined by these negative values of x belong to the graph of $S = 6x^2$, although they have no

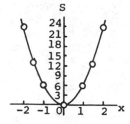

meaning in relation to the cube. The table of values from which the graph in the figure was constructed follows:

x	$S = 6x^2$	S
-2	$S = 6(-2)^2$ $= 6(4)$ $= 24$	24
$-\frac{3}{2}$	$S = 6\left(-\frac{3}{2}\right)^2$ $= 6\left(\frac{9}{4}\right)$ $= \frac{27}{2}$	$\frac{27}{2}$
-1	$S = 6(-1)^2$ $= 6(1)$ $= 6$	6

0	$S = 6(0)^2$ $= 6(0)$ $= 0$	0
1	$S = 6(1)^2$ $= 6(1)$ $= 6$	6
$\frac{3}{2}$	$S = 6\left(\frac{3}{2}\right)^2$ $= 6\left(\frac{9}{4}\right)$ $= \frac{27}{2}$	$\frac{27}{2}$
2	$S = 6(2)^2$ $= 6(4)$ $= 24$	24

Note that the axis of ordinates is labeled S. Moreover, units of different size are used on the two axes; this may be done if convenient, but should be avoided where possible.

● **PROBLEM 18-8**

Discuss the graph of the equation $y^2 = 12x$.

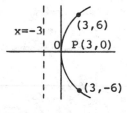

Solution: The equation written as $x = \frac{1}{12}y^2$ is a quadratic equation with the coefficient of the y^2 term positive. Therefore the graph is a parabola opening to the right. Since $f(x) = -f(x)$ the parabola is symmetric with respect to the x-axis. Point (0,0) satisfies the equation and lies on the axis of symmetry. Hence the vertex of the parabola

179

is at (0,0), (see figure). The focus of the parabola lies on the axis of symmetry, y = 0, at the point (p,0) where 4p = coefficient of x in the original equation: 4p = 12, p = 3. Therefore the focus is at (3,0). The directrix is the vertical line x = -p = -3. When x = 3, y = $\sqrt{12x}$ = $\sqrt{12(3)}$ = ±6. Therefore the points (3,6) and (3,-6) are points on the graph. The graph of this parabola is not the graph of a function since for any given value of x there is more than one corresponding value of y.

CIRCLES, ELLIPSES AND HYPERBOLAS

● PROBLEM 18-9

Discuss the graph of the equation $x^2 + y^2 = 25$.

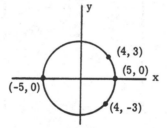

Solution: This is an equation of the form $x^2 + y^2 = r^2$, and therefore its graph is a circle with radius r = 5 and center at the origin (see figure). Note that the graph does not represent a function since, except for x = -5 or x = 5, each permissible value of x is associated with two values of y. For example, for x = 4, we have the ordered pairs (4,3) and (4,-3). The domain of this function is {x | -5 ≤ x ≤ 5}. The range of this function is {y | -5 ≤ y ≤ 5}.

● PROBLEM 18-10

Sketch the graph of the equation $x^2 + y^2 = 4$.

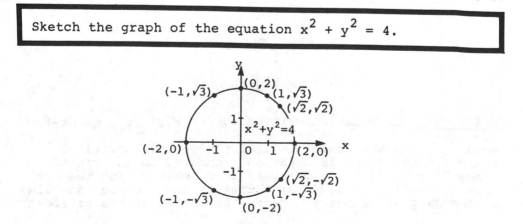

Solution: Substitute values for x and then find the corresponding values of y. This is done in the following table:

x	$y = \pm \sqrt{4 - x^2}$
-1	$\pm \sqrt{3} = \pm 1.73$
0	± 2
1	$\pm \sqrt{3} = \pm 1.73$
$\sqrt{2} = 1.41$	$\pm \sqrt{2} = \pm 1.41$

These points have been plotted and a smooth curve has been drawn through them in the figure. We could plot more points and then "fill in" the rest of the graph, but instead we will use some of our knowledge of the co-ordinate plane. Our given equation is equivalent to the equation $\sqrt{x^2 + y^2} = 2$. In the distance formula

$$d = \sqrt{(x_2 - x_1)^2 + (y_2 - y_1)^2},$$ where d is the distance be-

tween the points (x_1, y_1) and (x_2, y_2), let the origin or $(0,0) = (x_1, y_1)$ and let $(x,y) = (x_2, y_2)$. Therefore,

$$d = \sqrt{(x - 0)^2 + (y - 0)^2}$$

$$d = \sqrt{x^2 + y^2}.$$

Hence, the number $\sqrt{x^2 + y^2}$ is the distance between the point (x,y) and the origin. Thus, in words, our equation says, "The distance between the point (x,y) and the origin is 2." Clearly, the set of points that are two units from the origin is the circle whose center is the origin and whose radius is 2. This circle is therefore the graph of our given equation, and we have drawn it in the figure.

Most of the graphs of equations that we deal with in mathematics are "one-dimensional" figures, such as the circle we just drew. In these cases, we say that the graph is a curve. Not all simple looking equations in x and y, however, have graphs that are simple curves.

● **PROBLEM 18-11**

Find the equation for the circle whose center is at the origin and whose radius is 3.

Solution: A circle is the set of all points in a plane at a given distance from a fixed point. The fixed point is called the center of the circle and the measure of the given distance is called the radius of the circle. Thus to find the equation for the circle whose center

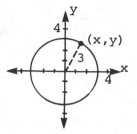

is at the origin and whose radius is 3, we wish to find the equation of all points at a distance of 3 from the origin, (0,0).

The distance formula for the distance between two points (x_1, y_1) and (x_2, y_2) is

$$d = \sqrt{(x_2 - x_1)^2 + (y_2 - y_1)^2}\,,$$

In our case $d = 3, (x_1, y_1) = (0,0)$. Thus

$$3 = \sqrt{(x - 0)^2 + (y - 0)^2}$$

$$3 = \sqrt{x^2 + y^2}$$

Squaring both sides, $x^2 + y^2 = 9$.

Hence the equation for the circle whose center is at the origin, with radius 3, is $x^2 + y^2 = 9$.

● **PROBLEM 18-12**

Discuss the graph of $\dfrac{x^2}{25} + \dfrac{y^2}{9} = 1$.

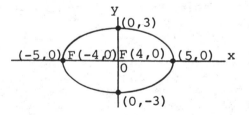

Solution: Since this is an equation of the form $\dfrac{x^2}{a^2} + \dfrac{y^2}{b^2} = 1$, with a = 5 and b = 3, it represents an ellipse. The simplest way to sketch the curve is to find its intercepts.

If we set x = 0, then

$$y = \sqrt{\left[1 - \frac{x^2}{25}\right]9} = \sqrt{\left[1 - \frac{0^2}{25}\right]9} = \pm 3$$

so that the y-intercepts are at (0,3) and (0,-3). Similarly, the x-intercepts are found for y = 0:

$$x = \sqrt{\left[1 - \frac{y^2}{9}\right]25}$$

$$= \sqrt{\left[1 - \frac{0^2}{9}\right]25}$$

$$= \pm 5$$

to be at (5,0) and (-5,0) (see figure). To locate the foci we note that

$$c^2 = a^2 - b^2 = 5^2 - 3^2$$

$$c^2 = 25 - 9 = 16$$

$$c = \pm\ 4.$$

The foci lie on the major axis of the ellipse. In this case it is the x-axis since a = 5 is greater than b = 3. Therefore, the foci are (+c,0), that is, at (-4,0) and (4,0). Therefore, the foci are at (-4,0) and (4,0). The sum of the distances from any point on the curve to the foci is 2a = 2(5) = 10.

● **PROBLEM** 18-13

Sketch the graph of the function $\{(x, 1/x^2)\}$.

Solution: Substitute different values of x and find the corresponding value of y or $1/x^2$.

x	$y = 1/x^2$
-2	$\frac{1}{(-2)^2} = \frac{1}{4}$
-1	$\frac{1}{(-1)^2} = \frac{1}{1} = 1$
$-\frac{1}{2}$	$\frac{1}{(-\frac{1}{2})^2} = \frac{1}{\frac{1}{4}} = 4$
$\frac{1}{2}$	$\frac{1}{(\frac{1}{2})^2} = \frac{1}{\frac{1}{4}} = 4$
1	$\frac{1}{1^2} = \frac{1}{1} = 1$
2	$\frac{1}{2^2} = \frac{1}{4}$

The graph is shown in the figure.

Draw the graph of   xy = 6.

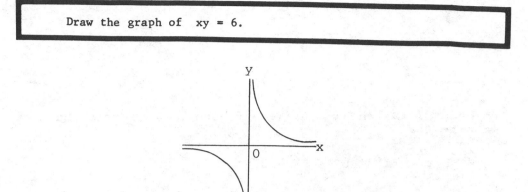

Solution: Since the product is positive the values of x and y must have the same sign, that is, when x is positive y must also be positive and when x is negative then y is also negative. Moreover, neither x nor y can be zero(or their product would be zero not 6), so that the graph never touches the coordinate axes. Solve for y and we obtain y = 6/x. Substituting values of x into this equation we construct the following chart:

x:	-6	-3	-2	-1	1	2	3	6
y:	-1	-2	-3	-6	6	3	2	1

The graph is obtained by plotting the above points and then joining them with a smooth curve, remembering that the curve can never cross a co-ordinate axis. The graph of the equation, xy = k, is a hyperbola for all nonzero real values of k. If k is negative, then x and y must have opposite signs, and the graph is in the second and fourth quadrants as opposed to the first and third.

Sketch the graph of the equation y = 2/x.

Solution: Substitute values for x and then find the cor-responding values for y. This is done in the following table.

x	$y = \dfrac{2}{x}$
-4	$-\dfrac{1}{2}$
-3	$-\dfrac{2}{3}$
-2	-1
-1	-2

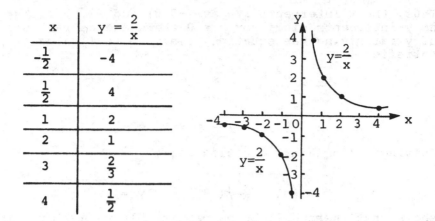

x	$y = \dfrac{2}{x}$
$-\dfrac{1}{2}$	-4
$\dfrac{1}{2}$	4
1	2
2	1
3	$\dfrac{2}{3}$
4	$\dfrac{1}{2}$

The graph is shown in the figure. This graph is an example of an equilateral hyperbola. Notice in the graph that, when x takes on larger and larger positive values, y gets closer and closer to 0. When x takes on larger and larger negative values, y also gets closer and closer to 0. Also, when x gets closer and closer to 0, y either takes on larger and larger positive values or larger and larger negative values. Note also that x cannot be 0, since $y = \dfrac{2}{x}$ = $\dfrac{2}{0}$ is not defined.

● **PROBLEM** 18-16

Discuss the graph of $\dfrac{x^2}{9} - \dfrac{y^2}{9} = 1$.

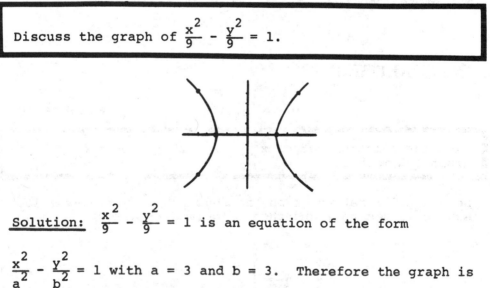

Solution: $\dfrac{x^2}{9} - \dfrac{y^2}{9} = 1$ is an equation of the form

$\dfrac{x^2}{a^2} - \dfrac{y^2}{b^2} = 1$ with a = 3 and b = 3. Therefore the graph is

a hyperbola. The x-intercepts are found by setting y = 0:

$$\frac{x^2}{9} - \frac{0^2}{9} = 1$$

$$x^2 = 9$$

$$x = \pm 3.$$

185

Thus, the x-intercepts are at (-3,0) and (3,0). There are
no y-intercepts since for x = 0 there are no real values
of y satisfying the equation, i.e., no real value of y
satisfies

$$\frac{0^2}{9} - \frac{y^2}{9} = 1$$

$$y^2 = -9, \quad y = \sqrt{-9}.$$

Solving the original equation for y:

$$y = \sqrt{\left(1 - \frac{x^2}{9}\right)(-9)} \quad \text{or} \quad y = \sqrt{x^2 - 9}$$

shows that there will be no permissible values of x in the
interval -3 < x < 3. Such values of x do not yield real
values for y. For x = 5 and x = -5 use the equation for y
to obtain the ordered pairs (5,4), (5,-4), (-5,4), and
(-5,-4) as indicated in the figure. The foci of the hyperbola are located at (±c,0), where

$$c^2 = a^2 + b^2$$

$$c^2 = 3^2 + 3^2 = 9 + 9 = 18$$

$$c = \pm\sqrt{18} = \pm 3\sqrt{2}.$$

Therefore, the foci are at $(-3\sqrt{2},0)$ and $(3\sqrt{2},0)$.

INEQUALITIES

● **PROBLEM 18-17**

Find the solution set of $x^2 - 6x + 10 > 0$ by the
graphical method.

Solution: First we graph the function $y = x^2 - 6x + 10$.
Assign values to x and then calculate y-values.

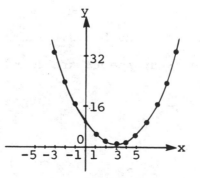

186

x	$x^2 - 6x + 10$	y
-3	$(-3)^2 - 6(-3) + 10$	37
-2	$(-2)^2 - 6(-2) + 10$	26
-1	$(-1)^2 - 6(-1) + 10$	17
0	$(0)^2 - 6(0) + 10$	10
1	$(1)^2 - 6(1) + 10$	5
2	$(2)^2 - 6(2) + 10$	2
3	$(3)^2 - 6(3) + 10$	1
4	$(4)^2 - 6(4) + 10$	2

See graph. The curve is the graph of $y = x^2 - 6x + 10$. Since the graph is entirely above the X axis, the

solution set of $x^2 - 6x + 10 > 0$ is the set of all real numbers.

CHAPTER 19

SYSTEMS OF QUADRATIC EQUATIONS

QUADRATIC/LINEAR COMBINATIONS

Solve the system

$$xy = 24, \tag{1}$$

$$y - 2x + 2 = 0. \tag{2}$$

<u>Solution:</u> This system is most easily solved by the method of substitution. Solve (2) for y in terms of x:

$$y = 2x - 2.$$

Substitute 2x - 2 for y in (1):

$$x(2x - 2) = 24,$$

$$2x^2 - 2x = 24,$$

$$2x^2 - 2x - 24 = 0,$$

$$x^2 - x - 12 = 0,$$

or factoring $(x+3)(x-4) = 0,$

Set each factor = 0 to find all values of x for which the product = 0.

$$
\begin{array}{c|c}
x + 3 = 0 & x - 4 = 0 \\
x = -3 & x = 4.
\end{array}
$$

In Equation (1): for x = -3, (-3)y = 24 or y = -8;

for x = 4, (4)y = 24 or y = 6.

In Equation (2): for x = -3, y - 2(-3) + 2 = 0 or
y = -8; for x = 4, y - 2(4) + 2 = 0 or y = 6.

Solve the following system:

$$x^2 + y^2 = 25 \qquad\qquad (1)$$

$$2x + y = 10 \qquad\qquad (2)$$

Solution: We solve equation (2) for y by adding - 2x to both sides:

$$y = 10 - 2x \qquad\qquad (3)$$

Replacing y by 10 - 2x in equation (1):

$$x^2 + (10 - 2x)^2 = 25$$

$$x^2 + 100 - 40x + 4x^2 = 25$$

$$5x^2 - 40x + 100 = 25$$

$$5x^2 - 40x + 75 = 0. \quad \text{Factoring out 5,}$$

$$5\left(x^2 - 8x + 15\right) = 0$$

Dividing both sides by 5,

$$x^2 - 8x + 15 = 0$$

Factoring,

$$(x - 5)(x - 3) = 0$$

Whenever the product of two numbers ab = 0, either a = 0 or b = 0; therefore

$$x - 5 = 0 \quad \text{or} \quad x - 3 = 0$$

$$x = 5 \quad \text{or} \quad x = 3$$

Replacing x by 5 in equation (3):

189

$$y = 10 - 2(5)$$

$$y = 10 - 10 = 0$$

Replacing x by 3 in equation (3):

$$y = 10 - 2(3)$$

$$y = 10 - 6$$

$$y = 4$$

Thus our solutions are $(5,0)$ and $(3,4)$. Check: Replacing (x,y) by $(5,0)$ in each equation:

$$x^2 + y^2 = 25 \qquad (1)$$

$$5^2 + 0^2 = 25$$

$$25 + 0 = 25$$

$$25 = 25$$

$$2x + y = 10 \qquad (2)$$

$$2(5) + 0 = 10$$

$$10 + 0 = 10$$

$$10 = 10$$

Replacing (x,y) by $(3,4)$ in each equation:

$$x^2 + y^2 = 25 \qquad (1)$$

$$3^2 + 4^2 = 25$$

$$9 + 16 = 25$$

$$25 = 25$$

$$2x + y = 10 \qquad (2)$$

$$2(3) + 4 = 10$$

$$6 + 4 = 10$$

$$10 = 10$$

Therefore the solution set is $\{(5,0), (3,4)\}$.

Obtain the simultaneous solution set of

$$x^2 + 2y^2 = 54 \qquad (1)$$

$$2x - y = -9. \qquad (2)$$

Solution: Equation (2) is readily solvable for y in terms of x, and so we proceed as follows:

$$-y = -9 - 2x$$

$$y = 2x + 9. \qquad (3)$$

$x^2 + 2(2x+9)^2 = 54$ replacing y by (2x+9) in equation (1)

$x^2 + 2(4x^2+36x+81) = 54$ squaring (2x+9)

$x^2 + 8x^2 + 72x + 162 = 54$ by the distributive law

$9x^2 + 72x + 108 = 0$ adding -54 to each member and combining terms

$x^2 + 8x + 12 = 0$ dividing by 9

$(x+6)(x+2) = 0$ factoring.

Whenever a product of two numbers ab = 0, either a = 0 or b = 0; thus either

$$x + 6 = 0 \quad \text{or} \quad x + 2 = 0 \quad \text{and}$$

$$x = -6 \quad \text{or} \quad x = -2.$$

To find y, we proceed as follows:

$y = 2(-6) + 9 = -12 + 9 = -3$ replacing x by -6 in equation (3)

$y = 2(-2) + 9 = -4 + 9 = 5$ replacing x by -2 in equation (3)

Therefore the simultaneous solution set is {(-6,-3), (-2,5)}.

Check. Replacing x and y by (-6) and (-3) in equations (1) and (2),

$$x^2 + 2y^2 = 54 \qquad (1)$$

$$(-6)^2 + 2(-3)^2 = 54$$

$$36 + 2(9) = 54$$

$$36 + 18 = 54$$

$$54 = 54$$

$$2x - y = -9 \qquad\qquad (2)$$

$$2(-6) - (-3) = -9$$

$$-12 + 3 = -9$$

$$-9 = -9.$$

Now replacing x and y by (-2) and (5) in equations (1) and (2),

$$x^2 + 2y^2 = 54 \qquad\qquad (1)$$

$$(-2)^2 + 2(5)^2 = 54$$

$$4 + 2(25) = 54$$

$$4 + 50 = 54$$

$$54 = 54$$

$$2x - y = -9 \qquad\qquad (2)$$

$$2(-2) - (5) = -9$$

$$-4 - 5 = -9$$

$$-9 = -9.$$

● **PROBLEM** 19-4

Find the solution set for the system:

$$3x - 5y = 13 \qquad\qquad (1)$$

$$y^2 = 4x \qquad\qquad (2)$$

Solution: Use the method of substitution to solve the system. From equation (2) we obtain:

$$x = \frac{y^2}{4}$$

Then upon substitution for x, equation (1) becomes:

$$3\left(\frac{y^2}{4}\right) - 5y = 13$$

Multiplying both sides of the equation by 4:

$$3y^2 - 20y = 52$$

The equation in standard quadratic form is:

$$3y^2 - 20y - 52 = 0$$

$$(3y - 26)(y + 2) = 0$$

$$3y - 26 = 0 \quad \text{or} \quad y + 2 = 0$$

$$y = \frac{26}{3} \quad \text{or} \quad y = -2$$

Returning to $x = \frac{y^2}{4}$, we see that

$y = \frac{26}{3}$ implies that $x = \frac{(26/3)^2}{4} = \frac{169}{9}$ and

$y = 2$ implies that $x = \frac{(-2)^2}{4} = 1$

Check to see if equation (1) is satisfied.

for $x = \frac{169}{9}$, $y = \frac{26}{3}$:

$$3\left(\frac{169}{9}\right) - 5\left(\frac{26}{3}\right) = \frac{169}{3} - \frac{130}{3} = \frac{39}{3} = 13$$

for $x = 1$, $y = -2$:

$$3(1) - 5(-2) = 3 + 10 = 13$$

Hence the solution set is

$$\left\{ \left(\frac{169}{9}, \frac{26}{3}\right), (1,-2) \right\}.$$

● **PROBLEM 19-5**

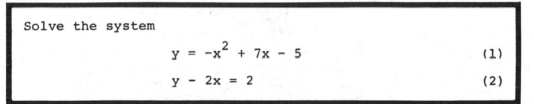

Solve the system

$$y = -x^2 + 7x - 5 \tag{1}$$

$$y - 2x = 2 \tag{2}$$

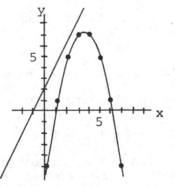

Solution: Solving Equation (2) for y yields an expression for y in terms of x. Substituting this expression in Equation (1),

$$2x + 2 = -x^2 + 7x - 5 \tag{3}$$

We have a single equation, in terms of a single variable, to be solved. Writing Equation (3) in standard quadratic form,

$$x^2 - 5x + 7 = 0 \tag{4}$$

Since the equation is not factorable the roots are not found in this manner. Evaluating the discriminant will indicate whether Equation (4) has real roots. The discriminant, $b^2 - 4ac$, of Equation (4) equals

$(-5)^2 - 4(1)(7) = 25 - 28 = -3$. Since the discriminant is negative, Equation (4) has no real roots, and therefore the system has no real solution. In terms of the graph, the figure shows that the parabola and the straight line have no point in common.

● PROBLEM 19-6

Solve the system

$$y = 3x^2 - 2x + 5 \qquad (1)$$

$$y = 4x + 2. \qquad (2)$$

Solution: To obtain a single equation with one unknown variable, x, substitute the value of y from Equation (2) in Equation (1),

$$4x + 2 = 3x^2 - 2x + 5. \qquad (3)$$

Writing Equation (3) in standard quadratic form,

$$3x^2 - 6x + 3 = 0. \qquad (4)$$

We may simplify Equation (4) by dividing both members by 3, which is a factor common to each term:

$$x^2 - 2x + 1 = 0. \qquad (5)$$

To find the roots, factor and set each factor = 0. This may be done since a product = 0 implies one or all of the factors must = 0.

$$(x - 1)(x - 1) = 0 \qquad (6)$$

$$x - 1 = 0 \quad | \quad x - 1 = 0$$

$$x = 1 \quad | \quad \quad x = 1$$

194

Equation (5) has two equal roots, each equal to 1. For x = 1, from Equation (2) we have y = 4(1) + 2 = 6. Therefore the system has but one common solution:

$$x = 1, \quad y = 6.$$

The figure indicates that our solution is probably correct. We may also check to see if our values satisfy Equation (1) as well:

Substituting in: $y = 3x^2 - 2x + 5$

$$6 \overset{?}{=} 3(1)^2 - 2(1) + 5$$

$$6 \overset{?}{=} 3 - 2 + 5$$

$$6 = 6.$$

● **PROBLEM** 19-7

Solve the system of equations

$$y = x^2 - 6x + 9 \qquad (1)$$

$$y = x + 3. \qquad (2)$$

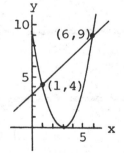

<u>Solution:</u> A single equation in terms of the one variable x may be obtained by the method of substitution. Substitute the value of y, x + 3, from Equation (2) for y in Equation (1).

$$x + 3 = x^2 - 6x + 9. \qquad (3)$$

Writing Equation (3) in the standard form of a quadratic equation,

$$x^2 - 7x + 6 = 0. \qquad (4)$$

Use the usual method of solving quadratic equations. Factor the equation. Then find the values of x for which each factor may = 0.

$$(x - 1)(x - 6) = 0 \qquad\qquad (5)$$

$$x - 1 = 0 \quad | \quad x - 6 = 0$$

$$x = 1 \quad | \qquad x = 6$$

The roots of Equation (4) are $x = 1$ and $x = 6$. Since $y = x + 3$, the solution of the given system is

$$x = 1, \ y = 4 \text{ and } x = 6, \ y = 9.$$

In the figure, the graph of the system, indicates that our solution is probably correct. We may prove that the solution is correct by substituting each solution in both equations of the given system, as usual. The values of y were obtained by satisfying equation (2). Now for Equation (1):

check for $x = 1$, $y = 4$	check for $x = 6$, $y = 9$
$y = x^2 - 6x + 9$	$y = x^2 - 6x + 9$
$4 \overset{?}{=} (1)^2 - 6(1) + 9$	$9 \overset{?}{=} (6)^2 - 6(6) + 9$
$4 \overset{?}{=} 1 - 6 + 9$	$9 \overset{?}{=} 36 - 36 + 9$
$4 = 4$	$9 = 9$

● **PROBLEM 19-8**

Solve the system
$$x^2 + y^2 = 10 \qquad\qquad (1)$$
$$x + 2y = 1 \qquad\qquad (2)$$

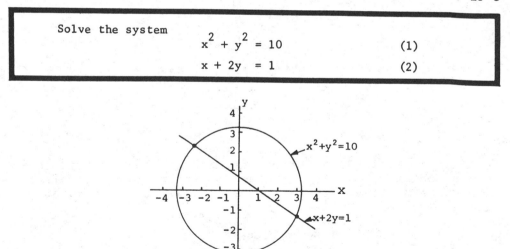

Solution: We solve the linear equation for x in terms of y by adding $-2y$ to both sides to obtain $x = 1 - 2y$. We substitute the result, $1 - 2y$, for x in the quadratic equation to obtain

$$(1 - 2y)^2 + y^2 = 10$$

Then we have
$$1 - 4y + 4y^2 + y^2 = 10$$
We add (-10) to both sides and combine terms:
$$5y^2 - 4y - 9 = 0$$
We factor,
$$(5y - 9)(y + 1) = 0$$

Whenever the product of two numbers $ab = 0$ either $a = 0$ or $b = 0$. Thus $(5y - 9)(y + 1) = 0$ implies either $5y - 9 = 0$ or $y + 1 = 0$
$$5y = 9 \qquad \text{or} \quad y = -1$$

Thus, $y = \frac{9}{5}$ or $y = -1$.

Substituting these values in turn in the linear equation, we find the corresponding values for x: $x + 2y = 1$, for $y = \frac{9}{5}$
$$x + 2\left(\frac{9}{5}\right) = 1, \ x = 1 - \frac{18}{5}, \ x = \frac{-13}{5}$$
and for $y = -1$
$$x + 2(-1) = 1, \ x - 2 = 1, \ x = 3.$$

The solutions of the system are therefore
$$\left(x = -\frac{13}{5}, \ y = \frac{9}{5}\right) \quad \text{and} \quad (x = 3, \ y = -1).$$

To consider the corresponding graphs of this system, we notice that $x^2 + y^2 = 10$ represents a circle with radius $\sqrt{10}$ and $x + 2y = 1$ is the line passing through the points $(1,0)$ and $(0,\frac{1}{2})$.

The two points where the circle and line intersect are the solution to our problem, $\left(\frac{-13}{5}, \frac{9}{5}\right)$ and $(3,-1)$, the points where $x^2 + y^2 = 10$ and $x + 2y = 1$ simultaneously.

● **PROBLEM 19-9**

Solve the system

$$x^2 + y^2 = 25, \tag{1}$$

$$x - y = 1. \tag{2}$$

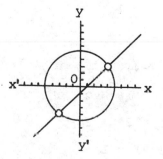

Solution: Solve (2) for y (the problem can be done similarly for x instead): The method of substitution is most easily employed in this example to solve the system.

$$y = x - 1.$$ (3)

Substitute x - 1 for y in (1):

$$x^2 + (x - 1)^2 = 25.$$ (4)

$$x^2 + x^2 - 2x + 1 = 25.$$

From (4)

$$2x^2 - 2x - 24 = 0,$$

or

$$x^2 - x - 12 = 0.$$ (5)

Solve (5) by factoring: $(x - 4)(x + 3) = 0$

$$x - 4 = 0 \quad x + 3 = 0$$

$$x = 4 \text{ or } -3.$$

Substituting 4 for x in (2), we obtain

$$4 - y = 1 \text{ or } y = 3.$$

Substituting -3 for x in (2), we obtain

$$-3 - y = 1 \text{ or } y = -4.$$

This gives $\begin{matrix} x = 4 \\ y = 3 \end{matrix}$ and $\begin{matrix} x = -3 \\ y = -4 \end{matrix}$ for the solutions.

Check:

for x = 4, y = 3

in Eq. (1): $(4)^2 + (3)^2 = 25$

$$16 + 9 = 25$$

$$25 = 25$$

in Eq. (2): $(4) - (3) = 1$

$$1 = 1$$

for x = -3, y = -4

in Eq. (1): $(-3)^2 + (-4)^2 = 25$

$$9 + 16 = 25$$

$$25 = 25$$

in Eq. (2): $(-3) - (-4) = 1$

$$-3 + \quad 4 = 1$$

$$1 = 1.$$

Graphical meaning of the two solutions. We may plot the graph for each of the equations (1) and (2). The graph of

$$x - y = 1$$

is the straight line shown in the figure, and the graph of

$$x^2 + y^2 = 25$$

is the circle there shown. To draw the graph of (1), the student may give various values to x and calculate the corresponding values for y from $y = \pm \sqrt{25 - x^2}$.

Any point on the straight line (2) has coordinates that satisfy Equation (2). Any point on the circle (1) has coordinates that satisfy Equation (1). The points (4,3) and (-3,-4) lie on both graphs and satisfy both Equations (1) and (2). That is to say, each point of intersection of the graph of (1) with the graph of (2) gives a pair of numbers that is a solution of the system.

● **PROBLEM 19-10**

Solve the system

$$x^2 + y^2 = 25, \tag{1}$$

$$x + y = 10, \tag{2}$$

and draw the graph to explain the fact that the solutions are not real.

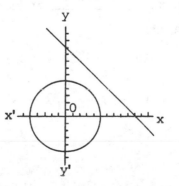

Solution: Use the method of substitution to obtain a single equation in terms of either one of the variables x or y. Solve Equation (2) for y (we could have chosen to solve for x). We get

$$y = 10 - x. \qquad\qquad (3)$$

Substitute this expression for y in Equation (1)

$$x^2 + (10 - x)^2 = 25$$

$$x^2 + 100 - 20x + x^2 = 25 \qquad \text{Expand the equation}$$

$$2x^2 - 20x + 100 = 25 \qquad \text{Combine like terms}$$

$$2x^2 - 20x + 75 = 0 \qquad \text{Put in standard quadratic form.}$$

This is a nonfactorable quadratic equation of the form $ax^2 + bx + c$ with a = 2, b = -20, c = 75. To find the roots of this equation use the formula

$$x = \frac{-b \pm \sqrt{b^2 - 4ac}}{2a}$$

substituting our values of a, b, and c we get

$$x = \frac{-(-20) \pm \sqrt{(-20)^2 - 4(2)(75)}}{2(2)}$$

$$x = \frac{20 \pm \sqrt{400 - 600}}{4} = \frac{20 \pm \sqrt{-200}}{4}$$

$$x = \frac{20 \pm \sqrt{(100)(2)(-1)}}{4} = \frac{20 \pm \sqrt{100} \cdot \sqrt{2} \cdot \sqrt{-1}}{4}$$

square roots of a product.

Recall $i = \sqrt{-1}$ then $x = \dfrac{20 \pm 10i\sqrt{2}}{4}$ reduces to $x = 5 \pm \dfrac{5i}{2}\sqrt{2}$.

Using Equation (3):

for $x = 5 + \dfrac{5i}{2}\sqrt{2}$, $y = 10 - x = 10 - \left(5 + \dfrac{5i}{2}\sqrt{2}\right)$

$$= 10 - 5 - \frac{5i}{2}\sqrt{2} = 5 - \frac{5i}{2}\sqrt{2}$$

for $x = 5 - \dfrac{5i}{2}\sqrt{2}$, $y = 10 - x = 10 - \left(5 - \dfrac{5i}{2}\sqrt{2}\right)$

$$= 10 - 5 + \frac{5i}{2}\sqrt{2} = 5 + \frac{5i}{2}\sqrt{2}$$

Check:

for $x = 5 + \dfrac{5i}{2}\sqrt{2}$, $y = 5 - \dfrac{5i}{2}\sqrt{2}$

Eq. (1): $x^2 + y^2 = 25$

$$\left(5 + \frac{5i}{2}\sqrt{2}\right)^2 + \left(5 - \frac{5i}{2}\sqrt{2}\right)^2 \overset{?}{=} 25$$

remember $i^2 = -1$

$$\left(25 + \frac{50i}{2}\sqrt{2} - \frac{50}{4}\right) + \left(25 - \frac{50i}{2}\sqrt{2} - \frac{50}{4}\right) \overset{?}{=} 25$$

$$50 \neq 25$$

These roots do not check. The roots are extraneous.

for $x = 5 - \frac{5i}{2}\sqrt{2}$, $y = 5 + \frac{5i}{2}\sqrt{2}$

Eq. (1): $x^2 + y^2 = 25$

$$\left(5 - \frac{5i}{2}\sqrt{2}\right)^2 + \left(5 + \frac{5i}{2}\sqrt{2}\right)^2 \overset{?}{=} 25$$

remember $i^2 = -1$

$$\left(25 - \frac{50i}{2}\sqrt{2} + \frac{50}{4}\right) + \left(25 + \frac{50i}{2}\sqrt{2} - \frac{50}{4}\right) \overset{?}{=} 25$$

$$50 \neq 25.$$

These roots do not check.

QUADRATIC/QUADRATIC (CONIC) COMBINATIONS

● **PROBLEM 19-11**

Solve the system:

$$x^2 + y^2 = 1 \qquad (1)$$

$$x^2 - 1 = y. \qquad (2)$$

<u>Solution:</u> Although the value of y in equation (2) can be substituted in equation (1), the result will be a fourth-degree equation. Hence, we substitute the value of x^2 from equation (2).

$$x^2 - 1 = y$$

$$x^2 = y + 1.$$

Replacing x^2 by $y + 1$ in equation (1),

$$y + 1 + y^2 = 1.$$

Add (-1) to both sides, $y^2 + y = 0$.
Factor out y, $\qquad\qquad y(y + 1) = 0$.

Whenever a product of two numbers $ab = 0$, either $a = 0$ or $b = 0$; hence

$$y = 0, \quad y + 1 = 0 \qquad \text{or}$$

$$y = 0, \qquad\quad y = -1.$$

Substituting $y = 0$ in equation (1),

$$x^2 + 0 = 1$$

$$x^2 = 1$$

$$x = \underline{+}1.$$

Two solutions are $(1,0)$ and $(-1,0)$.
Substituting $y = -1$ in equation (1),

$$x^2 + (-1)^2 = 1$$

$$x^2 + 1 = 1$$

$$x^2 = 0$$

$$x = 0.$$

The solution $(0,-1)$ is considered a double root in the sense that if $y = -1$, $x = \sqrt{0}$ or $x = -\sqrt{0}$. The solution set for the system is $\{(1,0), (-1,0), (0,-1)\}$.

Check: To verify that $(1,0)$ is a root, replace x by 1 and y by 0 in each equation.

$$x^2 + y^2 = 1 \qquad\qquad\qquad (1)$$

$$(1)^2 + 0^2 = 1$$

$$1 = 1$$

$$x^2 - 1 = y \qquad\qquad\qquad (2)$$

$$(1)^2 - 1 = 0$$

$$1 - 1 = 0$$

$$0 = 0.$$

To verify that (-1,0) is a root, replace x by -1 and y by 0 in each equation

$$x^2 + y^2 = 1 \qquad\qquad (1)$$

$$(1)^2 + 0 = 1$$

$$1 + 0 = 1$$

$$1 = 1$$

$$x^2 - 1 = y \qquad\qquad (2)$$

$$(-1)^2 - 1 = 0$$

$$1 - 1 = 0$$

$$0 = 0.$$

To verify that (0,-1) is a root, replace x by 0 and y by -1 in each equation,

$$x^2 + y^2 = 1 \qquad\qquad (1)$$

$$0 + (-1)^2 = 1$$

$$0 + 1 = 1$$

$$1 = 1$$

$$x^2 - 1 = y \qquad\qquad (2)$$

$$(0)^2 - 1 = -1$$

$$0 - 1 = -1$$

$$-1 = -1.$$

● **PROBLEM 19-12**

Solve the system of equations,
$$\begin{cases} x^2 + y^2 = 25, \\ xy = 12. \end{cases}$$

<u>Solution:</u> If the second equation of the system is multi-
plied by 2 and subtracted from the first we obtain
$x^2 - 2xy + y^2 = 1$, which can be written as $(x - y)^2 = 1$.
This last equation is equivalent to the two equations

x - y = 1 and x - y = -1 (since squaring both of these gives us back the original). Thus the solutions of the given system may be found by solving the two systems

$$(1)\begin{cases} xy = 12 \\ x - y = 1, \end{cases} \quad \text{and (2)} \quad \begin{cases} xy = 12 \\ x - y = -1. \end{cases}$$

For system (1):

$$xy = 12 \qquad \text{(a)}$$
$$x - y = 1 \qquad \text{(b)}$$

Solving equation (b) for x and then substituting this expression for x in equation (a), we obtain:

$$x = 1 + y \qquad \text{(b')}$$
$$(1 + y)y = 12 \qquad \text{(a')}$$
$$y + y^2 = 12$$
$$y^2 + y - 12 = 0$$

Factoring, $\qquad (y + 4)(y - 3) = 0$

Finding all values of y which make this product zero, we set each factor equal to zero:

$$(y + 4) = 0 \qquad\qquad (y - 3) = 0$$
$$y = -4 \quad \text{or} \quad y = 3$$

Then from (b'), $x = 1 + y = 1 + (-4) = -3$ or

$$x = 1 + y = 1 + 3 = 4$$

The results of the original system thus far are (-3, -4) and (4, 3). For system (2):

$$xy = 12 \qquad \text{(A)}$$
$$x - y = -1 \qquad \text{(B)}$$

Then, as for system (1):

$$x = y - 1 \qquad \text{(B')}$$
$$(y - 1)y = 12 \qquad \text{(A')}$$
$$y^2 - y = 12$$
$$y^2 - y - 12 = 0$$

Factoring, $(y - 4)(y + 3) = 0$

Setting each factor = 0,

$$(y - 4) = 0 \qquad \text{or} \quad (y + 3) = 0$$
$$y = 4 \qquad \text{or} \qquad y = -3$$

Then from (B'), $\quad x = y - 1 = 4 - 1 = 3$
$$x = y - 1 = -3 - 1 = -4$$

The results for system (2) are (3, 4) and (-4, -3).

Thus the results for systems (1) and (2) and for the original system are

$$(4, 3); \qquad (-3, -4); \qquad (-4, -3); \qquad (3, 4).$$

CHAPTER 20

EQUATIONS OF DEGREE GREATER THAN TWO

● **PROBLEM 20-1**

Remove fractional coefficients from the equation

$$2x^3 - \frac{3}{2} x^2 - \frac{1}{8} x + \frac{3}{16} = 0.$$

<u>Solution:</u> To rewrite this equation without fractional coefficients we must find a common denominator for all the terms of the equation. Observe that a common denominator is 16. Thus,

$$2x^3 - \frac{3}{2} x^2 - \frac{1}{8} x + \frac{3}{16} = 0$$

can be rewritten as:

$$\frac{2x^3}{1} - \frac{3x^2}{2} - \frac{x}{8} + \frac{3}{16} = 0 \qquad\qquad \text{or,}$$

$$\frac{32x^3 - 24x^2 - 2x + 3}{16} = 0. \text{ Multiplying both}$$

sides of the equation by 16 we obtain:

$$32x^3 - 24x^2 - 2x + 3 = 0. \quad \text{This is the required}$$
equation without fractional coefficients.

● **PROBLEM 20-2**

Solve the equation $x^3 - 16x = 0$.

<u>Solution:</u> Multiplying both sides by $\frac{1}{x}$, we have $x^2 - 16 = 0$. Factoring, we have $(x - 4)(x + 4) = 0$. Then all values of x which make

this product equal to 0 satisfy either $x - 4 = 0$ or $x + 4 = 0$. Thus $x = 4$ or $x = -4$. Both 4 and -4 satisfy the original equation since $(4)^3 - 16(4) = 0$ and $(-4)^3 - 16(-4) = 0$. However, so does the number 0, since $(0)^3 - 16(0) = 0$. From where did this root come?

There are several logical flaws in this solution. First, we cannot multiply both sides by $1/x$ if $x = 0$. But, basically, what is wrong is that $x^3 - 16x$ is not an equivalent expression to $x^2 - 16$.

We may undo this error by writing $x^3 - 16x = 0$ in factored form as $x(x + 4)(x - 4) = 0$.

Then $x = 0$ or $x + 4 = 0$ or $x - 4 = 0$

Hence $x = 0$ or $x = -4$ or $x = 4$

Therefore the solutions set is $\{-4, 0, 4\}$.

● **PROBLEM 20-3**

Find all solutions of the equation $x^3 - 3x^2 - 10x = 0$.

Solution: Factor out the common factor of x from the terms on the left side of the given equation. Therefore,

$$x^3 - 3x^2 - 10x = x(x^2 - 3x - 10) = 0.$$

Whenever $ab = 0$ where a and b are any two numbers, either $a = 0$ or $b = 0$. Hence, either $x = 0$ or $x^2 - 3x - 10 = 0$. The expression $x^2 - 3x - 10$ factors into $(x - 5)(x + 2)$. Therefore, $(x - 5)(x + 2) = 0$. Applying the above law again:

either $x - 5 = 0$ or $x + 2 = 0$
              $x = 5$ or $x = -2$.

Hence,

$$x^3 - 3x^2 - 10x = x(x - 5)(x + 2) = 0$$

Either $x = 0$ or $x = 5$ or $x = -2$.

The solution set is $X = \{0, 5, -2\}$.

We have shown that, if there is a number x such that $x^3 - 3x^2 - 10x = 0$, then $x = 0$ or $x = 5$ or $x = -2$. Finally, to see that these three numbers are actually solutions, we substitute each of them in turn in the original equation to see whether or not it satisfies the equation $x^3 - 3x^2 - 10x = 0$.

Check: Replacing x by 0 in the original equation,

$$(0)^3 - 3(0)^2 - 10(0) = 0 - 0 - 0 = 0 \checkmark$$

Replacing x by 5 in the original equation,

$$(5)^3 - 3(5)^2 - 10(5) = 125 - 3(25) - 50$$
$$= 125 - 75 - 50$$
$$= 50 - 50 = 0 \checkmark$$

Replacing x by -2 in the original equation,

$$(-2)^3 - 3(-2)^2 - 10(-2) = -8 - 3(4) + 20$$
$$= -8 - 12 + 20$$
$$= -20 + 20 = 0 \checkmark$$

● **PROBLEM 20-4**

Form the equation whose roots are 2, -3, and $\frac{7}{5}$.

<u>Solution:</u> The roots of the equation are 2, -3, and $\frac{7}{5}$. Hence, $x = 2$, $x = -3$, and $x = \frac{7}{5}$. Subtract 2 from both sides of the first equation:
$$x - 2 = 2 - 2 = 0.$$

Add 3 to both sides of the second equation:
$$x + 3 = -3 + 3 = 0.$$

Subtract $\frac{7}{5}$ from both sides of the third equation:
$$x - \frac{7}{5} = \frac{7}{5} - \frac{7}{5} = 0.$$

Hence, $(x - 2)(x + 3)\left(x - \frac{7}{5}\right) = (0)(0)(0) = 0$ or
$$(x - 2)(x + 3)\left(x - \frac{7}{5}\right) = 0.$$

Multiply both sides of this equation by 5:
$$5(x - 2)(x + 3)\left(x - \frac{7}{5}\right) = 5(0) \text{ or}$$

$$(x - 2)(x + 3)5\left(x - \frac{7}{5}\right) = 0 \text{ or}$$

$$(x - 2)(x + 3)(5x - 7) = 0$$

$$(x^2 + x - 6)(5x - 7) = 0$$

$$5x^3 - 7x^2 + 5x^2 - 7x - 30x + 42 = 0$$

$$5x^3 - 2x^2 - 37x + 42 = 0.$$

● **PROBLEM 20-5**

Graph the function $y = x^3 - 9x$.

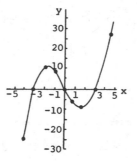

Solution: Choosing values of x in the interval $-4 \leq x \leq 4$, we have for $y = x^3 - 9x$,

x	-4	-3	-2	-1	0	1	2	3	4
y	-28	0	10	8	0	-8	-10	0	28

Notice that for each ordered pair (x,y) listed in the table there exists a pair (-x,-y) which also satisfies the equation, indicating symmetry with respect to the origin. To prove that this is true for all points on the curve, we substitute (-x,-y) for (x,y) in the given equation and show that the equation is unchanged. Thus

$$-y = (-x)^3 - 9(-x) = -x^3 + 9x$$

or, multiplying each member by -1,

$$y = x^3 - 9x$$

which is the original equation.

The curve is illustrated in the figure. The domain and range of the function have no restrictions in the set of real numbers. The x-intercepts are found from

$$y = 0 = x^3 - 9x$$

$$0 = x\left(x^2 - 9\right)$$

$$0 = x(x - 3)(x + 3)$$

$$x = 0 \quad | \quad x - 3 = 0 \quad | \quad x + 3 = 0$$
$$\qquad\qquad\quad x = 3 \qquad\quad x = -3.$$

The curve has three x-intercepts at x = -3, x = 0, x = 3. This agrees with the fact that a cubic equation has three roots. The curve has a single y-intercept at y = 0 since for x = 0, $y = 0^3 - 9(0) = 0$.

● **PROBLEM 20-6**

Locate the roots of $x^3 - 3x^2 - 6x + 9 = 0$.

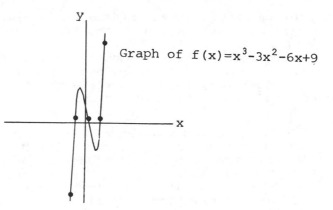

Graph of $f(x) = x^3 - 3x^2 - 6x + 9$

<u>Solution</u>:   If we let $f(x)$ be a function, then a solution of the equation $f(x) = 0$ is called a root of the equation.

In this particular case let the function $f(x) =$ $x^3 - 3x^2 - 6x + 9$ and set it equal to zero to find its roots. When $f(x) = 0$, the graph of this equation crosses the x-axis. These x-values are the roots of the function.

To locate the roots of $x^3 - 3x^2 - 6x + 9 = 0$, we consider the function $y = x^3 - 3x^2 - 6x + 9$, assign consecutive integers from -3 to 5 to x, compute each corresponding value of y, and record the results.

Table of Results

x	$x^3 - 3x^2 - 6x + 9$ $=$	y
-3	$(-3)^3 - 3(-3)^2 - 6(-3) + 9 =$	-27
-2	$(-2)^3 - 3(-2)^2 - 6(-2) + 9 =$	1
-1	$(-1)^3 - 3(-1)^2 - 6(-1) + 9 =$	11
0	$(0)^3 - 3(0)^2 - 6(0) + 9 =$	9
1	$(1)^3 - 3(1)^2 - 6(1) + 9 =$	1
2	$(2)^3 - 3(2)^2 - 6(2) + 9 =$	-7
3	$(3)^3 - 3(3)^2 - 6(3) + 9 =$	-9
4	$(4)^3 - 3(4)^2 - 6(4) + 9 =$	1
5	$(5)^3 - 3(5)^2 - 6(5) + 9 =$	29

Since $f(-3) = -27$ and $f(-2) = 1$, there is an odd number of roots between $x = -3$ and $x = -2$. Since $f(-3) = -27$ which is negative and $f(-2) = 1$ is positive, the graph must cross the x-axis at least once. The function is continuous; thus the curve must connect the two points. To do this, the curve must cross from the negative to the positive side of the x-axis. By the definition of continuity, in order for the curve to tra-

verse the axis it must intersect the axis. Each intersection point is called a zero or a root of the function.

Note that the curve must intersect the x-axis an odd
number of times if it is to pass from the negative side
to the positive, for if it traversed the axis an even
number of times it would end up on the side on which it
started.

Similarly, there is an odd number of roots between
$x = 1$ and $x = 2$, and between $x = 3$ and $x = 4$. Furthermore, since the equation is of degree 3, it has exactly
three roots. Observe that the curve crosses the x-axis
three times, indicating the three roots of the equation.
Therefore, exactly one root lies in each of the above
intervals.

CHAPTER 21

LOGARITHMS AND EXPONENTIALS

EXPRESSIONS

● **PROBLEM 21-1**

Find $\log_{10} 100$.

<u>Solution:</u> The following solution presents 2 methods for solving the given problem.

Method I. The statement $\log_{10} x = y$ is equivalent to $10^y = x$, hence $\log_{10} 100 = x$ is equivalent to $10^x = 100$. Since $10^2 = 100$, $\log_{10} 100 = 2$.

Method II. Note that $100 = 10 \times 10$; thus $\log_{10} 100 = \log_{10} (10 \times 10)$. Recall: $\log_x (a \times b) = \log_x a + \log_x b$, therefore

$$\log_{10} (10 \times 10) = \log_{10} 10 + \log_{10} 10$$

$$= \quad 1 \quad + \quad 1$$

$$= 2.$$

● **PROBLEM 21-2**

Find the logarithm of 3^2.

<u>Solution:</u> Recall that $\log_b x^y = y \log_b x$; thus

$$\log_{10} 3^2 = 2 \log_{10} 3$$

Referring to a table of common logarithms we find:

$\log_{10} 3 = .4771$; hence,

$$= 2(.4771)$$

$$= .9542 .$$

Thus, $\log_{10} 3^2 = .9542$.

We could have obtained the same result by noting that $3^2 = 9$. Using a log table to find $\log_{10} 9$, we observe:

$\log_{10} 9 = .9542$, as above.

● PROBLEM 21-3

Write $\frac{1}{2} = \log_9 3$ in exponential form.

Solution: The statement $\log_b x = y$ is equivalent to the statement $b^y = x$, where b is the base and y the exponent. The latter form is the exponential form. Thus, $\frac{1}{2} = \log_9 3$ in exponential form is $9^{\frac{1}{2}} = 3$, where the base is 9 and the exponent is $\frac{1}{2}$.

● PROBLEM 21-4

If $\log_3 N = 2$, find N.

Solution: The equation $\log_x a = y$ is equivalent to the equation $x^y = a$. Thus $\log_3 N = 2$ is equivalent to the equation $3^2 = N$. $3^2 = 9$, hence $N = 9$.

● PROBLEM 21-5

Find the value of x if $\log_4 64 = x$.

Solution:

$$\log_b u = v$$

is equivalent to,

$$b^v = u,$$

thus the exponential equivalent of

$$\log_4 64 = x \qquad \text{is } 4^x = 64.$$

Since,

$$4^3 = 4 \cdot 4 \cdot 4 = 64$$

$$\log_4 64 = 3.$$

That is,

$$x = 3.$$

● **PROBLEM** 21-6

Find $\log_3 729$.

Solution: Since we are working with log base 3, we check whether 729 has factors of 3.

$$729 = 3 \cdot 243 = 3 \cdot (3 \cdot 81) = 3 \cdot [3 \cdot (3 \cdot 27)] = 3[3 \cdot 3(3 \cdot 9)]$$
$$= [3 \cdot 3 \cdot 3 \cdot 3 \cdot (3 \cdot 3)]$$
$$= 3^6$$

Thus $\log_3 729 = \log_3 3^6 = 6$ (because $\log_b b^a = a$ is equivalent to the statement $b^a = b^a$).

Check: $\log_3 729 = 6$ is equivalent to $3^6 = 729$ which we have just seen to be true.

● **PROBLEM** 21-7

Find the value of N if $\log_8 N = \frac{2}{3}$.

Solution: The inverse of the logarithmic function, $y = \log_a N$, is the exponential function $N = a^y$. Then for

$$\log_8 N = \frac{2}{3},$$

$$N = 8^{2/3} = \sqrt[3]{(8)^2} = (\sqrt[3]{8})^2 = (2)^2 = 4$$

$$N = 4.$$

● **PROBLEM** 21-8

Express the logarithm of 7 to the base 3 in terms of common logarithms.

Solution: By definition, if $\log_b a = n$, then $b^n = a$. Therefore, if $\log_3 7 = x$, then $3^x = 7$. Take the logarithm of both sides:

$$\log 3^x = \log 7.$$

By the law of the logarithm of a power of a positive number which states that $\log a^n = n \log a$, $\log 3^x = x \log 3$. Hence, $x \log 3 = \log 7$. Divide both sides of this equation by $\log 3$:

$$\frac{x \log 3}{\log 3} = \frac{\log 7}{\log 3}.$$

Therefore, $x = \frac{\log 7}{\log 3} = \log_3 7$ is the logarithm of 7 to the base 3 expressed in terms of common logarithms.

● **PROBLEM 21-9**

What is the value of b in the relation $\log_b \frac{1}{25} = -2$?

Solution: Since the statement ,

$$\log_b x = y$$

is equivalent to,

$$b^y = x, \quad \log_b \frac{1}{25} = -2$$

is equivalent to

$$b^{-2} = \frac{1}{25}. \quad x^{-y} = \frac{1}{x^y}$$

thus,

$$b^{-2} = \frac{1}{b^2}.$$ Therefore $b^{-2} = \frac{1}{25}$ is equivalent to $\frac{1}{b^2} = \frac{1}{25}$. Cross multiply to obtain the equivalent equation ,

$$b^2 = 25.$$

Take the square root of both sides. Thus,

$$b = \pm 5$$

● **PROBLEM 21-10**

Express the logarithm of $\dfrac{\sqrt{a^3}}{c^5 b^2}$ in terms of log a, log b and log c.

214

<u>Solution:</u> We apply the following properties of logarithms:

$$\log_b(P \cdot Q) = \log_b P + \log_b Q$$

$$\log_b(P/Q) = \log_b P - \log_b Q$$

$$\log_b(P^n) = n \log_b P$$

$$\log_b(\sqrt[n]{P}) = \frac{1}{n} \log_b P$$

Therefore,

$$\log \frac{\sqrt{a^3}}{c^5 b^2} = \log \frac{a^{3/2}}{c^5 b^2}$$

$$= \log a^{3/2} - \log(c^5 b^2)$$

$$= 3/2 \log a - \left(\log c^5 + \log b^2\right)$$

$$= 3/2 \log a - \log c^5 - \log b^2$$

$$= 3/2 \log a - 5 \log c - 2 \log b \ .$$

● **PROBLEM 21-11**

If $\log_{10} 3 = .4771$ and $\log_{10} 4 = .6021$, find $\log_{10} 12$.

<u>Solution:</u> Since $12 = 3 \times 4$,

$$\log_{10} 12 = \log_{10}(3)(4).$$

Since $\log_b(xy) = \log_b x + \log_b y$

$$\log_{10}(3 \times 4) = \log_{10} 3 + \log_{10} 4$$

$$= .4771 + .6021$$

$$= 1.0792.$$

Thus $\log_{10} 12 = 1.0792$.

● **PROBLEM 21-12**

Given $\log_{10} 2 = 0.3010$, find $\log_{10} 32$.

<u>Solution:</u> Note that,

$$32 = 2 \cdot 2 \cdot 2 \cdot 2 \cdot 2 = 2^5.$$

Thus,

$$\log_{10} 32 = \log_{10} 2^5.$$

Recall the logarithmic property,

$$\log_b x^y = y \log_b x.$$

Hence,

$$\log_{10} 32 = \log_{10} 2^5 = 5 \log_{10} 2$$

$$= 5 \ (0.3010)$$

$$= 1.5050$$

● **PROBLEM 21-13**

Find $\log_{10}\left(10^2 \cdot 10^{-3} \cdot 10^5\right)$.

Solution: Recall $\log_x (a \cdot b \cdot c) = \log_x a + \log_x b + \log_x c$. Thus

$$\log_{10}\left(10^2 \cdot 10^{-3} \cdot 10^5\right) = \log_{10} 10^2 + \log_{10} 10^{-3} + \log_{10} 10^5$$

Recall $\log_b b^x = x$, since $b^x = b^x$; therefore, $\log_{10} 10^2 + \log_{10} 10^{-3} +$

$\log_{10} 10^5 = 2 + (-3) + 5 = 4$. Thus $\log_{10}\left(10^2 \cdot 10^{-3} \cdot 10^5\right) = 4$.

Another method of finding $\log_{10}\left(10^2 \cdot 10^{-3} \cdot 10^5\right)$ is to note

$10^2 \cdot 10^{-3} \cdot 10^5 = 10^{2+(-3)+5} = 10^4$ $\left(\text{because } a^x \cdot a^y \cdot a^z = a^{x+y+z}\right)$.

Thus $\log_{10}\left(10^2 \cdot 10^{-3} \cdot 10^5\right) = \log_{10} 10^4 = 4$.

● **PROBLEM 21-14**

Find the values of the following logarithims:

a) $\log_{10} 10$ b) $\log_{10} 100$ c) $\log_{10} 1$

d) $\log_{10} 0.1$ e) $\log_{10} 0.01$

Solution: The logarithmic expression $N = \log_b x$ is equivalent to $b^N = x$. Hence,

a) Let $N_1 = \log_{10} 10$. Then the logarithmic expression $N_1 = \log_{10} 10$ is equivalent to $10^{N_1} = 10$. Since
$10^1 = 10$, $N_1 = 1$. Therefore, $N_1 = 1 = \log_{10} 10$.

b) Let $N_2 = \log_{10} 100$. Then the logarithmic expression $N_2 = \log_{10} 100$ is equivalent to $10^{N_2} = 100$. Since
$10^2 = 100$, $N_2 = 2$. Therefore, $N_2 = 2 = \log_{10} 100$.

c) Let $N_3 = \log_{10}1$. Then the logarithmic expression $N_3 = \log_{10}1$ is equivalent to $10^{N_3} = 1$. Since $10^0 = 1$, $N_3 = 0$. Therefore, $N_3 = 0 = \log_{10}1$.

d) Let $N_4 = \log_{10}0.1 = \log_{10}\frac{1}{10}$. Then the logarithmic expression $N_4 = \log_1 0.1 = \log_{10}\frac{1}{10}$ is equivalent to $10^{N_4} = \frac{1}{10}$. Since $10^{-1} = \frac{1}{10^1} = \frac{1}{10}$, $N_4 = -1$. Therefore, $N_4 = -1 = \log_{10}0.1$.

e) Let $N_5 = \log_{10}0.01 = \log_{10}\frac{1}{100}$. Then the logarithmic expression $N_5 = \log_{10}0.01 = \log_{10}\frac{1}{100}$ is equivalent to $10^{N_5} = \frac{1}{100}$. Since $10^{-2} = \frac{1}{10^2} = \frac{1}{100}$, $N_5 = -2$. Therefore, $N_5 = -2 = \log_{10}0.01$.

● **PROBLEM 21-15**

Find $\log_9\left(\frac{1}{27}\right)$.

Solution: $\frac{1}{27} = 27^{-1}$, thus $\log_9\left(\frac{1}{27}\right) = \log_9 27^{-1}$. Recall $\log_x a^b = b \log_x a$ so:
$$\log_9 27^{-1} = (-1)\log_9 27 = -\log_9 27.$$

The statement $\log_x a = y$ is equivalent to $x^y = a$ thus $\log_9 27 = y$ is equivalent to $9^y = 27$. Observe that $9 = 3^2$ and $27 = 3^3$ therefore $(3^2)^y = 3^3$. Since $(a^x)^y = a^{xy}$, $3^{2y} = 3^3$. If $a^x = a^y$, $x = y$, thus
$$2y = 3$$
and
$$y = \frac{3}{2}$$
thus $\log_9 27 = \frac{3}{2}$ and $-\log_9 27 = -\frac{3}{2}$. Hence $\log_9\left(\frac{1}{27}\right) = -\frac{3}{2}$

● **PROBLEM 21-16**

Find the base b for which $\log_b 16 = \log_6 36$.

Solution: The statement $y = \log_b a$ is equivalent to the statement $b^y = a$. Thus, $x = \log_6 36$ is equivalent to $6^x = 36$. $6^2 = 36$, thus $x = 2$ and $\log_6 36 = 2$. Replacing

$\log_6 36$ by 2 we obtain $\log_b 16 = 2$, or equivalently $b^2 = 16$. Thus $b = \sqrt{16} = 4$.

● **PROBLEM** 21-17

Evaluate $\log_{10} \sqrt[3]{7}$.

<u>Solution:</u> Since $\sqrt[a]{x} = x^{1/a}$, $\sqrt[3]{7} = 7^{\frac{1}{3}}$, and

$$\log_{10} \sqrt[3]{7} = \log_{10} 7^{\frac{1}{3}}$$

Recall the property of logarithms: $\log_b x^a = a \log_b x$.

Thus, $\log_{10} 7^{\frac{1}{3}} = \frac{1}{3} \log_{10} 7$.

From the table of common logarithms we find that $\log_{10} 7 = .8451$, thus

$$\frac{1}{3} \log_{10} 7 = \frac{1}{3} (.8451) = .2817$$

Therefore, $\log_{10} \sqrt[3]{7} = .2817$.

● **PROBLEM** 21-18

Find the logarithm of 258, using a trig table.

<u>Solution:</u> Since our log tables only give values of logarithms between 1.00 and 9.99 we must express 258 in terms of some number between 1 and 9.99 multiplied by a power of ten. Hence

$$258 = 2.58 \times 100 = 2.58 \times 10^2$$

and $\quad \log 258 = \log\left(2.58 \cdot 10^2\right)$

since $\quad \log_a BC = \log_a B + \log_a C$

$$\log_{10}\left(2.58 \cdot 10^2\right) = \log_{10} 2.58 + \log_{10} 10^2 \ .$$

Since $\log_{10} x = a$ means by definition $10^a = x$,
we note $\log_{10} 10^2 = 2$ because $10^2 = 10^2$;
hence $\quad \log_{10}\left(2.58 \cdot 10^2\right) = \log_{10} 2.58 + 2$. From our trig. table we
read $\log 2.58 = .4116$. Hence $\log 258 = .4116 + 2 = 2.4116$.

Evaluate $\dfrac{\log_{10} 12}{\log_{10} 5}$.

Solution: First calculate $\log_{10} 12$.

$$\log_{10} 12 = \log_{10}(1.2 \times 10)$$

By the law of logarithms which states that $\log_b(x \cdot y) = \log_b x + \log_b y$,

$$\log_{10} 12 = \log_{10}(1.2 \times 10) = \log_{10} 1.2 + \log_{10} 10$$

$$= 0.0792 + 1$$

$$= 1.0792$$

The $\log_{10} 1.2$ was obtained from a table of common logarithms, base 10. Also, $\log_{10} 5 = 0.6990$. This value was also obtained from a table of common logarithms, base 10.

$$\frac{\log_{10} 12}{\log_{10} 5} = \frac{1.0792}{0.6990} = 1.544 \ .$$

Find the logarithm of 30,700.

Solution: First express 30,700 in scientific notation. $30,700 = 3.07 \times 10^4$. 4 is the characteristic. To find the mantissa, see a table of common logarithms of numbers The mantissa is 4871. Thus $\log 30,700 = 4 + .4871 = 4.4871$.

Find $\log 0.0364$.

Solution: $0.0364 = 3.64 \times 10^{-2}$. Therefore, the characteristic, the power of 10, is -2. From a table of logarithms, the mantissa for 3.64 is 0.5611. Therefore, $\log 0.0364 = -2 + 0.5611 = -1.4389$.

Find N if $\log N = 0.7917 - 3$.

<u>Solution:</u> Using a table of logarithms, the mantissa .7917 is found to correspond to the number 6.19. Therefore the antilogarithm is 6.19. Then, since the characteristic is -3,

$$N = 6.19 \times 10^{-3} = 0.00619.$$

● **PROBLEM 21-23**

What is the value of log 0.0148?

<u>Solution:</u> $0.0148 = 1.48 \times 10^{-2}$. The characteristic is the exponent of 10. Hence, the characteristic is -2. The mantissa for 148 can be found in a table of logarithms. The mantissa is 0.1703. Therefore, log 0.0148 = -2 + 0.1703 = -2.0000 + 0.1703 = -1.8297. Notice that the number 0.0148 is less than 1. Therefore, the value of log 0.0148 must be negative, as it was found to be.

● **PROBLEM 21-24**

Determine x when log x = 3.1818.

<u>Solution:</u> $\text{Log}_{10} x = 3.1818$ is equivalent to $10^{3.1818} = x$. Since $a^{x+y} = a^x \cdot a^y$, $x = 10^{3.1818} = 10^3 \cdot 10^{.1818}$

$= 1,000 \cdot 10^{.1818}$

We look in the body of the log table for the mantissa 0.1818 and find it in row 15 and column 2, so that the digits of x are 1.52. Thus

$$x = 1,000 \times 1.52$$

$$= 1520.$$

● **PROBLEM 21-25**

Find Antilog$_{10}$ 0.8762 - 2 .

<u>Solution:</u> Let N = Antilog$_{10}$ 0.8762 - 2. The following relationship between log and antilog exists: $\log_{10} x = a$ is the equivalent of $x = \text{antilog}_{10} a$. Therefore,

$$\log_{10} N = 0.8762 - 2.$$

The characteristic is -2. The mantissa is 0.8762. The number that cor-

220

responds to this mantissa is 7.52. This number is found from a table of common logarithms, base 10. Therefore,

$$N = 7.52 \times 10^{-2}$$

$$= 7.52 \times \left(\frac{1}{10^2}\right)$$

$$= 7.52 \times \left(\frac{1}{100}\right)$$

$$= 7.52(.01)$$

$$N = 0.0752 .$$

Therefore, $N = \text{Antilog}_{10}\ 0.8762 - 2 = 0.0752$.

● **PROBLEM 21-26**

Find the antilogarithm of 1.4349 to three significant figures.

Solution: The mantissa 4349 does not appear in a table of four place logarithms. However, it falls between the two listed mantissas:

4346, whose antilogarithm is 2.72

and   4362, whose antilogarithm is 2.73

Since the given mantissa is closer in value to the mantissa 4346, the three figure sequence of digits in the antilogarithm is 2.72. Using the characteristic 1, we have $2.72 \times 10' = 27.2$. Note that the characteristic is positive, (1), and is one less than the number of digits to the left of the decimal point. Thus there are two digits to the left of the decimal point, (27).

● **PROBLEM 21-27**

Find $\sqrt[5]{.2}$.

Solution: It is easier to perform this computation using logarithms.

Let $N = (.2)^{1/5}$. Then

$$\log N = \log (.2)^{1/5}$$

The characteristic of the common logarithm of any positive number less than 1 is negative and is one more than the number of zeros between the decimal point and the first digit.

To find the mantissa, see a table of common logarithms of numbers.

Thus for log (.2) = $\underbrace{.3010}_{\text{mantissa}} \overbrace{- 1}^{\text{characteristic}}$

Then: log N = $\frac{1}{5}$ log .2 = $\frac{.3010 - 1}{5}$.

If we proceed with the arithmetic at this point, we shall

find that log N = $\frac{- .6990}{5}$ = - .1398. But this last number

must be written in standard form before we can solve for N. It is easier to replace the number (.3010 - 1) with its equivalent expression (4.3010 - 5) before we divide by 5. Then

$$\log N = \frac{4.3010 - 5}{5} = .8602 - 1.$$

See a table to find the mantissa, 8602 and look for the corresponding number. We find 7248. Adjust the decimal point by its characteristic, - 1. Hence,

$$\sqrt[5]{.2} = .7248.$$

● **PROBLEM** 21-28

Evaluate

$$\frac{542.3\sqrt{0.1383}}{32.72}$$ using logarithms.

Solution: Let x denote the above expression. Then,

$$x = \frac{542.3\sqrt{0.1383}}{32.72} .$$

Take the logarithms of both sides to obtain:

$$\log x = \log \frac{542.3(0.1383)^{1/2}}{32.72}$$

Apply the following properties of logarithms:

$$\log\left(\frac{a}{b}\right) = \log a - \log b$$

$$\log(a \cdot b) = \log a + \log b$$

$$\log a^n = n \log a$$

Then,

$$\log x = \log 542.3(0.1383)^{1/2} - \log 32.72$$

$$= \log 542.3 + \log(0.1383)^{1/2} - \log 32.72$$

$$= \log 542.3 + \frac{1}{2} \log(0.1383) - \log 32.72$$

To find the characteristic and mantissa of each number, express each number in powers of 10. The exponent is the corresponding characteristic

$$542.3 = 5.423 \times 10^2$$
$$0.1383 = 1.383 \times 10^{-1}$$
$$32.72 = 3.272 \times 10^1$$

Note that these numbers are expressed as numbers between 1 and 10, multiplied by a power of ten. Look up the corresponding number in a table of common logarithms of numbers. This is the mantissa. Then,

$$\log 542.3 = 2.7343$$

$$\log 0.1383 = -1.1408.$$

The form 19.1408 - 20 is more convenient for computation.

$$\log 32.72 = 1.5148$$

Hence

$$\tfrac{1}{2} \log 0.1383 = \tfrac{1}{2}(19.1408 - 20) = 9.5704 - 10,$$

$$\log 542.3 = 2.7342$$

$$\tfrac{1}{2} \log 0.1383 + \log 542.3 \qquad = 9.5704\text{-}10 + 2.7342 = 2.3046$$

$$\log 32.72 = 1.5148$$

$$\log 542.3 + \tfrac{1}{2} \log(0.1383) - \log 32.72 \qquad = 2.3046 - 1.5148 = 0.7898$$

$$\log x = 0.7898$$

Look up the mantissa and we find the number is 6163. To adjust the decimal point, we note that the characteristic is 0. Since the characteristic is positive, it is one less than the number of digits to the left of the decimal point. Here, there is one digit to the left of the decimal point. Thus, the number is 6.163, and

$$x = 6.163.$$

Therefore,

$$\frac{542.3\sqrt{0.1383}}{32.72} = 6.163.$$

INTERPOLATION

● **PROBLEM** 21-29

Use linear interpolation to find log 5.723.

Solution: Since 5.723 is .3 of the way from 5.72 to 5.73, we argue that log 5.723 is approximately .3 of the way from log 5.72 to log 5.73.

This is the basic idea involved in linear interpolation. We obtain log 5.72 and log 5.73 from a table of common logarithms, and find the mantissas to be 7574 and 7582, respectively. We now use interpolation to find the mantissa for 5.723.

Number   Mantissa

Note: Observe that 5.73 - 5.72 = 0.1, and
5.723 - 5.72 = .003; but we can rewrite these as 1 and
.3 by shifting the decimal two places.

$$\frac{.3}{1} = \frac{x}{8}$$

$$x = 2.4 \stackrel{\sim}{\sim} 2$$

Thus, the mantissa of the given number is
7574 + 2 = 7576. Since the number is 5.723, and there is
one digit before the decimal point, we know that the
characteristic is one less than the number of digits, or
one less than one, or 0. Thus,

$$\log 5.723 = .7576.$$

● **PROBLEM 21-30**

Find log 0.7056.

Solution: First determine the characteristic by realiz-
ing that it will be one more than the number of zeros to
the right of the decimal point, with a negative sign
because the number is less than one. Thus, the characteristic is - 1. To compute the mantissa notice that the
number 7056 lies between 7050 and 7060, so that its
log will occur between the logs of those numbers. Inter-
polating we obtain

log

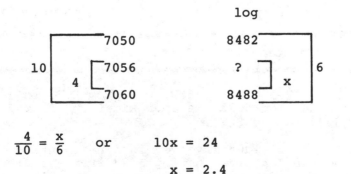

$$\frac{4}{10} = \frac{x}{6} \quad \text{or} \quad 10x = 24$$

$$x = 2.4$$

Now subtract this value from the higher mantissa

$$\begin{array}{r} 8488 \\ 2.4 \\ \hline 8485.6 \end{array}$$

The mantissa is always less than one so the decimal point must be moved four places to the left.

Now - 1 can be written as 9 - 10 for convenience, so our final answer becomes

$$\log 0.7056 = 9.84856-10$$

● **PROBLEM** 21-31

Determine log 51.83.

<u>Solution:</u> With the fourth digit dropped, the remaining three-digit number is 518, and the next larger one is 519. Schematically, we have

$$
\begin{array}{cc}
\text{Number} & \text{Log}
\end{array}
$$

$$
10\left[3\begin{array}{c}
\left[\begin{array}{cc}5180 & 7143\end{array}\right] \\
\left[\begin{array}{cc}5183 & x\end{array}\right] h \\
\begin{array}{cc}5190 & 7152\end{array}
\end{array}\right]9,
$$

We set up the proportion $\dfrac{h}{9} = \dfrac{1}{10}$. Cross multiplying we obtain

$$10h = 27$$

$$h = \frac{27}{10} \cong 3.$$

Thus x = 7143 + 3 = .7146.

Since $51.83 = 5.183 \times 10$

$$\log 51.83 = \log(5.183 \times 10)$$

$$= \log 5.183 + \log 10$$

$$= .7146 + 1$$

$$= 1.7146.$$

● **PROBLEM** 21-32

Find Antilog$_{10}$ 1.4850.

<u>Solution:</u> By definition, Antilog$_{10}$ a = N is equivalent to $\log_{10} N = a$.

Let Antilog$_{10}$1.4850 = N. Hence, Antilog$_{10}$1.4850 = N is equivalent to log$_{10}$N = 1.4850. The characteristic is 1. The mantissa is 0.4850. Therefore, the number that corresponds to this mantissa will be multiplied by 10^1 or 10. The mantissas which appear in a table of common logarithms and are closest to the mantissa 0.4850 are 0.4843 and 0.4857. The number that corresponds to the mantissa 0.4850 will be found by interpolation.

	Number	Logarithms
	3.05	0.4843
d $\bigg[$ x	0.4850 $\bigg]$ .0007
.01 $\bigg[$ 3.06	0.4857 $\bigg]$ .0014

Set up the following proportion.

$$\frac{d}{.01} = \frac{.0007}{.0014}$$

cross-multiplying, .0014d = (.01)(.0007), or d = .01$\left(\frac{.0007}{.0014}\right)$

$$= \left(1 \times 10^{-2}\right)\left(\frac{7 \times 10^{-4}}{1.4 \times 10^{-3}}\right)$$

$$= \frac{7 \times 10^{-6}}{1.4 \times 10^{-3}} = \frac{7}{1.4} \times \frac{10^{-6}}{10^{-3}} = 5 \times 10^{-6-(-3)}$$

$$= 5 \times 10^{-3} = 5 \times .001 = .005$$

Hence, d = 0.005

$\qquad$ x = d + 3.05

$\qquad$ = 0.005 + 3.050

$\qquad$ = 3.055

Hence, N = Antilog$_{10}$1.4850 = 3.055 $\times$ 10

$\qquad\qquad\qquad\qquad\qquad$ = 30.550

$\qquad\qquad\qquad\qquad\qquad$ = 30.55

Therefore Antilog$_{10}$1.4850 = 30.55.

● **PROBLEM 21-33**

Find Antilog 2.3625.

Solution: By definition, b = **Antilog** a, is equivalent to log b = a. Let N = **Antilog** 2.3625. Therefore, log N = 2.3625. The characteristic is 2. Hence, the number that corresponds to the mantissa 0.3625 will be multiplied by 10^2 or 100. In a table of four-place common logarithms, the mantissas 0.3617 and 0.3636 are those given that are closest to 0.3625. Therefore, since the mantissa 0.3625 does not appear in the table,

the number that corresponds to this mantissa will be found through interpolation.

Number		Log		
	2.30	0.3617		
.01 d	x	0.3625	.0008	.0019
	2.31	0.3636		

The following proportion is now established:

$$\frac{d}{.01} = \frac{.0008}{.0019}$$

Cross multiplying,

$$.0019d = (.01)(.0008)$$

$$d = .01\left(\frac{.0008}{.0019}\right)$$

$$= 1 \times 10^{-2}\left(\frac{8 \times 10^{-4}}{1.9 \times 10^{-3}}\right)$$

$$= \frac{8 \times 10^{-2+(-4)}}{1.9 \times 10^{-3}} = \frac{8 \times 10^{-6}}{1.9 \times 10^{-3}}$$

$$= \frac{8}{1.9} \times \frac{10^{-6}}{10^{-3}}$$

$$= 4.2 \times 10^{-6-(-3)}$$

$$= 4.2 \times 10^{-3}$$

$$d = .0042$$

Hence, $x = 2.30 + 0.0042 = 2.3042 \approx 2.304$. Therefore, **Antilog** 2.3625 =

$$N = 2.304 \times 10^2$$

$$= 2.304 \times 100$$

$$= 230.4$$

FUNCTIONS AND EQUATIONS

● **PROBLEM** 21-34

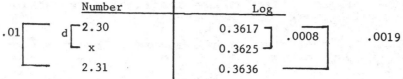

Write the following equations in logarithmic form.
(a) $3^4 = 81$ (b) $10^0 = 1$ (c) $M^k = 5$ (d) $5^k = M$

Solution: The expression $b^y = x$ is equivalent to the
logarithmic expression $\log_b x = y$. Hence,

a) $3^4 = 81$ is equivalent to the logarithmic expression
$\log_3 81 = 4$

b) $10^0 = 1$ is equivalent to the logarithmic expression

$$\log_{10} 1 = 0$$

c) $M^k = 5$ is equivalent to the logarithmic expression
$$\log_M 5 = k$$

d) $5^k = M$ is equivalent to the logarithmic expression
$$\log_5 M = k.$$

● **PROBLEM 21-35**

Show that $\log_{10} 10{,}000^{\frac{1}{2}} = \frac{1}{2} \log_{10} 10{,}000$.

<u>Solution:</u> We will evaluate both sides of this equation, and show them to be equal to the same quantity:

$$\underline{\log_{10} 10{,}000^{\frac{1}{2}}} \qquad\qquad \underline{\tfrac{1}{2}\log_{10} 10{,}000}$$

Since $x^{\frac{1}{2}} = \sqrt{x}$

$\log_{10} 10{,}000^{\frac{1}{2}} = \log_{10}\sqrt{10{,}000}$

$\qquad = \log_{10} 100$

$\qquad = 2$

$\tfrac{1}{2}\log_{10} 10{,}000 = \tfrac{1}{2}\log_{10} 10^4$

$\qquad = \tfrac{1}{2}\cdot 4$

$\qquad = 2$

Thus $\log_{10} 10{,}000^{\frac{1}{2}} = 2 = \tfrac{1}{2}\log_{10} 10{,}000$, and

$$\log_{10} 10{,}000^{1/2} = \tfrac{1}{2}\log_{10} 10{,}000.$$

● **PROBLEM 21-36**

Solve the equation $\log_3(x^2 - 8x) = 2$.

<u>Solution:</u> The expression $\log_b a = y$ is equivalent to $b^y = a$. Hence, $\log_3(x^2 - 8x) = 2$ is equivalent to $3^2 = x^2 - 8x$. Therefore,

$$3^2 = x^2 - 8x$$
or $\qquad 9 = x^2 - 8x$.

Subtract 9 both sides of this equation:

$$9 - 9 = x^2 - 8x - 9$$
$$0 = x^2 - 8x - 9.$$

Factoring this equation:

$$0 = (x - 9)(x + 1).$$

Whenever the product $ab = 0$ where a and b are any two numbers, either $a = 0$ or $b = 0$. Hence, either

$$x - 9 = 0 \quad \text{or} \quad x + 1 = 0$$
$$x = 9 \quad \text{or} \quad x = -1.$$

228

Solve the equation $2^x = 7$ for x.

Solution: By taking logarithms of both sides of the equation, we obtain the equation

$\log 2^x = \log 7$.

Using the rule $\log M^x = x \log M$, we obtain:

$x \log 2 = \log 7$

From a table on common logarithms the $\log 2 = .3010$ and the $\log 7 = .8451$. So our equation becomes $.3010x = .8451$. Hence,

$x = \dfrac{.8451}{.3010} = 2.808$.

Remark 1. Since $2^2 = 4$ and $2^3 = 8$, it should be obvious at the start that the solution of the equation $2^x = 7$ is a number between 2 and 3.

Remark 2. Since $x \log 2 = \log 7$, it follows that $x = \log 7/\log 2$. It should be emphasized that the expression $\log 7/\log 2$ is a quotient. We do not evaluate this quotient by looking up $\log 2$ and $\log 7$ in the table and subtracting; we look up the two numbers and divide. We can divide with the aid of logarithms, but it still will be division.

Solve the equation $2^x = 3^{x+1}$ for x.

Solution: We take logarithms of both sides of the equation to obtain the equation:

$$\log \left(2^x\right) = \log \left(3^{x+1}\right)$$

Using the rule $\log_b M^x = x \log_b M$, we obtain:

$$x \log 2 = (x + 1) \log 3.$$

Hence, $x \log 2 = x \log 3 + \log 3$, by distributing $\log 3$; and

$$x \log 2 - x \log 3 = \log 3,$$

or in other words $x(\log 2 - \log 3) = \log 3$

$$x = \frac{\log 3}{\log 2 - \log 3} \, .$$

Using a table of common logarithms we obtain:

$$x = \frac{.4771}{.3010 - .4771} = \frac{.4771}{- .1761} = - \, 2.709.$$

● **PROBLEM** 21-39

Express   y   in terms of   x   if

$$\log_b y = 2x + \log_b x \, .$$

<u>Solution:</u> Transposing $\log_b x$, we have

$$\log_b y - \log_b x = 2x,$$

A property of logarithms is that the logarithm of the quotient of two positive numbers S and T is equal to the difference of the logarithms of the numbers; that is,

$$\log_b \frac{S}{T} = \log_b S - \log_b T \, .$$

Therefore,

$$\log_b \frac{y}{x} = 2x \, .$$

Now use the definition of logarithm: The logarithm of N to the base b is $x = \log_b N$; and $b^x = N$ is an equivalent statement. Then,

$$2x = \log_b \frac{y}{x} \text{ is equivalent to}$$

$$b^{2x} = \frac{y}{x}$$

Solving for y we obtain:

$$y = x \cdot b^{2x}$$

● **PROBLEM** 21-40

Solve the equation 2 log x - log 10x = 0.

<u>Solution:</u> We can use a fundamental property of logarithms to simplify the left-hand side of this equation.

The logarithm of the product of two or more positive numbers is equal to the sum of the logarithms of the several numbers. If P, Q, and R are positive numbers, then log (P · Q · R) = log P + log Q + log R.

2 log x - log 10x = 2 log x - (log 10 + log x)

230

$$= 2 \log x - \log 10 - \log x$$

$$= \log x - \log 10.$$

But log 10 means that base 10 raised to what power = 10, or $10^? = 10$; and $10^1 = 10$. Thus, log 10 = 1, and the equation becomes: log x - 1 = 0.

Rewriting this equation:

$$\log x - 1 = 0$$

$$\log x = 1$$

Since the problem is in base 10, log x = 1 can be re-written as,

$$10^1 = x. \text{ Thus } x = 10.$$

● **PROBLEM** 21-41

Solve the equation log 2 + 2 log x = log(5x + 3).

<u>Solution :</u> By the law of the logarithm of a power of a positive number which states that

$$\log a^n = n \log a, \ 2 \log x = \log x^2.$$

Hence, $\log 2 + 2 \log x = \log 2 + \log x^2 = \log(5x + 3)$. Therefore, $\log 2 + \log x^2 = \log(5x + 3)$. By the law of the logarithm of a product of two numbers which states that $\log(a \cdot b) = \log a + \log b$, $\log 2 + \log x^2 = \log 2x^2$. Therefore, $\log 2x^2 = \log(5x + 3)$. Hence, $2x^2 = 5x + 3$. Subtract 5x from both sides to obtain:

$$2x^2 - 5x = \cancel{5x} + 3 - \cancel{5x}.$$

Combining terms, $2x^2 - 5x = 3$. Subtract 3 from both sides to obtain:

$$2x^2 - 5x - 3 = 3 - 3.$$

Combining terms, $2x^2 - 5x - 3 = 0$. Factoring the left side of this equation into two polynomial factors, $(2x + 1)(x - 3) = 0$. Whenever $a \cdot b = 0$ where a and b are any two real numbers, either a = 0 or b = 0. Therefore, either

$$2x + 1 = 0 \quad \text{or} \quad x - 3 = 0.$$

$$2x = -1$$

and $\qquad x = -\dfrac{1}{2}$ or $\qquad x = 3.$

231

Since the domain of the logarithmic function is the set of positive real numbers, it is important to check all proposed solutions of a logarithmic equation. In this example, the given equation is satisfied for x = 3, but $x = -\frac{1}{2}$ is not a solution since $\log\left(-\frac{1}{2}\right)$ is not defined in the relation

$$\log 2 + 2 \log \left(-\frac{1}{2}\right) = \log \frac{1}{2}.$$

● **PROBLEM** 21-42

Solve the equation $x^{\log x} = 100x$.

Solution: By taking logarithms of both sides of the equation, we obtain the equivalent equation

$$\log \left[x^{\log x}\right] = \log 100x.$$

But, by the law of exponents which states $\log x^p = p \log x$,

$$\log \left[x^{\log x}\right] = (\log x)(\log x) = (\log x)^2.$$

Also, by another law of exponents which states

$$\log (x \cdot y) = \log x + \log y,$$

$$\log 100x = \log 100 + \log x.$$

Now, since $\log 100$ can be equivalently written as $\log_{10} 100$, then $\log_{10} 100 = x$ or $10^x = 100$; and we can replace $\log 100$ by 2 ($10^2 = 100$).

Thus, we have: $2 + \log x$.

We can therefore write our equation as

$$(\log x)^2 = 2 + \log x,$$

and so it is equivalent to the equation

$$(\log x)^2 - \log x - 2, \quad \text{and factoring:}$$

$$= (\log x - 2)(\log x + 1) = 0.$$

Now, $\{(\log x - 2)(\log x + 1) = 0\}$

$$= \{x \mid \log x = 2 \text{ or } \log x = -1\}$$

$$= \{\log x = 2\} \cup \{\log x = -1\}.$$

Recall that when no base is expressed it is assumed to be 10. Thus, the equation $\log x = 2$ means $10^2 = x$, or $x = 100$; and $\log x = -1$ means $10^{-1} = x$, or $x = \frac{1}{10}$. Thus,

$$\{100\} \cup \left\{\frac{1}{10}\right\} = \left\{100, \frac{1}{10}\right\},$$

and this is the set of numbers that solves the given equation.

● **PROBLEM 21-43**

Solve the equation $27^{x^2+1} = 243$.

Solution: We seek all numbers which satisfy the equation. If x is such a number, then

$$27^{x^2+1} = 243$$

Then, taking logarithms to the base 3 of both sides we have

$$\log_3 27^{x^2+1} = \log_3 243$$

Since $\log_b x^r = r \log_b x$, it follows that

$$(x^2 + 1)\log_3 27 = \log_3 243.$$

Note that the expression $\log_b x = y$ is equivalent to $b^y = x$. Hence, $\log_3 27 = N$ is equivalent to $3^N = 27$. Therefore, $N = 3$ and $\log_3 27 = 3$. Also, $\log_3 243 = M$ is equivalent to $3^M = 243$. Therefore, $M = 5$ and $\log_3 243 = 5$. Hence,

$$(x^2 + 1)3 = 5$$

or, by the commutative property of multiplication,

$$3(x^2 + 1) = 5.$$

Divide both sides of the equation by 3.

$$\frac{3(x^2 + 1)}{3} = \frac{5}{3}$$

$$x^2 + 1 = \frac{5}{3}$$

Subtract 1 from both sides of the equation.

$$x^2 + 1 - 1 = \frac{5}{3} - 1$$

$$x^2 = \frac{5}{3} - 1 = \frac{5}{3} - \frac{3}{3} = \frac{2}{3}$$

Therefore, $x = \pm \sqrt{\dfrac{2}{3}}$, i.e., $x = \sqrt{\dfrac{2}{3}}$ or $x = -\sqrt{\dfrac{2}{3}}$.

To check that each of these numbers satisfies the given equation, substitute each number for x in the given equation. Substituting $\sqrt{\dfrac{2}{3}}$ for x:

$$(27)^{(\sqrt{2/3})^2 + 1} = (27)^{(2/3)+1} = 27^{5/3} = \sqrt[3]{27^5} = \left(\sqrt[3]{27}\right)^5$$
$$= (3)^5$$
$$= 243 \checkmark$$

Substituting $-\sqrt{\dfrac{2}{3}}$ for x:

$$(27)^{(-\sqrt{2/3})^2 + 1} = (27)^{(2/3)+1} = 27^{5/3} = \sqrt[3]{27^5} = \left(\sqrt[3]{27}\right)^5$$
$$= (3)^5$$
$$= 243 \checkmark$$

CHAPTER 22

DECIMAL / FRACTIONAL CONVERSIONS, SCIENTIFIC NOTATION

● **PROBLEM 22-1**

Use scientific notation to express each number.
(a) 4,375   (b) 186,000   (c) 0.00012   (d) 4,005

<u>Solution:</u> A number expressed in scientific notation is written as a product of a number between 1 and 10 and a power of 10. The number between 1 and 10 is obtained by moving the decimal point of the number (actual or implied) the required number of digits. The power of 10, for a number greater than 1, is positive and is one less than the number of digits before the decimal point in the original number. The power of 10, for a number less than 1, is negative and is one more than the number of zeros immediately following the decimal point in the original number. Hence,

(a) $4,375 = 4.375 \times 10^3$ (b) $186,000 = 1.86 \times 10^5$

(c) $0.00012 = 1.2 \times 10^{-4}$ (d) $4,005 = 4.005 \times 10^3$

● **PROBLEM 22-2**

Express $\dfrac{6,400,000}{400}$ in scientific notation.

<u>Solution:</u> In order to solve this problem, we express the numerator and denominator as the product of a number between 1 and 10 and a power of 10. This is known as scientific notation. Thus

$$6,400,000 = 6.4 \times 1,000,000 = 6.4 \times 10^6$$
$$400 = 4 \times 100 = 4 \times 10^2$$

Thus,

$$\frac{6,400,000}{400} = \frac{6.4 \times 10^6}{4.0 \times 10^2}$$

Since $\dfrac{ab}{cd} = \dfrac{a}{c} \cdot \dfrac{b}{c}$: $= \dfrac{6.4}{4.0} \times \dfrac{10^6}{10^2}$

Since $\dfrac{a^x}{a^y} = a^{x-y}$: $= 1.6 \times 10^4$

● **PROBLEM 22-3**

Write $\dfrac{2}{7}$ as a repeating decimal.

Solution: To write a fraction as a repeating decimal divide the numerator by the denominator, until a pattern of repeated digits appears.

$$2 \div 7 = .285714285714...$$

Identify the entire portion of the decimal which is repeated. The repeating decimal can then be written in the shortened form:

$$\dfrac{2}{7} = .\overline{285714}$$

● **PROBLEM 22-4**

Find the common fraction form of the repeating decimal 0.4242....

Solution: Let x represent the repeating decimal.

$$x = 0.4242...$$

$$100x = 42.42... \quad \text{by multiplying by 100}$$

$$\underline{x = 0.42...}$$

$$99x = 42 \qquad \text{(1) by subtracting x from 100x}$$

Divide both sides of equation (1) by 99.

$$\dfrac{99x}{99} = \dfrac{42}{99}$$

$$x = \dfrac{42}{99} = \dfrac{14}{33}$$

The repeating decimal of this example had 2 digits that repeated. The first step in the solution was to multiply both sides of the original equation by the 2nd power of 10 or 10^2 or 100. If there were 3 digits that repeated, the first step in the solution would be to multiply both sides of the original equation by the 3rd power of 10 or 10^3 or 1000.

Find $0.25\overline{25}$ as a quotient of integers.

Solution: Let $x = 0.25\overline{25}$.(1) Multiply both sides of this equation by 100:

$$100x = 100(0.25\overline{25})$$

Multiplying by 100 is equivalent to moving the decimal two places to the right, and since the digits 25 are repeated we have:

$$100x = 25.25\overline{25} \qquad (2)$$

Now subtract equation (1) from equation (2):

$$100x = 25.25\overline{25}$$
$$- \quad x = \quad 0.25\overline{25}$$
$$\overline{99x = 25.0000}$$

or $99x = 25$ (3)

(Note that this operation eliminates the decimal)
Dividing both sides of equation (3) by 99:

$$\frac{99x}{99} = \frac{25}{99}$$

$$x = \frac{25}{99}$$

Therefore,

$$0.25\overline{25} = x = \frac{25}{99}$$

Also, note that the given repeating decimal, $0.25\overline{25}$, was multiplied by 100 or 10^2, where the power of 10 (which is 2) is the same as the number of repeating digits (namely, 2) for this problem. In general, for problems of this type, if the repeating decimal has n repeating digits, then the repeating decimal should be multiplied by 10^n.

Write the repeating decimal $14.\overline{23}$ as a quotient of two integers, $\frac{p}{q}$.

Solution: Let $x = 14.\overline{23}$. (1) Multiply both sides of this equation by 100:

$$100x = 100(14.\overline{23})$$

$$100x = 1423.\overline{23} \qquad (2)$$

Subtract equation (1) from equation (2):

$$100x = 1423.\overline{23}$$

$$- \quad x = \quad 14.\overline{23}$$

$$99x = 1409.00$$

or $\qquad 99x = 1409 \qquad\qquad (3)$

(Note that this operation eliminates the decimal.) Dividing both sides of equation (3) by 99:

$$\frac{99x}{99} = \frac{1409}{99}$$

$$x = \frac{1409}{99}.$$

Therefore,

$$14.\overline{23} = x = \frac{1409}{99}.$$

Also, note that the given repeating decimal, $14.\overline{23}$, was multiplied by 100 or 10^2, where the power of 10 (which is 2) is the same as the number of repeating digits (namely, 2) for this problem. In general, for problems of this type, if the repeating decimal has n repeating digits, then the repeating decimal should be multiplied by 10^n.

CHAPTER 23

AREAS AND PERIMETERS

● **PROBLEM 23-1**

Find the area of a rectangle with base of length 12 and diagonal of length 13.

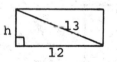

Solution: First find h, the length of the altitude of the rectangle.

In a right triangle, the square of the hypotenuse equals the sum of the squares of the legs.

Hence, $(\text{leg})^2 + (\text{leg})^2 = (\text{hypotenuse})^2$

$$h^2 + 12^2 = 13^2$$

$$h^2 + 144 = 169$$

$$h^2 = 25, \ h = 5$$

Since the area of a rectangle is the product of the base and altitude, the area of the rectangle = 12(5) = 60.

● **PROBLEM 23-2**

One side of a rectangle is twice the length of the other side, and the perimeter is 36. Find the area of the rectangle.

Solution: Since one side of the rectangle is twice the other side, w and 2w can be used to represent the width and the length of the rectangle.

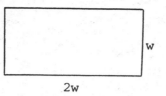

2w

Since the perimeter = 36,

$$2w + 2w + w + w = 36$$

$$6w = 36, \ w = 6$$

Hence, the width = 6 and the length = 12.

Since the area of a rectangle is the product of the length and width, the area = 12(6) = 72.

● **PROBLEM 23-3**

The area of a square is 9. The square and an equilateral triangle have equal perimeters. Find the length of a side of the triangle.

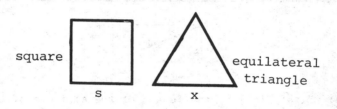

Solution: The area of a square is the square of a side; hence, if s is the side of the square,
$$s^2 = 9$$

Take the square root of each side.

$$s = 3$$

The perimeter of the square is 4 times a side. Hence, the perimeter of the square = 4(3) = 12.

The perimeter of the equilateral triangle is 3 times a side, that is, 3x.

Since the perimeters are equal, 3x = 12 and x = 4. Hence the length of a side of the triangle is 4.

● **PROBLEM 23-4**

The diagonals of a rhombus are represented by n and n + 3. Express the area of the rhombus in terms of n.

Solution: The area of a rhombus equals one-half the product of the diagonals.

240

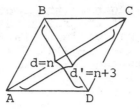

If K = area of rhombus,

   K = ½dd'

Substitute n for d and (n+3) for d'.

   $K = \frac{1}{2}n(n + 3)$ or $\frac{1}{2}(n^2 + 3n)$ or $\frac{n^2 + 3n}{2}$.

● **PROBLEM 23-5**

The area of a rhombus is equal to the area of a square whose side is 6. If the length of one diagonal of the rhombus is 8, how long is the other diagonal?

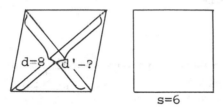

Solution: Since the side, s, of the square is 6, the area of the square = s^2 = 36. Therefore,

   area of rhombus = 36.

The area of a rhombus equals one-half the product of its diagonals. Hence, ½dd' = 36.

Substitute 8 for d.

   ½(8)d' = 36

   4d' = 36

   d' = 9

● **PROBLEM 23-6**

A square parcel of land has twice the area of a rectangular parcel whose length is 9 feet less and whose width is 40 feet less. What are the dimensions of the square parcel of land?

Solution: Let x = the side of the square parcel of land.

Then $x - 9$ is the length of the rectangular parcel, and $x - 40$ is the width of the rectangular parcel. Since the area of the square parcel is x^2, and the area of the rectangular parcel is $(x - 9)(x - 40)$, the equation relating the two areas is then

$$x^2 = 2(x - 9)(x - 40) \qquad\qquad (1)$$

$$x^2 = 2x^2 - 98x + 720 \qquad\qquad (2)$$

or $\quad x^2 - 98x + 720 = 0 \qquad\qquad (3)$

In factored form, we have

$$(x - 90)(x - 8) = 0 \qquad\qquad (4)$$

So that $x = 90$ and $x = 8$.

From the statement of the problem $x = 8$ must be rejected as the side of the square parcel, because the dimensions of the rectangular parcel are 9 feet and 40 feet less than the side of the square parcel. That is, if $x = 8$ were accepted as the side of the square, then the rectangular parcel would have negative dimensions, which is impossible.

● **PROBLEM 23-7**

Find the dimensions of a rectangular piece of metal whose area is 35 square inches and whose perimeter is 24 inches.

Solution: Let x = width and y = length. The area of a rectangle is equal to width times length. The perimeter of a rectangle is equal to 2 times the width plus 2 times the length. Therefore, the area may be expressed as $xy = 35$, while the perimeter can be written as $2x + 2y = 24$. Since area and perimeter are simultaneous properties of a rectangle we have the system:

$$xy = 35$$
$$2x + 2y = 24$$

The computation can be arranged in the following manner: From $xy = 35$ we obtain

$$y = \frac{35}{x} .$$

Using this expression for y, and substituting, $2x + 2y = 24$ becomes,

$$2x + 2\left(\frac{35}{x}\right) = 24$$

Multiplying both sides of the equation by x: (this is allowed since $x \neq 0$ because width can't = 0)

$$2x^2 + 70 = 24x$$

Put in standard quadratic form and solve for x by factoring:

$$2x^2 - 24x + 70 = 0$$
$$x^2 - 12x + 35 = 0$$

$$(x - 5)(x - 7) = 0$$
$$x - 5 = 0 \quad \text{or} \quad x - 7 = 0$$
$$x = 5 \quad \text{or} \quad x = 7$$

Solve for y using the area equation, xy = 35:

when x = 5, 5(y) = 35; thus, y = 7

when x = 7, 7y = 35; thus, y = 5. Then check using the perimeter equation:

$$x = 5, \, y = 7 : \quad 2(5) + 2(7) = 24$$
$$x = 7, \, y = 5 : \quad 2(7) + 2(5) = 24$$

Hence the solution set is $\{(5,7),(7,5)\}$. Thus the dimensions of the piece of metal are 5 by 7 inches.

● **PROBLEM 23-8**

The bases of a trapezoid are 10 inches and 20 inches. If the area of the trapezoid is 60 square inches, find the number of inches in the length of the altitude of the trapezoid.

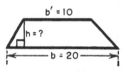

Solution: Find altitude h as follows:

The area of a trapezoid equals one-half the product of the altitude and the sum of the bases.

If K = area of the trapezoid,

$$K = \frac{h}{2}(b + b')$$

Substitute 60 for K, 20 for b, and 10 for b'.

$$60 = \frac{h}{2}(20 + 10) = \frac{h}{2}(30)$$

$$60 = 15h, \quad h = 4; \text{ thus the altitude is } 4 \text{ inches.}$$

● **PROBLEM 23-9**

In parallelogram ABCD, AB = 8 inches, AD = 6 inches, and angle A = 30°. Find the number of square inches in the area of the parallelogram.

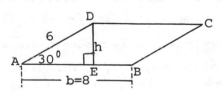

<u>Solution:</u> In right $\triangle ADE$, h is opposite 30°. Since a leg opposite 30° equals one-half the hypotenuse,

$$h = \frac{6}{2} = 3$$

The area of a parallelogram equals the product of the base and the altitude.

Area of $\square ABCD$ = bh

Substitute 8 for b and 3 for h.

Area of $\square ABCD$ = 8(3) = 24

● **PROBLEM** 23-10

The area of a circle is 49π. Find the circumference of the circle in terms of π.

Area = 49π

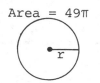

<u>Solution:</u> First find the radius, r, as follows:

The area of a circle equals the product of π and the square of the radius.

If K = the area of the circle, then

$$K = \pi r^2$$

Substitute 49π for K.

$$49\pi = \pi r^2$$

Divide each side by π and then take the square root of each side.

$$7 = r$$

Find C, the circumference, as follows:

The circumference of a circle equals the product of 2π and the radius.

Hence, C = 2πr

$$= 2\pi(7) = 14\pi \ .$$

● **PROBLEM** 23-11

The circumference of a circle is 8π. What is the area of the circle in terms of π ?

<u>Solution:</u> First find the radius, r, as follows:

The circumference of a circle equals the product of 2π and the radius.

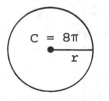

If C = the circumference of the circle, then

$$2\pi r = C$$

Substitute 8π for C.

$$2\pi r = 8\pi$$

Divide each side by 2π.

$$r = 4$$

Now, since area = πr^2, area = $\pi 4^2 = 16\pi$.

● **PROBLEM 23-12**

In the accompanying figure, the large rectangle has been divided into a square and three smaller rectangles. If the areas of the square and two of the rectangles are k^2, 4k, and 8k, respectively, what is the numerical value of the area of the shaded rectangle?

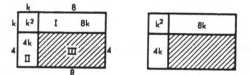

Solution: Since the area of the square is k^2, the length of each side is k.

The area of rectangle I is 8k, and its altitude is k, a side of the square. Hence, its base is 8.

The area of rectangle II is 4k and its base is k, a side of the square. Hence, its altitude is 4.

Since the base and altitude of rectangle III are 8 and 4, its area is the product of 8 and 4, or 32.

● **PROBLEM 23-13**

Given quadrilateral ABCD with vertices at A(-3,0), B(9,0), C(9,9), and D(0,12). Find the area of quadrilateral ABCD.

Solution: As shown in the figure the area of quadrilateral ABCD is the sum of the areas of △AOD and trapezoid OBCD.

Recall that the area of a triangle is ½bh, where b = the base and h = the altitude. In the figure note that the base of △AOD is 3 units and h = 12. Thus,

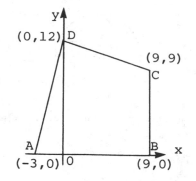

$$\text{area of triangle} = \tfrac{1}{2}bh$$

$$= \tfrac{1}{2}(3)(12) = 18$$

Now recall that the area of a trapezoid is $\dfrac{h}{2}(b + b')$, where h = altitude and b, b' = bases. In the figure note that the height of trapezoid OBCD = 9 units, and b and b' = 12 and 9. Thus,

$$\text{area of trapezoid} = \frac{h}{2}(b + b')$$

$$= \frac{9}{2}(12 + 9) = \frac{9}{2}(21) = 94\tfrac{1}{2}$$

Area of quadrilateral ABCD = area of triangle + area of trapezoid
= 18 + 94½ = 112½.

● **PROBLEM 23-14**

Side AB of ΔABC is 5 inches and side AC is 6 inches. If the number of degrees in angle A varies, what is the largest possible area, in square inches, of ΔABC?

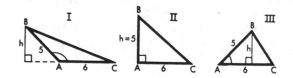

<u>Solution:</u> If the size of ∠A varies, it may be an obtuse angle, a right angle, or an acute angle. Note the three triangles in the diagram. In ΔI, ∠A is an obtuse angle; in ΔII, ∠A is a right angle; and in ΔIII, ∠A is an acute angle. In each case, ∠A is included between sides of 5 and 6 inches.

Determine the maximum area by applying the following principle:

The area of a triangle equals one-half the product of a side and the altitude drawn to that side.

The largest altitude that can be drawn to side AC occurs when ∠A is a right angle, as in ΔII. In ΔI and ΔIII, note that the altitude, h, is less than 5.

Hence, as ∠A varies, the largest possible area is obtained when ∠A is a right angle. The area of ΔII = ½(6)(5) = 15.

● **PROBLEM 23-15**

A rectangle 4 in. by 8 in. is completely bordered by a strip x in. wide. If the perimeter of the larger rectangle is twice that of the smaller rectangle, what is the value of x?

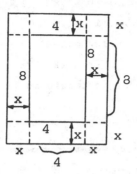

Solution: Observe the accompanying figure. The perimeter of a rectangle is the sum of the lengths of its sides. Thus, the perimeter of the larger rectangle is

$$(4+x+x) + (8+x+x) + (4+x+x) + (8+x+x) = 24 + 8x,$$

and the perimeter of the smaller or inner rectangle is 8 + 4 + 8 + 4 = 24. We are told that the perimeter of the larger rectangle is twice that of the smaller, thus

$$24 + 8x = 2 \cdot 24$$
$$24 + 8x = 48$$
$$8x = 24$$
$$x = 3 \text{ in.}$$

● **PROBLEM 23-16**

A rectangle is twice as long as it is wide. If it is bordered by a strip 2 ft. wide, its area is increased by 160 sq. ft. What are its dimensions?

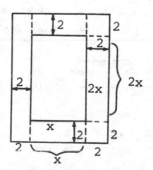

247

<u>Solution:</u> Observe the accompanying figure.

Let x = the width of the inner rectangle
Let 2x = the length of the inner rectangle.

The area of a rectangle is its length multiplied by its width. Thus, the area of the inner rectangle is $2x \cdot x = 2x^2$.

The length of the outer rectangle is $2 + 2x + 2 = 2x + 4$ and the width of the outer rectangle is $2 + x + 2 = x + 4$.

Thus, the area of the outer rectangle is $(2x+4)(x+4)$. We are told that the outer rectangle has an area of 160 sq. ft. greater than the inner, thus

$$(x+4)(2x+4) = 2x^2 + 160$$
$$2x^2 + 12x + 16 = 2x^2 + 160$$
$$12x + 16 = 160$$
$$12x = 144$$
$$x = 12, \quad 2x = 24.$$

Thus, the width of the inner rectangle is 12 ft. and the length is 24 ft.

● **PROBLEM** 23-17

A supermarket, rectangular in shape and 200 feet by 300 feet, is to be built on a city block that contains 81,600 square feet. There will be a uniform strip around the building for parking. How wide is the strip?

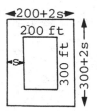

<u>Solution:</u> If the strip is s feet wide, the dimensions of the super-market will be 200 + 2s by 300 + 2s (see figure). Its area, the product of the width and length, is (200 + 2s)(300 + 2s) square feet. But the area is given as 81,600 square feet. Thus, we have

$$(200 + 2s)(300 + 2s) = 81,600$$
$$60,000 + 1000s + 4s^2 = 81,600$$
$$4s^2 + 1000s - 21,600 = 0 \quad \text{Standard Quadratic Form}$$
$$s^2 + 250s - 5400 = 0 \quad \text{Dividing by 4}$$

Using the quadratic formula

$$s = \frac{-b \pm \sqrt{b^2 - 4ac}}{2a} \quad \text{with a = 1, b = 250, and}$$

c = -5400, we have:

$$s = \frac{-250 \pm \sqrt{250^2 + 21,600}}{2}$$

248

$$s = \frac{-250 \pm 290}{2}$$

$$s = 20 \quad \text{or} \quad s = -270$$

The strip is 20 feet wide, since it is impossible for a strip to be a negative width.

Check: If the strip is 20 feet wide, then the block is 340 by 240 feet, and its area must be (340)(240) = 81,600 square feet.

● **PROBLEM** 23-18

A rectangle has its length 2 feet greater than its width. If the length is increased by 3 feet and the width by one foot, the area of the new rectangle will be twice the area of the old. What is the length and width of the original rectangle?

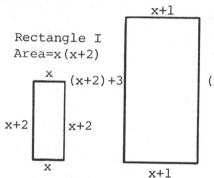

Rectangle I
Area=x(x+2)

Rectangle II
Area={ (x+1) [(x+2)+3] }

(x+2)+3

Solution: We designate the original rectangle by Rectangle I, and the new rectangle by Rectangle II. Let x = the number of feet in the width of Rectangle I.

If x represents the number of feet in the width of the original rectangle, the number of feet in the length is x + 2. (This is obtained from the first and last sentence.) From the second sentence we gain the basic equation

(area of new rectangle) = 2(area of original rectangle)   (1)

Since the area of a rectangle is the product of the width and the length the area of the new rectangle is
(x + 1)[(x + 2) + 3] = (x + 1)(x + 5), and the area of the old rectangle is x(x + 2). (See Figures). Substituting these values into equation (1), we have

$$(x + 1)(x + 5) = 2[x(x + 2)].$$

$$x^2 + 6x + 5 = 2(x^2 + 2x)$$

$$x^2 + 6x + 5 = 2x^2 + 4x$$

$$6x + 5 = x^2 + 4x$$

$$5 = x^2 - 2x$$

$$x^2 - 2x - 5 = 0.$$

To find the roots of an equation in the form $ax^2 + bx + c = 0$ we use the quadratic formula $x = \dfrac{-b \pm \sqrt{b^2 - 4ac}}{2a}$. In our case $a = 1$, $b = -2$, $c = -5$. Replacing these values in the quadratic formula we have

$$x = \frac{-(-2) \pm \sqrt{(-2)^2 - 4(1)(-5)}}{2}$$

$$= \frac{2 \pm \sqrt{4 + 20}}{2}$$

$$= \frac{2 \pm \sqrt{24}}{2}$$

$$= \frac{2 \pm \sqrt{4 \cdot 6}}{2}$$

$$= \frac{2 \pm \sqrt{4}\,\sqrt{6}}{2}$$

$$= \frac{2 \pm 2\sqrt{6}}{2}$$

$$= \frac{2(1 \pm \sqrt{6})}{2}$$

$$= 1 \pm \sqrt{6}$$

Since $\sqrt{6} \cong 2.45$

$$x = 1 + 2.45 + 3.45 \text{ and } x = 1 - 2.45 = -1.45.$$

We reject the negative value, as there are no rectangles with negative sides. Thus, the width of the original rectangle, x, is 3.45 ft., and the length, x + 2, is 5.45 ft.

Check: The area of rectangle I is $x(x + 2)$. Replacing x by 3.45 we have

$$x(x + 2) = 3.45(3.45 + 2) = (3.45)(5.45) = 18.80.$$

The area of rectangle II is $(x + 1)[(x + 2) + 3]$. Replacing x by 3.45 we have

$$(x + 1)[(x + 2) + 3] = (3.45 + 1)(3.45 + 5) = (4.45)(8.45)$$

$$= 37.60$$

$$37.60 = 2(18.80).$$

Thus area rectangle II = 2(area rectangle I), and 3.45 is the correct value of x.

CHAPTER 24

MOTION

Two cars traveled the same distance. One car traveled at 50 mph and the other car traveled at 60 mph. It took the slower car 50 minutes longer to make the trip. How long did it take the faster car to make the trip?

<u>Solution:</u> Step. 1. Read problem again. Step 2. If we let t represent the number of hours the faster car travels, we can construct the following table from the given statements.

Note: The 50 minutes must be converted to $\frac{5}{6}$ hr.

This is done by the following:

$$\frac{50 \text{ minutes}}{60 \text{ minutes}} \times 1 \text{ hour} = \frac{50}{60} \text{ hours} = \frac{5}{6} \text{ hour.}$$

Step 3

	Distance	Rate	Time
Faster car	D	60 mph	t
Slower car	D	50 mph	t + 5/6

Note: Since the two cars travelled the same distance, the distance for both cars is D, as indicated in the above table.

Step 4

Formula D = rt,

where D is distance, r is rate, and t is time.

251

$$D = 60t$$
$$D = 50\left(t + \frac{5}{6}\right)$$

Since the distances are the same, we can set the two expressions for D equal as in Step 5.

Step 5

$$60t = 50\left(t + \frac{5}{6}\right) \qquad (1)$$

Multiply each term within the parentheses by 50 to eliminate the parentheses.

$$60t = 50t + \frac{250}{6} \qquad (2)$$

Subtract 50t from both sides of equation (2).

$$60t - 50t = 50t + \frac{250}{6} - 50t$$

Therefore: $60t - 50t = \frac{250}{6}$.

Therefore: $10t = \frac{250}{6} \qquad (3)$.

Multiply both sides of equation (3) by $\frac{1}{10}$.

$$\frac{1}{\cancel{10}}(\cancel{10}t) = \frac{1}{\cancel{10}}_{1}\left(\frac{\cancel{250}^{25}}{6}\right)$$

$$t = \frac{25}{6} = 4\frac{1}{6} \text{ hours} = 4 \text{ hours } 10 \text{ minutes.}$$

Thus, it took the faster car 4 hours 10 minutes to make the trip.

● **PROBLEM 24-2**

Two cars are traveling 40 and 50 miles per hour, respectively. If the second car starts out 5 miles behind the first car, how long will it take the second car to overtake the first car?

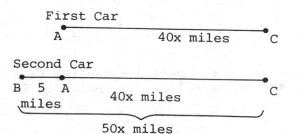

Solution: Let x = number of hours it takes the second car to overtake the first car. See table.

252

	Rate (in mph)	Time (hours)	Distance (miles)
First Car	40	x	40x
Second Car	50	x	50x

$$\text{Distance} = \text{rate} \times \text{time}$$

Then

$$50x = \text{distance second car travels in } x \text{ hours,}$$

and

$$40x = \text{distance first car travels in } x \text{ hours.}$$

Since the second car must travel an additional 5 miles (from B to A in diagram),

$$40x + 5 = 50x$$

Simplify,

$$-10x = -5$$

Divide by -10,

$$x = \frac{1}{2}$$, number of hours it takes the second car to overtake the first car.

Check:

$$40\left(\frac{1}{2}\right) + 5 = 50\left(\frac{1}{2}\right),$$

$$25 = 25.$$

● PROBLEM 24-3

One plane flies at a ground speed 75 miles per hour faster than another. On a particular flight, the faster plane requires 3 hours and the slower one 3 hours and 36 minutes. What is the distance of the flight?

Solution: If the velocity of the fast plane is v_1 and that of the slow plane is v_2, we have

$$v_1 = 75 + v_2 \qquad (1)$$

since the fast plane is 75 miles per hour faster. The distance is the same for each plane. The distance is $d = v \cdot t$, where v is the velocity and t is the time. Note that the time for the slower plane expressed in hours is

$$3\frac{36}{60} = 3\frac{3}{5} \text{ hours.}$$

Hence,

$$3v_1 = 3\frac{3}{5} v_2 \qquad (2)$$

Equations (1) and (2) constitute a system of two equations in two variables. Solving equation (2) for v_1, we have

$$v_1 = \frac{6}{5} v_2$$

Substituting this value in equation (1), we have

$$\frac{6}{5} v_2 = 75 + v_2$$

$$\frac{1}{5} v_2 = 75$$

$$v_2 = 375$$

$$v_1 = 75 + 375 = 450$$

Hence, the length of the trip is $3 \cdot 450 = 1,350$ miles.

Check: The fast plane, velocity 450 miles per hour, is 75 miles per hour faster than the slow one, velocity 375 miles per hour. In 3 hours the fast plane travels $3 \cdot 450 = 1,350$ miles. In 3 hours 36 minutes the slow plane travels the same distance; that is, $3\frac{3}{5} \cdot 375 = 1,350$ miles.

● **PROBLEM 24-4**

An airplane with an air speed of 300 miles per hour flies against a head wind, and flies 900 miles in 4 hours. What is the speed of the head wind?

Solution: Let x = number of miles per hour in the rate of the head wind.

Then since the head wind is detracting from the speed of the airplane, let

$300 - x$ = number of miles per hour in the ground speed of the airplane.

Applying the formula, Rate X Time = Distance, with rate = $(300 - x)$, Time = 4, Distance = 900, we obtain:

$$(300 - x)(4) = 900$$

Distributing 4, we have:

$$1200 - 4x = 900.$$

Subtract 1200 from both sides:

$$-4x = -300.$$

Divide by -4, $\quad x = 75$, number of miles per hour in the rate of the head wind.

Check: $\quad 4(300 - 75) = 900,$

$$900 = 900.$$

Two airfields A and B are 400 miles apart, and B is due east of A. A plane flew from A to B in 2 hours and then returned to A in 2½ hours. If the wind blew with a constant velocity from the west during the entire trip, find the speed of the plane in still air and the speed of the wind.

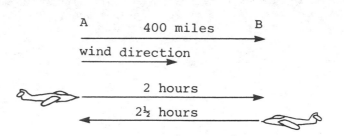

Solution: The essential point in solving this problem is that the wind helps the plane in flying from A to B and hinders it in flying from B to A. We therefore have the basis for two equations that involve the speed of the plane, the speed of the wind, and the time for each trip. We let

x = speed of plane in still air, in miles per hour
y = speed of wind, in miles per hour

Then, since the wind blew constantly from the west,

$x + y$ = speed of plane from A to B (wind helping)
$x - y$ = speed of plane from B to A (wind hindering)

The distance traveled each way was 400 miles, and so we have the following equations based on the formula distance/rate = time:

$$\frac{400}{x+y} = 2 = \text{time required for eastward trip} \qquad (8)$$

$$\frac{400}{x-y} = 2\tfrac{1}{2} = \text{time required for westward trip} \qquad (9)$$

We solve these equations simultaneously for x and y

$$400 = 2x + 2y \quad \text{multiplying (8) by } x + y \qquad (10)$$

$$800 = 5x - 5y \quad \text{multiplying (9) by } 2(x - y) \qquad (11)$$

$$2,000 = 10x + 10y \quad \text{multiplying (10) by 5} \qquad (12)$$

$$\underline{1,600 = 10x - 10y} \quad \text{multiplying (11) by 2} \qquad (13)$$

$$3,600 = 20x \quad \text{adding equations (12) and (13)}$$

$$x = 180 \qquad \text{solving for } x$$
$$400 = 360 + 2y \quad \text{replacing } x \text{ by } 180 \text{ in (10)}$$
$$2y = 40$$
$$y = 20$$

Therefore the solution set of equations (8) and (9) is $\{(180,20)\}$, and it follows that the speed of the plane in still air is 180 miles per hour and the speed of the wind is 20 miles per hour.

Check:

$$\frac{400}{180 + 20} = \frac{400}{200} = 2 \qquad\qquad \text{from (8)}$$

$$\frac{400}{180 - 20} = \frac{400}{160} = \frac{5}{2} = 2\tfrac{1}{2} \qquad\qquad \text{from (9)}$$

CHAPTER 25

MIXTURES/FLUID FLOW

How many gallons of a liquid that is 74 percent alcohol
must be combined with 5 gallons of one that is 90 percent
alcohol in order to obtain a mixture that is 84 percent
alcohol?

Solution: If we let x represent the number of gallons
needed of the first liquid and remember that 74 percent of
x is 0.74x, then the table (see table) shows all the data
given in this problem.

	Number of gallons	Percentage of alcohol	Number of gallons of alcohol
First liquid	x	74	0.74x
Second liquid	5	90	0.90(5) = 4.5
Mixture	x + 5	84	0.84(x + 5)

We are told that we are combining the number of gallons of alcohol in the 74 percent alcohol (0.74x) with the
number of gallons of alcohol in the 90 percent alcohol
(4.5) to obtain the number of gallons of alcohol in the 84
percent alcohol [0.84(x + 5)]. Thus

$$.74x + 4.5 = .84(x + 5)$$

Multiplying both sides by 100,

$$74x + 450 = 84(x + 5)$$
$$74x + 450 = 84x + 420$$
$$30 = 10x$$
$$x = 3$$

Therefore, 3 gallons of liquid that is 74 percent alcohol must be combined with 5 gallons of one that is 90 percent alcohol to obtain a mixture of 84 percent alcohol.

● **PROBLEM** 25-2

How much water must be added to 500 gallons of alcohol that is 70 per cent pure to make a mixture that is 60 per cent pure?

Solution: Let x = number of gallons of water to be added.

Let x + 500 = number of gallons of liquid in the 60% pure mixture.

We can thus formulate the following chart:

AMOUNT OF LIQUID $\times$ % ALCOHOL	=	NUMBER OF GALLONS OF ALCOHOL
500 gallons	.70	500(.70)
500 + x gallons	.60	(500+x)(.60)

We form the equation:

$$(0.60)(500 + x) = (0.70)(500)$$

and we wish to solve for x.

Distribute, $300 + 0.60x = 350.$

Subtract 300 from both sides,

$$0.60x = 350 - 300.$$

Collect terms, $0.60x = 50.$

Divide by 0.60, $x = 83\frac{1}{3}$, number of gallons of water to be added.

● **PROBLEM** 25-3

A grocer mixes two grades of coffee which sell for 70 cents and 80 cents per pound, respectively. How much of each must he take to make a mixture of 50 pounds which he can sell for 76 cents per pound?

Solution: Let x = the number of pounds of 70-cent coffee. Since the mixture is to contain 50 pounds and there are x pounds of 70 cent coffee , then 50 - x = number of pounds of 80 cent coffee. [Thus the total number of pounds in the mixture is x pounds (of 70-cent coffee) + (50 - x) pounds (of 80-cent coffee) = x - x + 50 = 50 lbs, our desired amount]. Using our formula:

	Number of Pounds ×Price per Pound (in cents)	= Total Price
70¢/lb. coffee	x	70	70x
80¢/lb. coffee	50-x	80	80(50-x)
76¢/lb.	50	76	76(50)

The total price of the 70¢ coffee, 70x and total price of the 80¢ coffee, 80(50 - x) equals total price of the 76¢ coffee, (76)(50).

Therefore $70x + 80(50 - x) = (50)(76).$

Using the distributive law, we obtain:

$$70x + 4000 - 80x = 3800.$$

Subtract 4000 from both sides,

$$70x - 80x = 3800 - 4000.$$

Collect terms, $- 10x = -200.$

Divide by –10, $x = 20,$ number of pounds of 70-cent coffee.

Then $50 - x = 30,$ number of pounds of 80-cent coffee.

Check: $(70)(20 + (80)(30) = (50)(76),$

$$1400 + 2400 = 3800,$$

$$3800 = 3800.$$

● **PROBLEM 25-4**

How many ounces of silver alloy which is 28% silver must be mixed with 24 ounces of silver which is 8% silver to produce a new alloy which is 20% silver?

Solution: Let x = number of ounces of 28% silver to be used. The relationship used to set up the equation is

Volume of 28% silver + Volume of 8% silver = Volume of silver in mixture.

$$.28x + .08(24) = .20(x + 24)$$
$$28x + 8(24) = 20(x + 24)$$
$$8x = 288$$
$$x = 36 \text{ ounces of silver}$$

Check: Volume of 28% silver = (.28)(36) = 10.08
Volume of 8% silver = (.08)(24) = 1.92

Total amount of silver = 12 ounces
The total mixture contains 24 + 36 = 60 ounces, and 12 ounces
is 20% of 60 ounces.

● PROBLEM 25-5

How much water must be evaporated from 120 pounds of solution which
is 3% salt to make a solution of 5% salt?

Solution: Let x = number of pounds of salt to be evaporated.
The relationship used to set up the equation is

Amount of salt in new mixture = Amount of salt in old mixture.

$$.05(120 - x) = .03(120)$$
$$5(120 - x) = 3(120)$$
$$600 - 5x = 360$$
$$x = 48 \text{ pounds of water}$$

Check: Water in new mixture is 120 - 48 = 72 pounds. Of this

3% of 120 or 3.6 pounds is salt.

$$\frac{3.6}{72} = 5\%.$$

● PROBLEM 25-6

A chemist has 24 ounces of a 25% solution of argyrol. How much
water must he add to reduce the strength of the argyrol to 20%?

Solution: Let x = number of ounces of water to be added.
The relationship used to set up the equation is (since only water is
added)

Amount of argyrol in new mixture = Amount of argyrol in old
mixture.

$$.20(24 + x) = .25(24)$$
$$4.8 + .2x = 6$$
$$2x = 12$$
$$x = 6 \text{ ounces of water}$$

Check: The new mixture has 30 ounces. Of this, 6 ounces or 20% of the
mixture is argyrol.

● PROBLEM 25-7

How many quarts of pure alcohol must be added to 40 quarts of a
mixture that is 35% alcohol to make a mixture that will be 48% alcohol?

Solution: Let x = number of quarts of pure alcohol to be added.
The relationship used to set up the equation is

Amount of alcohol in new mixture = Amount of alcohol in old
mixture + Amount of alcohol added

$$.48(40 + x) = (.35)(40) + x$$
$$19.2 + .48x = 14 + x$$
$$x = 10 \text{ quarts of alcohol}$$

Check: Amount of alcohol in new mixture = 14 quarts + 10 quarts =
24 quarts. New mixture contains a total of 40 + 10 = 50 quarts.

$$\frac{24}{50} = 48\% .$$

● PROBLEM 25-8

A storekeeper has two kinds of cookies, one worth $.75 a pound and
the other worth $.50 a pound. How many pounds of each should he use to
make a mixture of 60 pounds worth $.55 a pound?

Solution: Let x = number of pounds of cookies at 75 cents. Then
$(60 - x)$ = the number of cookies at 50 cents a pound.

The relationship used to set up the equation is:

Value of 75 cent cookies + Value of 50 cent cookies = Value of
mixture.

$$75x + 50(60 - x) = 60(55)$$
$$75x + 3000 - 50x = 3300$$
$$25x = 300$$
$$x = 12 \text{ pounds of 75 cent cookies}$$
$$60 - x = 48 \text{ pounds of 50 cent cookies}$$

Check: The value of 12 pounds of cookies at 75 cents a pound is $9.00.
The value of 48 pounds of cookies at 50 cents a pound is $24.00. The
resulting mixture contains 60 pounds worth $33.00. If 60 pounds of
cookies are sold for $33.00 then each pound is sold for $.55.

● PROBLEM 25-9

A chemist has an 18% solution and a 45% solution of a disinfectant.
How many ounces of each should be used to make 12 ounces of a 36%
solution?

Solution: Let x = Number of ounces from the 18% solution
         And y = Number of ounces from the 45% solution

(1) $x + y = 12$

(2) $.18x + .45y = .36(12) = 4.32$

Note that .18 of the first solution is pure disinfectant and that
.45 of the second solution is pure disinfectant. When the proper
quantities are drawn from each mixture the result is 12 gallons of
mixture which is .36 pure disinfectant, i.e., the resulting mixture
contains 4.32 ounces of pure disinfectant.

When the equations are solved, it is found that
$$x = 4 \quad \text{and} \quad y = 8.$$

In a chemical laboratory one carboy contains 12 gallons of acid and 18 gallons of water. Another carboy contains 9 gallons of acid and 3 gallons of water. How many gallons must be drawn from each carboy and combined to form a solution that is 7 gallons acid and 7 gallons water?

<u>Solution:</u> Let x = Number of gallons taken from first carboy
And y = Number of gallons taken from second carboy

(1) $x + y = 14$

(2) $\frac{12x}{30} + \frac{9y}{12} = 7$

In forming the second equation, it should be observed that $\frac{12}{30}$ of the liquid drawn from the first carboy is acid and $\frac{9}{12}$ of the liquid drawn from the second carboy is acid. The two quantities of liquid drawn from the two carboys yield 7 gallons of acid in the mixture.
When the equations are solved, it is found that
$$x = 10 \quad \text{and} \quad y = 4$$

What quantities of silver 60 per cent and 82 per cent pure must be mixed together to give 12 ounces of silver 70 per cent pure?

<u>Solution:</u> Let x = number of ounces of 60 per cent silver, and

y = number of ounces of 82 per cent silver.

We use the following table to describe the given information:

	Number of ounces	% Pure Silver	Number of Ounces of Pure Silver
Silver (60%)	x	60	.60x
Silver (82%)	y	82	.82y
Silver (70%)	12	70	.70(12)

From the information obtained in the table we have the following

equations:
$$.60x + .82y = .70(12) \tag{1}$$

$$x + y = 12 \tag{2}$$

Multiplying each term of equation (1) by 100, we obtain:

$$60x + 82y = 70(12) \tag{3}$$

Equation (2) multiplied by 60 gives:

$$60x + 60y = (12)(60). \tag{4}$$

Then equation (3)-(4) gives:

$$\begin{array}{r} 60x + 82y = 840 \\ -60x - 60y = -720 \\ \hline 22y = 120 \end{array} \; ;$$

dividing both sides by 22, $\quad y = \dfrac{120}{22} = \dfrac{60}{11} = 5\dfrac{5}{11}$.

Substituting $5\dfrac{5}{11}$ for y in (2) gives

$$x + 5\frac{5}{11} = 12, \text{ or } \quad x + \frac{60}{11} = \frac{132}{11}$$

Therefore, $\qquad\qquad\qquad x = \dfrac{72}{11} = 6\dfrac{6}{11}$.

Thus, we must mix $6\dfrac{6}{11}$ ounces of 60 per cent pure silver and $5\dfrac{5}{11}$

ounces of 82 per cent pure silver to obtain 12 ounces of silver 70

per cent pure.

Check: Substituting $6\dfrac{6}{11}$ for x and $5\dfrac{5}{11}$ for y in (3) gives

$$\left(6\frac{6}{11}\right)(60) + \left(5\frac{5}{11}\right)(82) = (70)(12)$$

Convert $6\dfrac{6}{11}$ and $5\dfrac{5}{11}$ to fractions, $\dfrac{72}{11}(60) + \dfrac{60}{11}(82) = 840.$

Multiply, $\dfrac{4320}{11} + \dfrac{4920}{11} = 840$

Add fractions, $\dfrac{9240}{11} = 840$

$$840 = 840 \quad .$$

Substituting in (2) gives

$$6\frac{6}{11} + 5\frac{5}{11} = 12$$

$$12 = 12.$$

CHAPTER 26

NUMBERS, DIGITS, COINS, AND CONSECUTIVE INTEGERS

The sum of two numbers is 23. One of the numbers is 7 more than the other number. What are the numbers?

<u>Solution:</u> Let x = one of the numbers, and x + 7 = the other number.
Since we are given that the sum of the two numbers is 23,

$$x + (x + 7) = 23.$$

By the associative law of addition:

$$x + (x + 7) = 23$$

is the same as

$$(x + x) + 7 = 23,$$

or

$$2x + 7 = 23.$$

Subtract 7 from both sides:

$$2x = 23-7.$$

Collect terms,

$$2x = 16.$$

Divide by 2,

$$x = 8, \text{ one of the numbers.}$$

Then solving for our other number x + 7, we substitute 8 for x .
Hence,

$$x + 7 = 8 + 7 = 15, \text{ the other number .}$$

Therefore, the two numbers are 8 and 15. We can verify this result by observing that the sum of the two numbers is indeed 23, and 15 is 7 more than 8, 8 + 7 = 15.

The sum of a number and its reciprocal is $\frac{65}{28}$. What is the number?

<u>Solution:</u> Given a number x. Its reciprocal is written as $\frac{1}{x}$. The sum of x and its reciprocal $\frac{1}{x}$, that is $x + \frac{1}{x}$, equals $\frac{65}{28}$. We have: $x + \frac{1}{x} = \frac{65}{28}$.

Multiplying both sides of this equation by 28x, the least common denominator, we obtain:

$$28x^2 + 28 = 65x$$
$$28x^2 - 65x + 28 = 0$$
$$(7x - 4)(4x - 7) = 0$$

$$7x - 4 = 0 \qquad\qquad 4x - 7 = 0$$
$$x = \frac{4}{7} \qquad\qquad\qquad x = \frac{7}{4}$$

Note: The two possible values of the number are reciprocals so a single check will suffice to show the number could be either $\frac{4}{7}$ or $\frac{7}{4}$.

Check: $\quad \frac{4}{7} + \frac{7}{4} = \frac{16}{28} + \frac{49}{28} = \frac{65}{28}$.

● **PROBLEM 26-3**

The sum of two numbers is 24; one number is 3 more than twice the other. Find the numbers.

<u>Solution:</u> Let x = one of the numbers
      Let y = the other number
Since the sum of the two numbers is 24,

$$x + y = 2x \qquad\qquad\qquad (1)$$

and since one of the numbers is 3 more than twice the other,

$$x = 2y + 3 \qquad\qquad\qquad (2)$$

Thus we have 2 equations in 2 unknowns and we solve for x and y:
Since x = 2y + 3, we may replace x by (2y + 3) in equation (1),

$$(2y + 3) + y = 24$$
$$3y + 3 = 24$$
$$3y = 21$$
$$y = 7$$

To solve for x we replace y by 7 in equation (2)

$$x = 2(7) + 3$$
$$x = 14 + 3$$
$$x = 17$$

Thus the two numbers are 17 and 7.

Check: The sum of the two numbers is 24:
$$x + y = 17 + 7 = 24$$
One of the numbers is 3 more than twice the other:
$$17 = 2(7) + 3$$
$$17 = 14 + 3$$
$$17 = 17$$

● **PROBLEM 26-4**

The sum of two numbers is 25 and the difference of their squares is 225. Find the numbers.

Solution: Let x = one of the two numbers.
Let y = the other number.

Since the sum of the two numbers is 25,
$$x + y = 25 \qquad (1)$$
and since the difference of their squares is 225,
$$x^2 - y^2 = 225 \qquad (2)$$
Thus we now have 2 equations in 2 unknowns:
$$x + y = 25 \qquad (1)$$
$$x^2 - y^2 = 225 \qquad (2)$$
Solving equation (1) for y we obtain
$$y = 25 - x \qquad (3)$$
To solve for x, we substitute this value of y into equation (2),
$$x^2 - (25 - x)^2 = 225$$
$$x^2 - (625 - 50x + x^2) = 225$$
$$x^2 - 625 + 50x - x^2 = 225$$
$$50x - 625 = 225$$
$$50x = 850$$
$$x = 17$$
To solve for y, we substitute this value of x into equation (1)
$$17 + y = 25$$
$$y = 8$$
Thus the two numbers are 17 and 8.

Check: Replace x and y by 17 and 8 in equations (1) and (2):
$$x + y = 25 \qquad (1)$$
$$17 + 8 = 25$$
$$25 = 25$$
$$x^2 - y^2 = 225 \qquad (2)$$
$$(17)^2 - (8)^2 = 225$$
$$289 - 64 = 225$$
$$225 = 225$$

Find the number which, increased by its reciprocal, is equal to 37/6.

Solution: Let x = The number

Then $\frac{1}{x}$ = The reciprocal

$$x + \frac{1}{x} = \frac{37}{6}$$

$$6x^2 + 6 = 37x$$

$$6x^2 - 37x + 6 = 0$$

$$(6x - 1)(x - 6) = 0$$

$$6x - 1 = 0$$

$$x = \frac{1}{6}$$

$$x - 6 = 0$$

$$x = 6$$

The number may be taken as 1/6 and the reciprocal as 6, or the number may be taken as 6 and the reciprocal as 1/6.

Check: If the number is 6, the reciprocal is 1/6. Then

$$6 + \frac{1}{6} = \frac{37}{6} \; .$$

The units digit of a two digit number is two larger than the tens digit. When the digits are reversed, the new two digit number is equal to seven times the sum of the digits. What is the original number?

Solution: When dealing with number problems that are concerned with the digits of a number, we must utilize position values and write a two digit number as 10a + b, a three digit number as 100x + 10y + z, and so on.

Let x represent the digit in the tens position, then the digit in the units position must be x + 2. The original two digit number is of the form 10a + b where a = digit in tens position and b = digit in the units position. Therefore, the original number is

10x + (x + 2) or 10x + x + 2 or 11x + 2.

When the digits are reversed, the new number can be expressed as

10(x + 2) + x or 11x + 20.

The sum of the digits is x + (x + 2) = 2x + 2.
Setting the new number equal to seven times the sum of the digits, we have:

$$11x + 20 = 7(2x + 2)$$

$$11x + 20 = 14x + 14$$

$$20 - 14 = 14x - 11x$$

$$6 = 3x$$

$$x = 2, \quad x + 2 = 4$$

The original number 10x + (x + 2) = 10(2) + 4 = 24.

If the digits are reversed, we get 42, and this is the product of seven and the sum of the digits (six).

● PROBLEM 26-7

The sum of the digits of a two-digit number is 9. The number is equal to 9 times the units' digit. Find the number.

Solution: (1) t + u = 9

(2) 10t + u = 9u

If these two equations are solved simultaneously, t = 4 and u = 5 and the number is 45.

● PROBLEM 26-8

A purse contains 19 coins worth $3.40. If the purse contains only dimes and quarters, how many of each coin are in the purse?

Solution: Let x = the number of dimes in the purse
Then 19 - x = the number of quarters in the purse
10x = the value of the dimes
25(19 - x) = the value of quarters

The relationship used in setting up the equation is:

The value of the dimes + the value of the quarters = $3.40
$$10x + 25(19 - x) = 340$$
$$10x + 475 - 25x = 340$$
$$x = 9$$

There are 9 dimes and 10 quarters in the purse.

Check: The dimes are worth $.90 and the quarters are worth $2.50, making a total of $3.40.

A toy savings bank contains $17.30 consisting of nickels, dimes, and quarters. The number of dimes exceeds twice the number of nickels by 3 and the number of quarters is 4 less than 5 times the number of nickels. How many of each coin are in the bank?

Solution: Let x = the number of nickels
Then 2x + 3 = the number of dimes
And 5x - 4 = the number of quarters
The relationship used in setting up the equation is:

Value of nickels + Value of dimes + Value of quarters = 1730.

$5x + 10(2x + 3) + 25(5x - 4) = 1730$; $x = 12$

There are 12 nickels, 27 dimes and 56 quarters in the bank.

Check: The nickels are worth $.60, the dimes are worth $2.70, and the quarters are worth $14.00, making a total of $17.30.

The sum of three consecutive odd numbers is 45. Find the numbers.

Solution: If we look at a series of odd numbers 1,3,5,7,9,11... we note that each consecutive odd number is 2 more than the one before it.

i.e.,
$$3 = 1 + 2$$
$$5 = 3 + 2$$
$$7 = 5 + 2 \quad \text{etc.}$$

Therefore, if x is the first odd number,

x + 2 is the second odd number,

and $(x + 2) + 2 = x + (2 + 2) = x + 4$

is the third odd number. Therefore

Let   x = the first odd number,

x + 2 = the second odd number,

x + 4 = the third odd number.

Then, since the sum of these numbers is 45, we have:

$$x + (x + 2) + (x + 4) = 45.$$

Using the Associative and Commutative Laws of Addition:

$$3x + 6 = 45.$$

Subtract 6 from both sides:

$$3x = 45 - 6.$$

Collect terms, $3x = 39.$

Divide by 3,   x = 13, the first odd number.

Replace   x by 13,   x + 2 = 15, the second odd number.

Replace   x by 13,   x + 4 = 17, the third odd number.

Check: 13 + 15 + 17 = 45,

                        45 = 45.

The sum of four consecutive even numbers is 140. What are the numbers?

<u>Solution:</u> An even number can be represented by 2n, where n is an integer. Consecutive even integers (or odd integers) differ by 2. Therefore, four consecutive even integers can be represented by the following:

the first even integer is 2n,

the next even integer is 2n + 2

the next even integer is (2n + 2) + 2 = 2n + 4, and

the next or fourth even integer is (2n + 4) +2=2n+6.

Hence, the four consecutive even integers are 2n, 2n + 2, 2n + 4, and 2n + 6. Then

$$2n + (2n + 2) + (2n + 4) + (2n + 6) = 140$$

$$8n + 12 = 140$$

$$8n = 128$$

$$n = 16$$

Therefore:

the first even integer = 2n = 2(16) = 32
the next even integer = 2n + 2 = 2(16) + 2 = 32 + 2 = 34
the next even integer= 2n + 4 = 2(16) + 4 = 32 + 4 = 36
and the next or fourth even integer
                = 2n + 6 = 2(16) + 6 = 32 + 6 = 38

Note: The sum of these four consecutive even integers=

32 + 34 + 36 + 38 = 66 + 36 + 38 = 102 + 38 = 140.

The product of two consecutive odd integers is 35. Find the integers.

<u>Solution:</u> Let x represent the first odd integer. Then x + 2 represents the next odd integer. The product x(x + 2) equals 35.

Thus, we solve the following equation.

$$x(x + 2) = 35.$$

$$x^2 + 2x = 35 \qquad \text{Distributing}$$

$$x^2 + 2x - 35 = 0 \qquad \text{Subtracting 35 from both members}$$

$$(x + 7)(x - 5) = 0 \qquad \text{Factoring}$$

In order for this product to $= 0$, either $(x + 7) = 0$ or $(x - 5) = 0$. Therefore,

$$x = -7 \quad \text{or} \quad x = 5$$

Since x represents the first odd integer, we see that there are two solutions.

When $x = -7$, $x + 2 = -5$, and $(-7) \cdot (-5) = 35$.
When $x = 5$, $x + 2 = 7$, and $5 \cdot 7 = 35$.
The two integers are 5 and 7 or -7 and -5.

● **PROBLEM 26-13**

Find two numbers such that twice the first added to the second equals 19, and three times the first is 21 more than the second.

Solution: Let $x =$ the first number and $y =$ the second number. The equations are

$$2x + y = 19 \quad \text{(twice the first added to the second equals 19)}$$

$$3x = y + 21 \quad \text{(three times the first is 21 more than the second)}$$

To solve this system

$$2x + y = 19$$

$$3x = y + 21$$

obtain all the variables on one side of the equations.

$$2x + y = 19 \qquad (1)$$

$$3x - y = 21 \qquad (2)$$

Add (2) to (1)

$$2x + y = 19 \qquad (1)$$

$$\underline{3x - y = 21} \qquad (2)$$

$$5x \quad = 40 \qquad (3)$$

Divide by 5 to obtain x

271

x = 8

Substitute x = 8 into (1) or (2).

(1)   2x + y = 19

2(8) + y = 19

16 + y = 19

y = 3

The solution of this system is

x = 8, the first number

y = 3, the second number

To check the solution, show that the two numbers satisfy the conditions of the problem.

Twice the first number is 2(8) = 16. Add this result to the second is 16 + 3 = 19. Thus 19 = 19. Then three times the first number is 3(8) =24 which is 21 more than 3. That is 24 = 21 + 3;   24 = 24.

● **PROBLEM 26-14**

Find two numbers such that the sum of twice the larger and the smaller is 64. But, if 5 times the smaller be subtracted from four times the larger the result is 16.

Solution: Let x = the larger number
And y = the smaller number
Then 2x + y = 64
4x - 5y = 16

When these equations are solved simultaneously the larger number is found to be 24 and the smaller number 16.

● **PROBLEM 26-15**

Separate 120 into two parts such that the larger exceeds three times the smaller by 12.

Solution: Let x = the larger number
And y = the smaller number
Then x + y = 120
x = 3y + 12

When these equations are solved simultaneously the larger number is found to be 93 and the smaller 27.

Find two real numbers whose sum is 10 such that the sum of the larger and the square of the smaller is 40.

<u>Solution:</u> Let x = the smaller number
Let y = the larger number

The sum of the numbers is 10, therefore

$$x + y = 10 \qquad\qquad (1)$$

The sum of the larger and the square of the smaller is 40, therefore

$$y + x^3 = 40 \qquad\qquad (2)$$

Solving for y in equation (1) by adding (-x) to both sides we obtain

$$y = 10 - x \qquad\qquad (3)$$

Replacing this value of y in equation (2) we obtain

$$(10 - x) + x^2 = 40$$

Adding -40 to both sides,
$$10 - x + x^2 - 40 = 0$$

$$x^2 - x - 30 = 0$$

Factoring,
$$(x - 6)(x + 5) = 0$$

Whenever the product of two numbers ab = 0, either a = 0 or b = 0. Thus, either

$$x - 6 = 0 \quad or \quad x + 5 = 0$$

and

$$x = 6 \qquad or \quad x = -5.$$

To find the corresponding y values we replace x by each of these values in equation (3):
Replacing x by 6:
$$y = 10 - 6$$
$$y = 4$$

Replacing x by -5:
$$y = 10 - (-5)$$
$$y = 10 + 5$$
$$y = 15$$

Thus the two possible solutions are (6,4) and (-5,15).
Since we assumed x to be the smaller number, and 6 is greater than 4, not smaller than it, we reject (6,4). To check if (-5,15) fits the conditions of this problem, we replace (x,y) by (-5,15) in equations (1) and (2):

$$x + y = 10 \qquad\qquad (1)$$
$$-5 + 15 = 10$$
$$10 = 10$$

$$y + x^3 = 40 \qquad\qquad (2)$$
$$15 + (-5)^2 = 40$$
$$15 + 25 = 40$$
$$40 = 40$$

Thus the pair of numbers whose sum is ten such that the sum of the larger and the square of the smaller is 40 is (-5,15).

If 3 is subtracted from the numerator of a certain fraction, the value of the fraction becomes 3/5. If 1 is subtracted from the denominator of the same fraction then the value of the fraction becomes 2/3. Find the original fraction.

Solution: Let x = the numerator of the fraction
And y = the denominator of the fraction

Then (1) $\dfrac{x - 3}{y} = \dfrac{3}{5}$, 5x - 15 = 3y

(2) $\dfrac{x}{y - 1} = \dfrac{2}{3}$, 3x = 2y - 2

(3) 5x - 3y = 15

(4) 3x - 2y = -2

When these equations are solved simultaneously x is found to be 36 and y is found to be 55. Therefore, the original fraction is 36/55.

The units' digit of a two-digit number is 4 less than 3 times the tens' digit. If the digits are reversed, a new number is formed which is 12 less than twice the original number. Find the number.

Solution: (1) u = 3t - 4

(2) 10u + t = 2(10t + u) - 12

If these equations are solved simultaneously t = 4 and u = 8 and the number is 48.

Max has $1.45 in coins. He has fourteen coins in nickels, dimes, and quarters. There are two more nickels than dimes and quarters combined. How many of each kind of coin does he have?

Solution: Let the number of nickels be n, dimes d, and quarters q. The total value of the coins yields one equation.

$$0.05n + 0.10d + 0.25q = 1.45 \tag{1}$$

The total number of coins yields another.

$$n + d + q = 14 \tag{2}$$

The number of nickels yields a third.

$$n = d + q + 2 \tag{3}$$

Substituting the value of n from (3) in (2),

$$d + q + 2 + d + q = 14$$
$$2d + 2q + 2 = 14$$
$$d = 6 - q$$

Substituting this value of d in (2),

$$n + 6 - q + q = 14$$
$$n = 8$$

Substituting n = 8 and d = 6 - q in (1),

$$0.05(8) + 0.10(6 - q) + 0.25q = 1.45$$

$$0.40 + 0.60 - 0.10q + 0.25q = 1.45$$

$$0.15q = 0.45$$
$$q = 3$$

Since d = 6 - q, d - 3. Therefore, Max has q = 3 quarters, d = 3 dimes, and n = 8 nickels.

● **PROBLEM 26-20**

The three angles of a triangle are together equal to 180°. The smallest angle is half as large as the largest one, and the sum of the largest and smallest angles is twice the third angle. Find the three angles.

Solution: Let x = the smallest angle,

y = the largest angle,

z = the third angle.

From the given information we formulate the following equations:

$$x + y + z = 180 \qquad (1)$$
$$x = \frac{y}{2} \qquad (2)$$
$$x + y = 2z \qquad (3)$$

We wish to solve for x, y and z . Multiply both sides of equation (2) by 2. Thus, $2x = 2\left(\frac{y}{2}\right)$

$$2x = y$$

Now, subtract y from both sides. Thus,

$$2x - y = y - y,$$

or $\qquad 2x - y = 0$. $\qquad (4)$

Subtract 2z from both sides of equation (3):

$$x + y - 2z = 2z - 2z ,$$

or $\qquad x + y - 2z = 0$. $\qquad (5)$

Equation (1) multiplied by 2 gives

$$2x + 2y + 2z = 360 . \qquad (6)$$

Equation (5) + (6) gives

$$x + y - 2z = 0$$
$$\underline{+ \ (2x + 2y + 2z = 360)}$$
$$3x + 3y = 360 \qquad\qquad (7)$$

Equation (4) multiplied by 3 gives
$$6x - 3y = 0 \ . \qquad\qquad (8)$$
Equation (7) + (8) gives
$$3x + 3y = 360$$
$$\underline{+ \ (6x - 3y = 0)} \quad ;$$
$$9x = 360$$

therefore, $\qquad x = 40°$

Substituting $40°$ for x in (2) gives $40 = \frac{y}{2}$. Multiply both sides

by 2: $80° = y$. Substituting $40°$ for x and $80°$ for y in (1)
gives
$$40° + 80° + z = 180° \ .$$

Subtract 120 from both sides: $\qquad z = 60°$.

Thus, the angles are $40°$, $80°$, and $60°$.

Check: Substituting $40°$ for x, $80°$ for y, $60°$ for z gives:
$$40° + 80° + 60° = 180°$$
$$40° = \frac{80°}{2}$$
$$40° + 80° = 2(60°) \ .$$

● **PROBLEM 26-21**

Show that the sum of any positive number and its reciprocal cannot be less than 2.

Solution: Express the given example as a mathematical statement, recalling the reciprocal of x = 1/x . Write "the sum of any positive number and its reciprocal cannot be less than 2" as
$$a + \frac{1}{a} \nless 2,$$

where a represents the positive number. Thus, the sum of any positive number and its reciprocal can be greater than or equal to 2. We are to show that
$$a + \frac{1}{a} \geq 2, \quad a > 0.$$

If this relation is true, the following inequalities will also hold:

$a^2 + 1 \geq 2a$, Multiply both members of the inequality
$\qquad\qquad$ by a ,

$a^2 - 2a + 1 \geq 0$, Transpose 2a

$(a - 1)^2 \geq 0$, $\qquad$ Factor

Now this simple relation is easily shown to be true, for, whether
a - 1 is positive, negative, or zero, its square must be non-negative.

276

This is therefore a suitable starting point, and our synthesis, constituting the actual proof, is as follows. Since
$$(a - 1)^2 \geq 0,$$

for the reason just stated, expansion of the left member gives us the equivalent relations

$$a^2 - 2a + 1 \geq 0 , \qquad \text{Expanding}$$

$$a^2 + 1 \geq 2a , \qquad \text{Transposing } 2a$$

$$a + \frac{1}{a} \geq 2 , \qquad \text{Divide both sides of the inequality by } a, \text{ with } a > 0 .$$

We see, incidentally, that the equality holds only if $a = 1$; if $0 < a < 1$, or if $a > 1$, the inequality holds.

● **PROBLEM 26-22**

Find 3 consecutive positive integers such that when 5 times the largest be subtracted from the square of the middle one the result exceeds three times the smallest by 7.

Solution: Let x = The smallest number

Then $x + 1$ = The next larger number

And $x + 2$ = The largest number

$$(x + 1)^2 - 5(x + 2) = 3x + 7$$
$$x^2 + 2x + 1 - 5x - 10 = 3x + 7$$
$$x^2 - 6x - 16 = 0$$
$$(x - 8)(x + 2) = 0$$
$$x = -2 \text{ reject}$$

$x = 8$
$x + 1 = 9$
$x + 2 = 10$

Check: $(9)^2 - 5(10) = 3(8) + 7$
$81 - 50 = 24 + 7, \quad 31 = 31$

● **PROBLEM 26-23**

If the largest of four consecutive odd integers is represented by n, what is the smallest of these integers represented by?

Solution: Smaller consecutive odd integers are obtained by subtracting 2 from each successive odd integer. For example, the sequence 17, 15, 13 may be extended to include 11 and 9.

Hence, if n is the largest of four consecutive odd integers, then the three smaller ones found by subtracting 2 are $(n - 2)$, $(n - 4)$, and $(n - 6)$. The smallest of these is $(n - 6)$.

Can the sum of three consecutive odd integers be (a) 25? (b) 45?

Solution: Notice that all consecutive odd integers differ by 2:

1, 1 + 2 = 3, 3 + 2 = 5, 5 + 2 = 7, 7 + 2 = 9, ...

Thus, if we let x = the first consecutive odd integer
             x + 2 = the 2nd consecutive odd integer
and
  (x+2) + 2 = x + 4 = the 3rd consecutive odd integer,

(a) We take the sum of these three numbers and determine if it can be 25:

$$x + (x+2) + (x+4) = 25$$
$$3x + 6 = 25$$
$$3x = 19$$
$$x = \frac{19}{3} .$$

Since 19/3 is not an integer, there are no such odd integers.

(b) If 25 is replaced by 45, the equation takes the form

$$x + (x+2) + (x+4) = 45$$
$$3x + 6 = 45$$
$$3x = 39$$
$$x = \frac{39}{3} = 13$$

$$x + 2 = 13 + 2 = 15$$
$$x + 4 = 13 + 4 = 17$$

Thus, the three consecutive odd integers are 13, 15, 17.

In general, if the sum of three consecutive odd integers is to be the number N, then N must be an integral multiple of 3.

CHAPTER 27

AGE AND WORK

John is 4 times as old as Harry. In six years John will be twice as old as Harry. What are their ages now?

<u>Solution</u>: Let x represent Harry's age now. John's age now is then represented by 4x. In six years their respective ages will be (x + 6) and (4x + 6). In tabular form our data is:

	Now	In Six Years
John's Age	4x	4x + 6
Harry's Age	x	x + 6

From the statement six years from now John will be twice as old as Harry, we can write the equation necessary to solve the problem. To form an equation from this inform-ation we must multiply Harry's age in six years by 2, to account for John's age being 2 times Harry's. Thus, we have: 4x + 6 = 2(x + 6), or

$$4x + 6 = 2x + 12.$$

We now want to solve for x to obtain Harry's age. To do this we proceed as follows: Subtract 2x from both sides of the equation, 4x + 6 = 2x + 12. We obtain:

$$4x - 2x + 6 = 2x - 2x + 12$$
$$2x + 6 = 12. \tag{1}$$

Now, subtracting 6 from both sides of Equation (1), we have:

$$2x + 6 - 6 = 12 - 6$$
$$2x = 6. \tag{2}$$

Finally, dividing both sides of Equation (2) by 2, we obtain:

$$\frac{2x}{2} = \frac{6}{2} \text{ or, } x = 3.$$

279

Therefore, Harry's age now is 3 years, and John's is 4(3) = 12 years.

We can verify these values by observing that in six years Harry will be (3 + 6) or 9 years old and John will be [4(3) + 6] or 18 years old. Therefore, John will then be twice as old as Harry, which was given above.

A mother is now 24 years older than her daughter. In 4 years, the mother will be 3 times as old as the daughter. What is the present age of each?

Solution: Let x = the age of the daughter
Then x + 24 = the age of the mother
x + 4 = the age of the daughter in 4 years
x + 24 + 4 = x + 29 = the age of the mother in 4 years

The relationship used in setting up the equation is:
In 4 years, the mother will be 3 times as old as the daughter.

$$x + 28 = 3(x + 4); \quad x = 8$$

Check: The daughter is now 8 years old and the mother is 32 years old. In 4 years, the daughter will be 12 years old and the mother will be 36 years old. At this time, the mother will be 3 times as old as the daughter.

A man is now 6 times as old as his son. In two years, the man will be 5 times as old as his son. Find the present ages of the man and his son.

Solution: Let x = the present age of the son.
Then let 6x = the present age of the father.
x + 2 = the son's age in 2 years.
6x + 2 = the father's age in 2 years.

The relationship used in setting up the equation is:
In two years the father will be five times as old as the son.
$$6x + 2 = 5(x + 2)$$
$$6x + 2 = 5x + 10$$
$$x = 8$$

Check: The son is now 8 and the father is now 48.
In two years, the son will be 10 and the father will be 50.
At this time, the father will be 5 times as old as the son.

John is now 18 years old and his brother, Charles, is 14 years old. How many years ago was John twice as old as Charles?

280

Solution: Let x = the number of years ago John was twice as old as Charles.

　　Then 18 - x = John's age x years ago.

　　And 14 - x = Charles' age x years ago.

The relationship used in setting up the equation is:

　　x years ago, John was twice as old as Charles

$$18 - x = 2(14 - x); \quad x = 10$$

Check: 10 years ago, John was 8 and Charles was 4. At this time, John was twice as old as Charles.

● **PROBLEM 27-5**

How long will it take Jones and Smith working together to plow a field which Jones can plow alone in 5 hours and Smith alone in 8 hours?

Solution: Here we have

　　(1)　How long will it take Jones and Smith working together to plow a field?

　　(2)　Jones and Smith working together plow a field.

　　(3)　Jones can plow it alone in 5 hours.

　　(4)　Smith can plow it alone in 8 hours.

These sentences become, in turn:

　　(1')　Let x = number of hours that it takes Jones and Smith to plow the field.

　　(2')　(Jones's fractional part of the work) + (Smith's fractional part of the work) = 1, since they do 1 job together

　　(3')　Since Jones does the job alone in 5 hours, we can write 1 job = 5 hours work. Divide both sides of this equation by 5:

$$\frac{1}{5} \text{ job} = \frac{5 \text{ hours work}}{5}$$

$$\frac{1}{5} \text{ job} = 1 \text{ hour work.} \tag{1}$$

Hence, Jones does 1/5 of the job in 1 hour. Note that the numerator of the fraction on the left side of equation (1) is equal to the number of hours; i.e., 1 = 1. Therefore, in x hours, Jones does x/5 of the job.

　　(4')　Similarly, in one hour Smith does 1/8 of the job and, in x hours, x/8 of the job. Hence, we have

$$\frac{x}{5} + \frac{x}{8} = 1 \tag{2}$$

Obtaining a common denominator of 40 for the two fractions on the right side of equation (2):

$$\frac{8(x)}{8(5)} + \frac{5(x)}{5(8)} = 1$$

$$\frac{8x}{40} + \frac{5x}{40} = 1$$

$$\frac{8x + 5x}{40} = 1$$

$$\frac{13x}{40} = 1 \qquad\qquad (3)$$

Multiply both sides of equation (3) by 40/13,

$$\frac{40}{13}\left(\frac{13x}{40}\right) = \frac{40}{13} \quad (1)$$

$$x = \frac{40}{13} \text{ hours} = 3\frac{1}{13} \text{ hours} \approx 3 \text{ hours } 5 \text{ min-}$$

utes. Therefore, it takes Jones & Smith 3 hours 5 minutes to plow the field.

● **PROBLEM 27-6**

If A can do a job in 8 days and B can do the same job in 12 days, how long would it take the two men working together?

<u>Solution:</u> Let x = the number of days it would take the two men working together.

Then $\frac{x}{8}$ = the part of the job done by A

and $\frac{x}{12}$ = the part of the job done by B

The relationship used in setting up the equation is:

Part of job done by A + Part of job done by B = 1 job

$$\frac{x}{8} + \frac{x}{12} = 1$$

$$3x + 2x = 24$$

$$x = 4\frac{4}{5} \text{ days}$$

Check: $\dfrac{4\frac{4}{5}}{8} + \dfrac{4\frac{4}{5}}{12} = 1$

$$\dfrac{\frac{24}{5}}{8} + \dfrac{\frac{24}{5}}{12} = 1$$

$$\frac{3}{5} + \frac{2}{5} = 1$$

● **PROBLEM 27-7**

A mechanic and his helper can repair a car in 8 hours. The mechanic works 3 times as fast as his helper. How long would it take the helper to make the repair, working alone?

<u>Solution:</u> Let x = Number of hours it would take the mechanic working alone.

Then 3x = Number of hours it would take the helper working alone.

The relationship used in setting up the equation is:

Part of job done by mechanic + Part of job done by helper = 1

282

job.

$$\frac{8}{x} + \frac{8}{3x} = 1$$

$$x = 10\frac{2}{3} \text{ hours by mechanic}$$

$$3x = 32 \text{ hours by helper .}$$

Check: $\frac{8}{10\frac{2}{3}} + \frac{8}{32} = 1$

$$\frac{24}{32} + \frac{1}{4} = 1$$

$$\frac{3}{4} + \frac{1}{4} = 1$$

A man can do a job in 9 days and his son can do the same job in 16 days. They start working together. After 4 days the son leaves and the father finishes the job alone. How many days did the man take to finish the job alone?

Solution: Let x = the number of days it takes the man to finish the job.

Note that the man actually works (x + 4) days, and the son actually works 4 days.

The relationship used to set up the equation is:
Part of job done by man + Part of job done by boy = 1 job

$$\frac{x + 4}{9} + \frac{4}{16} = 1$$

$$16(x + 4) + 4(9) = 144$$

$$x = 2\frac{3}{4} \text{ days}$$

Check: $\frac{2\frac{3}{4} + 4}{9} + \frac{4}{16} = 1$

$$\frac{3}{4} + \frac{1}{4} = 1$$

A tank can be filled in 9 hours by one pipe, in 12 hours by a second pipe, and can be drained when full, by a third pipe, in 15 hours. How long would it take to fill the tank if it is empty, and if all pipes are in operation?

Solution: Let x = the number of hours the pipes are in operation

Then $\frac{x}{9}$ = part of tank filled by first pipe

and $\frac{x}{12}$ = part of tank filled by second pipe

and $\frac{x}{15}$ = part of tank emptied by third pipe

The relationship used in setting up the equation is:

Part of tank filled by first pipe + Part of tank filled by second pipe - Part of tank emptied by third pipe = 1 Full tank.

$$\frac{x}{9} + \frac{x}{12} - \frac{x}{15} = 1$$

$$20x + 15x - 12x = 180$$

$$x = 7\frac{19}{23} \text{ hours}$$

Check: $\dfrac{7\frac{19}{23}}{9} + \dfrac{7\frac{19}{23}}{12} - \dfrac{7\frac{19}{23}}{15} = 1$

$$\left(\frac{180}{23} \cdot \frac{1}{9}\right) + \left(\frac{180}{23} \cdot \frac{1}{12}\right) - \left(\frac{180}{23} \cdot \frac{1}{15}\right) = 1$$

$$\frac{20}{23} + \frac{15}{23} - \frac{12}{23} = 1$$

CHAPTER 28

RATIOS, PROPORTIONS AND VARIATIONS

RATIOS AND PROPORTIONS

● **PROBLEM 28-1**

Solve the proportion $\dfrac{x + 1}{4} = \dfrac{15}{12}$.

<u>Solution:</u> Cross multiply to determine x; that is, multiply the numerator of the first fraction by the denominator of the second, and equate this to the product of the numerator of the second and the denominator of the first.

$$(x + 1)12 = 4 \cdot 15$$

$$12x + 12 = 60$$

$$x = 4.$$

● **PROBLEM 28-2**

On a map, $\dfrac{3}{16}$ inch represents 10 miles. What would be the length of a line on the map which represents 96 miles?

<u>Solution:</u> The lengths of line segments on the map are proportional to the actual distances on the earth. If L represents the length of the line segment on the map corresponding to a distance of 96 miles, then

$$\frac{\frac{3}{16} \text{ inches}}{\text{L inches}} = \frac{10 \text{ miles}}{96 \text{ miles}}$$

$$\frac{3}{16}(96) = 10L \qquad \text{by cross multiplying}$$

$$L = \frac{(3)(96)}{(16)(10)} = \frac{3(6)}{10}$$

$$L = \frac{18}{10}$$

$$L = 1\frac{4}{5} \text{ inches.}$$

DIRECT VARIATION

● **PROBLEM** 28-3

If y varies directly with respect to x and y = 3 when x = -2, find y when x = 8.

Solution: If y varies directly as x then y is equal to some constant k times x; that is, y = kx where k is a constant. We can now say $y_1 = kx_1$ and $y_2 = kx_2$ or

$\frac{y_1}{x_1} = k$, $\frac{y_2}{x_2} = k$ which implies $\frac{y_1}{x_1} = \frac{y_2}{x_2}$ which is a proportion.

We use the proportion $\frac{y_1}{x_1} = \frac{y_2}{x_2}$. Thus $\frac{3}{-2} = \frac{y_2}{8}$. Now solve for y_2:

$$8\left(\frac{3}{-2}\right) = 8\left(\frac{y_2}{8}\right)$$

$$-12 = y_2.$$

When x = 8, y = -12.

● **PROBLEM** 28-4

According to Hooke's Law, the length of a spring, S, varies directly as the force, F, applied on the spring. In a spring to which Hooke's Law applies, a force of 18.6 lb stretches the spring by 1.27 in. Find k, the proportionality constant.

Solution: The direct variation of the length of the spring, S, and the force applied on it, F, is expressed symbolically as

F = kS, where k is the constant of proportionality.

We are given that F = 18.6 lb and S = 1.27 in. Thus, it is necessary merely to substitute the given values in the equation F = kS, obtaining

$$18.6 = k(1.27),$$

from which k = 18.6/1.27 = 14.65 lb/in.

● **PROBLEM** 28-5

The area of a sphere is directly proportional to the square of the radius. If a sphere of radius 3 inches has an area of 36π square inches, deduce the formula for the area of a sphere.

Solution: If a quantity x is directly proportional to another quantity y, x is the product of a constant k and y; that is, x = ky. Let a = the area of a sphere and let r = the radius of the sphere. Since the area a of a sphere is directly proportional to the square of the radius r, the following equation can be written:

$$a = kr^2 \qquad\qquad (1)$$

When the area a is 36π square inches, the radius is 3 inches. Then, using equation (1):

$$36\pi = k(3)^2$$

$$36\pi = k(9)$$

$$36\pi = 9k$$

Divide both sides of this equation by 9:

$$\frac{36\pi}{9} = \frac{9k}{9}$$

$$4\pi = k$$

Substituting this value for the constant k in equation (1):
$a = (4\pi)r^2$, is the equation which represents the formula for the area of a sphere.

INVERSE VARIATION

● **PROBLEM** 28-6

Express y in terms of x if y is inversely proportional to x and y = 2 when x = 3.

<u>Solution:</u> y is inversely proportional to x means there exists a number k such that y = k/x. Our problem will be solved when we determine the number k. If we substitute 3 for x and 2 for y in the equation y = k/x, we find 2 = k/3. Multiplying both sides by 3 we obtain k = 6. Thus, the equation relating x and y is y = 6/x.

If y varies inversely as the cube of x, and y = 7 when x = 2, express y as a function of x.

<u>Solution:</u> The relationship "y varies inversely with respect to x" is expressed as,

$$y = \frac{k}{x}.$$

The inverse variation is now with respect to the cube of x, x^3 and we have,

$$y = \frac{k}{x^3}$$

Since y = 7 and x = 2 must satisfy this relation, we replace x and y by these values,

$$7 = \frac{k}{2^3} = \frac{k}{8},$$

and we find k = 7 · 8 = 56. Substitution of this value of k in the general relation gives,

$$y = \frac{56}{x^3},$$

which expresses y as a function of x. We may now, in addition find the value of y corresponding to any value of x. If we had the added requirement to find the value of y when x = 1.2, x = 1.2 would be substituted in the function so that for x = 1.2, we have,

$$y = \frac{56}{(1.2)^3} = \frac{56}{1.728} = 32.41$$

Other expressions in use are "is proportional to" for "varies directly," and "is inversely proportional to" for "varies inversely."

The cube root of x varies inversely as the square of y; if x = 8 when y = 3, find x when y = 1½.

<u>Solution:</u> If x varies inversely as y, then $x = \frac{m}{y}$, and

in this case $\sqrt[3]{x}$ varies inversely as y^2, thus,

$\sqrt[3]{x} = \dfrac{m}{y^2}$, where m is constant.

Putting x = 8, y = 3, we have $\sqrt[3]{8} = \dfrac{m}{3^2}$ or, $2 = \dfrac{m}{9}$;

therefore, m = 18.

Now, we want to find x when $y = 1\frac{1}{2} = \dfrac{3}{2}$. We know

from above that m = 18, and since $\sqrt[3]{x} = \dfrac{m}{y^2}$, by sub-

stitution we obtain:

$$\sqrt[3]{x} = \dfrac{18}{\left(\dfrac{3}{2}\right)^2}$$

$$\sqrt[3]{x} = \dfrac{18}{\dfrac{9}{4}}$$

$\sqrt[3]{x} = 18 \left(\dfrac{4}{9}\right) = 8$. Now cubing both sides we obtain:

x = 8^3 or x = 512.

JOINT AND COMBINED DIRECT - INVERSE VARIATION

● **PROBLEM 28-9**

If y varies jointly as x and z, and 3x:1 = y:z, find the constant of variation.

<u>Solution:</u> A variable s is said to vary jointly as t and v if s varies directly as the product tv; that is, if s = ctv where c is called the constant of variation.

Here the variable y varies jointly as x and z with k as the constant of variation.

$$y = kxz$$
$$3x:1 = y:z$$

Expressing these ratios as fractions.

$$\dfrac{3x}{1} = \dfrac{y}{z}$$

Solving for y by cross-multiplying,

$$y = 3xz$$

Equating both relations for y we have:

$$kxz = 3xz$$

Solving for the constant of variation, k, we divide both sides by xz, $k = 3$

● **PROBLEM 28-10**

The current, i, in amperes in an electric circuit varies directly as the electromotive force, E, in volts and inversely as the resistance, R, in ohms. If, in a certain circuit, i = 30 amperes when R = 15 ohms and E = 450 volts, find i when R = 20 ohms and E = 200 volts.

<u>Solution:</u> The relation "i varies directly as E and inversely as R" may be expressed as $i = \frac{kE}{R}$ where k is the proportionality constant. k must be determined before i can be found as desired.

$i = kE/R$ and so

$$30 = \frac{k \cdot 450}{15} \quad \text{or, } k = 30\left(\frac{15}{450}\right)$$

$$= \frac{15}{15}$$

$$= 1.$$

Hence $i = E/R$ and when R = 20 and E = 200, we have i = = 200/20 = 10 amperes.

● **PROBLEM 28-11**

The weight W of an object above the earth varies inversely as the square of the distance d from the center of the earth. If a man weighs 180 pounds on the surface of the earth, what would his weight be at an altitude of 1000 miles? Assume the radius of the earth to be 4000 miles.

<u>Solution:</u> W varies inversely with d^2; therefore $W = \frac{k}{d^2}$ where k is the proportionality constant. Similarly,

$W_1 = \frac{k}{d_1^2}$, $W_2 = \frac{k}{d_2^2}$ and, solving these two equations for k,

$W_1 d_1^2 = k$ and $W_2 d_2^2 = k$. Hence,

$$k = W_1 d_1^2 = W_2 d_2^2$$

$$\text{or} \quad \frac{W_1 d_1^2}{W_2} = \frac{\cancel{W_2} d_2^2}{\cancel{W_2}}$$

$$\frac{W_1 d_1^2}{W_2} = d_2^2$$

$$\frac{W_1 \cancel{d_1^2}}{W_2 \cancel{d_1^2}} = \frac{d_2^2}{d_1^2}$$

$$\frac{W_1}{W_2} = \frac{d_2^2}{d_1^2} \tag{1}$$

Letting d_1 = radius of the earth, 4000, then d_2 = 4000 + 1000 = 5000.

Substituting the given values in Equation (1):

$$\frac{180}{W_2} = \frac{5000^2}{4000^2} = \frac{(5 \times 1000)^2}{(4 \times 1000)^2} = \frac{5^2 \times \cancel{1000^2}}{4^2 \times \cancel{1000^2}}$$

$$= \frac{5^2}{4^2}$$

$$= \frac{25}{16}$$

$$\frac{180}{W_2} = \frac{25}{16}$$

$$\cancel{W_2}\left(\frac{180}{\cancel{W_2}}\right) = W_2\left(\frac{25}{16}\right)$$

$$180 = \frac{25}{16}W_2$$

$$\frac{16}{\cancel{25}} \overset{36}{(\cancel{180})} = \frac{\cancel{16}}{25}\left(\frac{25}{\cancel{16}} W_2\right)$$
$$\underset{5}{}$$

$$\frac{576}{5} = W_2$$

$$115\tfrac{1}{5} \text{ pounds} = W_2$$

$$\text{or } 115.2 \text{ pounds} = W_2$$

The pressure of wind on a sail varies jointly as the area of the sail and the square of the wind's velocity. When the wind is 15 miles per hour, the pressure on a square foot is one pound. What is the velocity of the wind when the pressure on a square yard is 25 pounds?

Solution: Let p = pressure of the wind, in pounds
v = the velocity of the wind, in miles per hour
a = the area of the sail, in square feet.

Pressure, p, varies jointly as the area of the sail, a, and the square of the wind's velocity, v^2. Therefore p varies directly as the product av^2 times a proportionality constant, k. k must be determined before we can proceed to find v as desired. Use the given information a = 1 and p = 1 when v = 15 to determine the proportionality constant, k.

$$p = kav^2.$$

$$1 = k(1)(225).$$

$$k = \frac{1}{225}, \text{ value of the proportionality constant.}$$

Now we can find v using $k = \frac{1}{225}$ when p = 25 and a = 9 (1 yard = 3 feet, 1 square yard = 9 square feet).

$$p = \frac{1}{225}av^2.$$

$$25 = \frac{1}{225}(9)v^2.$$

$$v^2 = \frac{(25)(225)}{9}$$

$$v = \sqrt{\frac{(25)(225)}{9}} = \frac{(5)(15)}{3}$$

v = 25, number of miles per hour.

The elongation, E, of a steel wire when a mass, m, is hung from its free end varies jointly as m and the length, x, of the wire and inversely as the cross sectional area A, of the wire. Given that E = 0.001 inches when m = 20 pounds, x = 10 inches, and A = 0.01 square inches, find E when m = 40 pounds, x = 15.5 inches, and A = 0.015 square inches.

<u>Solution:</u>   If E is directly proportional to m and x and inversely proportional to A, our equation is

$$E = \frac{kmx}{A}$$

where k is a constant which we can determine from the given information.

Since, when m = 20, x = 10, and A = .01, E = .001, we can use this information to solve for k. Substituting we obtain:

$$0.001 = \frac{k(20)(10)}{.01}$$, and multiplying both

sides by $\frac{.01}{(20)(10)}$ we obtain:

$$k = \frac{(.001)(.01)}{200} = \frac{.00001}{200} \cdot$$

Multiplying numerator and denominator by 100,000 (move the decimal 5 places to the right) we obtain:

$$\frac{1}{20,000,000}$$

Hence, $E = \frac{1}{20,000,000} \frac{mx}{A}$

and when m = 40, x = 15.5, and A = 0.015, we have:

$$E = \frac{1}{20,000,000} \frac{40(15.5)}{0.015}$$

= 0.00207 inches (approximately).

● **PROBLEM 28-14**

A certain beam L ft. long has a rectangular cross section b in. in horizontal width and d in. in vertical depth. It is found that, when the beam is supported at the ends, the deflection D at the center varies directly as the fourth power of L, inversely as b, and inversely as the cube of d. If the length is decreased by 10 per cent but the width kept the same, by how much should the depth be changed in order that the same deflection D be obtained?

<u>Solution:</u> A quantity m varies directly as another q quantity n if m equals the product of a constant and n; that is, m = cn where c is the constant. Also, a quantity p varies inversely as another quantity q if p equals the product of a constant and the reciprocal of q; that is, p = c(1/q) = c/q where c is the constant. From the statement of the problem, we see that the combined variation is given by

$$D = \frac{kL^4}{bd^3} \quad , \text{ where } k \text{ is a constant.}$$

Since corresponding values of the four variables are not known, we cannot determine the value of the constant of proportionality k. But if one set of variables is designated with the subscript 1, and the new set with the subscript 2, we have

$$D_1 = \frac{kL_1^4}{b_1 d_1^3} \quad , \quad D_2 = \frac{kL_2^4}{b_2 d_2^3} \quad .$$

Since it is desired to obtain a relationship between d_1 and d_2, carry out the following procedure in order to isolate d_1 and d_2 on different sides of the equation.

Divide D_2 by D_1:

$$\frac{D_2}{D_1} = \frac{kL_2^4/b_2 d_2^3}{kL_1^4/b_1 d_1^3} \tag{1}$$

Since division by a fraction is equivalent to multiplication by that fraction's reciprocal, equation (1) becomes:

$$\frac{D_2}{D_1} = \frac{kL_2^4}{b_2 d_2^3} \cdot \frac{b_1 d_1^3}{kL_1^4} = \frac{L_2^4 b_1 d_1^3}{b_2 d_2^3 L_1^4} = \frac{L_2^4 b_1 d_1^3}{L_1^4 b_2 d_2^3}$$

or

$$\frac{D_2}{D_1} = \frac{L_2^4 b_1 d_1^3}{L_1^4 b_2 d_2^3}$$

In this problem we have $D_2 = D_1$, $L_2 = 0.9L_1$, and $b_2 = b_1$. Therefore we get

$$\frac{D_1}{D_1} = \frac{\left(0.9L_1\right)^4 b_1 d_1^3}{L_1^4 b_1 d_2^3}$$

$$1 = \frac{(0.9)^4 L_1^4 b_1 d_1^3}{L_1^4 b_1 d_2^3}$$

$$1 = (0.9)^4 \frac{d_1^3}{d_2^3}$$

Multiplying both sides by d_2^3:

$$d_2^3(1) = d_2^3 (0.9)^4 \frac{d_1^3}{d_2^3}$$

$$d_2^3 = (0.9)^4 d_1^3$$

Take the cube root of each side:

$$\sqrt[3]{d_2^3} = \sqrt[3]{(0.9)^4 d_1^3}$$

$$d_2 = \sqrt[3]{(0.9)^4}\ \sqrt[3]{d_1^3}$$

$$d_2 = \sqrt[3]{(0.9)^4}\ d_1$$

$$d_2 = (0.9)^{4/3}\ d_1$$

$$d_2 = \left[(0.9)^{1/3}\right]^4 d_1$$

$$d_2 = \left[\sqrt[3]{0.9}\right]^4 d_1$$

$$d_2 \approx (.966)^4\ d_1$$

$$d_2 \approx .871\ d_1$$

Hence, the new depth, d_2 is only $.871\ d_1$. Subtracting $.871\ d_1$ from $1\ d_1$:

$$
\begin{array}{r}
1.000\ d_1 \\
-\ 0.871\ d_1 \\
\hline
0.129\ d_1
\end{array}
$$

Therefore, the depth has been decreased by an amount of $.129$ or

$$\frac{129}{1000} = \frac{129}{10} \times \frac{1}{100}$$

$$= \frac{129}{10}\ \%\ \text{since "hundredths means per cent"}$$

$$= 12.9\%.$$

Hence, the depth has been decreased approximately 13%.

CHAPTER 29

COSTS

Reserved seat tickets to a football game are $6 more than general admission tickets. Mr. Jones finds that he can buy general admission tickets for his whole family of five for only $3 more than the cost of reserved seat tickets for himself and Mrs. Jones. How much do the general admission tickets cost?

Solution: Let x = the cost of general admission tickets.

Let $x + 6$ = the cost of reserved seat tickets.

Thus, $5x$ is the cost of five general admission tickets and $2(x+6)$ is the cost of two reserved seat tickets. Since the five tickets cost three dollars more than the two reserved tickets,

$$5x = 2(x + 6) + 3$$
$$5x = 2x + 12 + 3$$
$$5x = 2x + 15$$
$$3x = 15$$
$$x = 5,$$

and
$$x + 6 = 5 + 6 = 11$$

Thus, general admission tickets are $5.00, and reserve tickets are $11.00.

● PROBLEM 29-2

A television set cost a dealer $102. At what price should he mark the set so that he can give a discount of 15% from the marked price and still make a profit of 20% on the selling price?

Solution: Let x = The marked price

Then $.85x$ = The selling price

296

The relationship used to set up the equation is:

Selling price = Cost + Profit

$$.85x = 102 + (.20)(.85x)$$
$$.85x = 102 + .17x$$
$$.68x = 102$$
$$x = \$150$$

Check: The marked price = \$150. The selling price is 15% less or \$127.50. Since the cost is \$102, the profit is \$25.50. The profit (\$25.50) is 20% of the selling price (\$127.50).

● **PROBLEM 29-3**

At a movie showing there were 356 paid admissions. The total receipts were \$287.40. If orchestra seats sold for \$.90 and balcony seats for \$.65, how many of each kind were sold?

<u>Solution:</u>   Let x = The number of \$.90 seats sold

Then (356 - x) = The number of \$.65 seats sold

The relationship used to set up the equation is:

Orchestra receipts + Balcony receipts = Total receipts or \$287.40

$$.90x + .65(356 - x) = 287.40$$
$$90x + 65(356 - x) = 287.40$$
$$90x + 23140 - 65x = 287.40$$
$$25x = 5600$$
$$x = 224 \text{ orchestra seats sold}$$
$$356 - x = 132 \text{ balcony seats sold}$$

Check: 224 at \$.90 = \$201.60
132 at \$.65 = \$85.80
356 tickets for \$287.40

● **PROBLEM 29-4**

A dealer can buy a certain number of ties for \$30. If 5 more could be bought for the same money, the price would be \$3.60 less per dozen. What is the price per dozen?

<u>Solution:</u>   Let x = The number of ties the dealer can buy for \$30.

Then $\dfrac{30}{x}$ = The cost per tie

And $\dfrac{30}{x + 5}$ = The supposed cost per tie

The relationship used to set up the equation is:

The supposed cost per dozen = The old cost per dozen minus \$3.60

$$12\left(\frac{30}{x + 5}\right) = 12\left(\frac{30}{x}\right) - \frac{18}{5}$$

$$12(30)(5x) = 12(30)(5)(x + 5) - 18(x)(x + 5)$$

$$1,800x = 1,800x + 9,000 - 18x^2 - 90x$$

$$18x^2 + 90x - 9,000 = 0$$

$$x^2 + 5x - 500 = 0$$

$$(x + 25)(x - 20) = 0$$

$$x = -25 \text{ reject}, \quad x = 20$$

The man bought 20 ties for $30, which is at the rate of $18 per dozen.

Check: The man bought 20 ties for $30, paying $1.50 per tie or $18 per dozen. Had he bought 25 ties for $30 he would have paid $1.20 per tie or $14.40 per dozen. This would have been a saving of $3.60 per dozen.

● **PROBLEM 29-5**

A haberdasher sold 3 shirts and 4 ties to one customer for $18.70. Another customer bought 4 shirts and 7 ties of the same quality for $27.75. What was the price per shirt and price per tie?

Solution: Let x = Cost of one shirt
And y = Cost of one tie

(1) $3x + 4y = 1870$
(2) $4x + 7y = 2775$

When the equations are solved simultaneously it is found that x = 398, i.e., the price of a shirt is $3.98 and y = 169, i.e., the price of a tie is $1.69.

● **PROBLEM 29-6**

A merchant paid $1,800 for a group of men's suits. He sold all but 5 of the suits at $20 more per suit than he paid, thereby making a profit of $200 on the transaction. How many suits did the merchant buy?

Solution: Let x = The number of suits the merchant bought
Then $\dfrac{1,800}{x}$ = The cost of each suit

The relationship used to set up the equation is:

The number of suits sold × The selling price of each suit

$$= \$1,800 + \$200$$

$$(x - 5)\left(\frac{1,800}{x} + 20\right) = 2,000$$

$$1,800 + 20x - \frac{9,000}{x} - 100 = 2,000$$

$$20x - \frac{9,000}{x} = 300$$

$$20x^2 - 300x - 9,000 = 0$$

$$x^2 - 15x - 450 = 0$$

$$(x - 30)(x + 15) = 0$$

$$x = 30, \quad x = -15 \text{ reject}$$

The merchant bought 30 suits.

Check: The merchant bought 30 suits at $60 each. He sold 25 suits at $80 each, thus taking in $2,000.

● **PROBLEM 29-7**

A real estate dealer received $1,200 in rents on two dwellings last year, and one of the dwellings brought $10 per month more than the other. Find the monthly rental on each if the more expensive house was vacant for 2 months.

<u>Solution:</u> On inspecting the problem we see that there are two basic relations involved, the relation between the separate rentals, and the relation between the monthly rentals and the income per year. Since the monthly rentals differ by $10, we let

    x = monthly rental of the more expensive house in dollars
    y = monthly rental of the less expensive house in dollars

and we write $x = y + 10$

    or $x - y = 10$ (1)

Furthermore, since the first of the two houses was rented for 10 months and the other was rented for 12 months, we know that $10x + 12y$ is the total annual income. Hence

$$10x + 12y = 1,200 \qquad (2)$$

We now solve Eq. (1) and (2) simultaneously by eliminating y:

  $12x - 12y = 120$ multiplying (1) by 12
  <u>$10x + 12y = 1,200$</u>   (2) recopied
  $22x \qquad = 1,320$ equating the sums of corresponding members
        $x = 60$ solving for x
   $60 - y = 10$ replacing x by 60 in (1)
        $y = 50$ solving for y

Therefore, the solution set $\{(x, y)\} = \{(60, 50)\}$, and it follows that the monthly rentals are $60 and $50, respectively.

We check the obtained values by substituting in equations (1) and (2). Thus

$$x - y = 10 \qquad (1)$$
$$60 - 50 = 10$$
$$10 = 10$$

$$10x + 12y = 1200 \qquad (2)$$
$$10(60) + 12(50) = 1200$$
$$600 + 600 = 1200$$
$$1200 = 1200$$

● **PROBLEM** 29-8

A wholesale outlet has room in its radio and television section for not more than 150 radio and television sets. A radio set weighs 50 pounds and a television set weighs 100 pounds, and the floor is limited by the city inspector to a total weight of 10,000 pounds. The profit on a radio set is $50, and the profit on a television set is $75. In order to realize a maximum profit, how many of each shall be stocked? We shall assume, of course, that radio sets and television sets sell equally well.

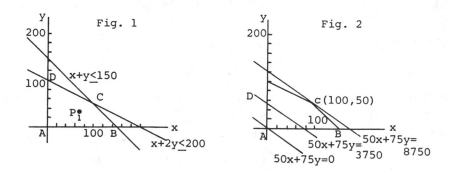

Solution: Let x = the number of radio sets and y = the number of television sets. Since each radio weighs 50 pounds and each television weighs 100 pounds: Let $50x =$ total weight contributed by the radios and $100y =$ total weight contributed by the television sets. Because of the limitation on weight, we have the first constraint

$$50x + 100y \leq 10,000 \qquad (1)$$

Since at most 150 sets can be stocked, the second constraint is

$$x + y \leq 150 \qquad (2)$$

Since the number of sets of either kind cannot be less than zero, we have two more constraints

$$x \geq 0 \qquad\qquad (3)$$
$$y \geq 0 \qquad\qquad (4)$$

The graph of this system (noting that inequality 1 can be reduced to $x + 2y \leq 200$) is shown in Figure 1. It is clear that only points such as P_1 which lie within or on the boundary of the polygon will satisfy the given constraints, and are therefore called feasible points.

We now consider the profit equation also
$$50x + 75y = P \qquad\qquad (5)$$

where $50x$ = total profit on all radio sets and $75x$ = total profit on all television sets.

For all values of P, Equation 5 represents a system of parallel lines, as shown in Figure 2. We note further that as P increases, the lines move to the right. Of particular significance is the fact that the maximum profit occurs at the vertex C, since no feasible points exist beyond this point. This can be shown by substituting other points of the polygon into the profit equation. For example, given the point (40,8), then $P = \$8000$. The coordinates of C are found by solving the system of equations, derived from the first two constraints, since this is their point of intersection. The equations are:
$$x + y = 150$$
$$x + 2y = 200 \qquad\qquad (6)$$

Subtracting the first equation from the second we obtain:
$$x = 100, \text{ the number of radio sets}$$
$$y = 50, \text{ the number of television sets}$$

Thus, the maximum profit is

$$P = 100(50) = 50(75) = \$8750.$$

CHAPTER 30

PROGRESSIONS AND SEQUENCES

ARITHMETIC

• **PROBLEM** 30–1

If the 6th term of an arithmetic progression is 8 and the 11th term is - 2, what is the 1st term? What is the common difference?

<u>Solution:</u> An arithmetic progression is a sequence of numbers where each term excluding the first is obtained from the preceding one by adding a fixed quantity to it. This constant amount is called the common difference. Let a = value of first term, and d = common difference

Term of
sequence: 1st 2nd 3^{thrd} 4th ... n^{th}

Value of
term: a   a+d   a+2d   a+3d ... a+(n-1)d

Use the formula for the nth term of the sequence to write equations for the given 6th and 11th terms, to determine a and d.

11th term: a + (11 - 1)d = - 2

6th term: a + (6 - 1)d = 8. Simplifying the above equations we obtain:

a+ 10d = - 2   (1)
a+ 5d = 8   (2)

5d = - 10 Subtracting (2) from (1)
d = - 2 Substituting in (1)
a + 10(- 2) = - 2
a = 18

The first term is 18 and the common difference is - 2.

• **PROBLEM** 30–2

Find a_n for the sequence 1, 4, 7, 10,...

<u>Solution:</u> An arithmetic progression (A.P.) is a sequence of numbers each of which, after the first, is obtained by adding to the preceding number a constant number, d, called the common difference. Thus 1, 4, 7, 10,... is an arithmetic progression because each term is obtained by adding 3 to the preceding number. The nth term, a_n, of an A.P. is:

$$a_n = a_1 + (n-1)d$$

where a_1 = first term of the progression; d = common difference; n = number of terms.

Thus, with $a_1 = 1$ and $d = 3$,

$$a_n = 1 + (n-1)3 = 1 + 3n - 3$$

$$a_n = 3n - 2$$

It is easily verified by substitution that $a_n = 3n - 2$ will suffice, i.e. $a_1 = 3(1) - 2 = 1$

$$a_2 = 3(2) - 2 = 4$$

$$a_3 = 3(3) - 2 = 7$$

$$a_4 = 3(4) - 2 = 10$$

$$a_5 = 3(5) - 2 = 13 = a_4 + d = 10 + 3$$

by definition of an A.P. etc.

• **PROBLEM 30-3**

Find the first term of an arithmetic progression if the fifth term is 29 and d is 3.

Solution: The nth term, or last term, of an arithmetic progression (A.P.) is:

$$\ell = a_1 + (n-1)d \qquad (1)$$

where a_1 = first term of the progression

    d = common difference

    n = number of terms

    $\ell = n^{th}$ term, or last term.

Using this formula we can find the first term of an A.P. whose fifth term is 29 and d is 3. Since $\ell = a_5 = 29$, $d = 3$, and $n = 5$, substituting into equation (1) gives:

$$29 = a_1 + (5 - 1)3$$

$$29 = a_1 + 12$$

$$a_1 = 29 - 12 = 17.$$

Thus, the first term is 17.

• **PROBLEM 30-4**

If the first term of an arithmetic series is -4 and the twelfth term is 32, find the common difference.

Solution: Since the first and last terms and the number of terms are known, the formula for the nth term, or last term of the series

$$\ell = a_1 + (n-1)d$$

where a_1 = first term of the series

    n = number of terms

    d = common difference

    $\ell = n^{th}$ term, or last term

can be solved for d.

$$\ell = a_1 + (n-1)d \text{ with } a_1 = -4, \ n = 12, \ \ell = 32 \text{ gives}$$

$$32 = -4 + (12 - 1)d$$

$$36 = 11 \ d$$

$$\frac{36}{11} = d$$

• **PROBLEM** 30–5

Find the twelfth term of the arithmetic sequence

$$2, \ 5, \ 8, \ \ldots \ .$$

<u>Solution:</u> It is given that the sequence is an arithmetic sequence. The common difference d is obtained by subtracting any term from the succeeding term;

$$d = 5 - 2 = 3$$

The twelfth term, a_{12}, can be obtained by substituting $a_1 = 2$, $d = 3$, and $n = 12$ in the expression for the nth term:

$$a_1 + (n - 1)d$$

Thus,

$$a_{12} = a_1 + (n - 1)d = 2 + (12 - 1)3 = 35$$

This can be checked by completing the sequence to the twelfth term.

$$2, \ 5, \ 8, \ 2+(4-1)3, \ 2+(5-1)3, \ 2+(6-1)3, \ \ldots \ , \ 2+(11-1)3, \ 35$$
$$2, \ 5, \ 8, \ 11, \ 14, \ 17, \ 20, \ 23, \ 26, \ 29, \ 32, \ 35$$

• **PROBLEM** 30–6

Given that the first term of an arithmetic sequence is 56 and the seventeenth term is 32, find the tenth term and the twenty-fifth term.

<u>Solution:</u> The formula for the nth term, or last term, of an arithmetic sequence is:

$$\ell = s_1 + (n-1)d$$

where s_1 = first term of the sequence

    d = common difference

    n = number of terms

    ℓ = nth term, or last term.

Since we are given the first and seventeenth term of the sequence we can use this information, with $n = 17$, to find d before we proceed to find the tenth and twenty-fifth terms. Thus we find d by

$$s_{17} = s_1 + (17 - 1)d,$$

$$32 - 56 = 16d$$

$$16d = -24$$

$$d = -\frac{3}{2}$$

Now we can find the tenth term, s_{10}, as

$$s_{10} = 56 + (10 - 1)\left(-\frac{3}{2}\right) = 56 - \frac{27}{2} = \frac{85}{2}$$

and the twenty-fifth term, s_{25}, as

$$s_{25} = 56 + (25 - 1)\left(-\frac{3}{2}\right) = 56 - 36 = 20$$

• **PROBLEM** 30–7

The 54th and 4th terms of an arithmetic progression are − 61 and 64; find the 23rd term.

<u>Solution:</u> An arithmetic progression is a sequence of numbers, each of which, after the first, is obtained by adding a constant to the preceding term. This constant is called the 'common difference'. Let a be the first term, and d the common difference; then the sequence looks as follows:

a, a + d, (a + d) + d, (a + d + d) + d, ...   or,

a, a + d, a + 2d, a + 3d, ...

Notice that, 1st. term = a = a + (1 − 1)d

2nd. term = a + 1d = a + (2 − 1)d

3rd. term = a + 2d = a + (3 − 1)d

4th. term = a + 3d = a + (4 − 1)d

Thus, we obtain the formula for any term of an A.P. (arithmetic progression). Let us call this general term n. Then the nth. term = a + (n − 1)d. Therefore,

− 61 = the 54th term = a + 53d;

and   64 = the 4th term = a + 3d.

We now solve these two equations for d by subtracting the second from the first. Thus,

a + 53d = − 61

a +   3d = 64
_____

a − a + 53d − 3d = − 61 − 64   or

$$50d = - 125, \text{ or } d = \frac{-5}{2}$$

Thus, substituting for d in equation two we have:

$$a + 3 \left(- \frac{5}{2}\right) = 64$$

$$a - \frac{15}{2} = 64$$

$$a = \frac{128}{2} + \frac{15}{2} = \frac{143}{2} .$$

Thus, the 23rd term = a + 22d, and substituting for a and d we have:

$$\frac{143}{2} + 22\left(-\frac{5}{2}\right) = \frac{143}{2} - \frac{110}{2} = \frac{33}{2} \,.$$

• **PROBLEM** 30–8

If the first term of an arithmetic progression is 7, and the common difference is -2, find the fifteenth term and the sum of the first fifteen terms.

Solution: An arithmetic progression is a sequence of numbers each of which is obtained from the preceding one by adding a constant quantity to it, the common difference, d. If we designate the first term by a and the common difference by d, then the terms can be expressed as follows:

terms of
  series   1   2   3   .....   n

value of
  term   a   a + d   a + 2d ℓ = a + (n-1)d

In this example a = 7, and d = -2. To find the fifteenth term, we have n = 15. The nth term is a + (n-1)d. For n = 15, a + (n-1)d = 7 + (15 - 1)(-2) = 7 - 28 = -21. To find the sum of the first fifteen terms apply the following formula:

$$S_n = \frac{n}{2}(a + \ell)$$

$$S_{15} = \frac{15}{2}[7 + (-21)] = \frac{15}{2}(-14) = -105.$$

• **PROBLEM** 30–9

Find the sum of the first sixteen terms of the arithmetic series whose first term is $\frac{1}{4}$ and common difference is $\frac{1}{2}$.

Solution: The sum of the first n terms of an arithmetic series is

$$S_n = \frac{n}{2}\left[2a_1 + (n - 1)d\right]$$

where a_1 = first term of the series

  d = common difference
  n = number of terms
  S_n = sum of first n terms

Hence, the sum of the first sixteen terms of the arithmetic series with $a_1 = \frac{1}{4}$, d = $\frac{1}{2}$, and n = 16, is

$$S_{16} = \frac{16}{2}\left[2\left(\frac{1}{4}\right) + (16 - 1)\frac{1}{2}\right]$$

$$= 8\left(\frac{1}{2} + \frac{15}{2}\right)$$

$$= 8\left(\frac{16}{2}\right)$$
$$= 8(8)$$
$$= 64$$

Find the sum of the first 20 terms of the arithmetic progression -9, -3, 3, ...

Solution: An arithmetic progression is a sequence in which each term after the first is formed by adding a fixed amount, called the common difference, to the preceding term. The common difference of -9, -3, 3, ... is 6 since $-9 + 6 = -3$, $-3 + 6 = 3$, etc. If a is the first term, d is the common difference, and n is the number of terms of the arithmetic progression, then the last term (or n^{th} term) ℓ is given by

$$\ell = a + (n-1)d \qquad (1)$$

and the sum S_n of the n terms of this progression is given by

$$S_n = \frac{n}{2}[a + \ell] \qquad (2)$$

In this example,

$$a = -9, \quad d = 6, \quad n = 20. \quad \text{By equation (1):}$$

$$\ell = -9 + (19)(6)$$
$$= -9 + 114$$
$$= 105.$$

By equation (2): $\quad S_{20} = \frac{20}{2}\left(-9 + 105\right)$

$$= 10(96)$$
$$= 960.$$

Thus, the sum of the first 20 terms is 960.

Find the sum of the arithmetic series

$$5 + 9 + 13 + \ldots + 401$$

Solution: The common difference is $d = 9 - 5 = 4$, and the nth term, or last term, is $\ell = a + (n-1)d$, where
 a = first term of the progression
 d = common difference
 n = number of terms
 ℓ = nth term, or last term.

Hence, $401 = 5 + (n-1)4$. Solving for the number of terms n, we have n = 100. The required sum is

$$S = 5 + 9 + 13 + \ldots + 393 + 397 + 401$$

Written in reverse order, this sum is

$$S = 401 + 397 + 393 + \ldots + 13 + 9 + 5$$

Adding the two expressions for S, we have

$$2S = (5 + 401) + (9 + 397) + (13 + 393) + \dots$$
$$+ (393 + 13) + (397 + 9) + (401 + 5)$$

Each term in parentheses is equal to the sum of the first and last terms; 5 + 401 = 406. There is a parenthetic term corresponding to each term of the original series; that is, there are 100 terms. Hence,

$$2S = 100(5 + 401) = 40,600 \text{ and } S = \frac{40,600}{2} = 20,300$$

In general, the sum of the first n terms of an arithmetic series is:
$$S = \frac{n}{2}(a + \ell) = \frac{n}{2}[2a + (n-1)d]$$

For this problem,

$$S = \frac{100}{2}(5 + 401) = \frac{100}{2}[2(5) + (100-1)4] = 20,300$$

● **PROBLEM** 30–12

Find the sum of the first 100 positive integers.

Solution: The first 100 positive integers is an arithmetic progression (A.P.), because each number after the first is obtained by adding 1, called the common difference, to the preceding number. For an A.P., the sum of the first n terms is

$$S_n = \frac{n}{2}\left(a + \ell\right)$$

where a = first number of the progression
n = number of terms
$\ell = n^{th}$ term, or last term
S_n = sum of first n terms.

Concerning the first 100 positive integers: there are 100 terms; hence n = 100. The first term is 1; hence, a = 1. The last term is 100; hence, ℓ = 100.

$$S_{100} = \frac{100(1 + 100)}{2} = 5050$$

● **PROBLEM** 30–13

Find the sum of the first 25 even integers.

Solution: The even integers form an arithmetic progression which is a sequence of numbers each of which is obtained from the preceding one by adding a constant quantity to it. This constant quantity is called the common difference, d. The first term of an arithmetic progression is a and the nth term is ℓ = a + (n-1)d. In this case:

a = 2, n = 25, d = 2.

ℓ = 2 + (25 - 1)2

= 50

308

To find the sum of the n terms of an arithmetic progression, we apply the formula

$$S_n = \frac{n}{2}(a + \ell).$$

$$S_{25} = \frac{25}{2}(2 + 50)$$

$$= 25(26)$$

$$= 650.$$

• **PROBLEM** 30–14

Find the sum of the first p terms of the sequence whose nth term is 3n - 1.

Solution: By putting n = 1, and n = p, respectively, in 3n - 1, we obtain

    1st term = 3(1) - 1 = 2

    last term = pth term = 3p - 1.

We can now apply the formula for the sum of the terms of an arithmetic progression, which states:

$$S_n = \frac{n}{2}(a + \ell), \text{ where}$$

n = the number of terms

a = the first term

ℓ = the last term

S_n = sum of first n terms.

By subtitution,

$$S_p = \text{sum of first p terms} = \frac{p}{2}(2 + 3p - 1) =$$

$$\frac{p}{2}(3p + 1).$$

• **PROBLEM** 30–15

How many terms of the sequence - 9, - 6, - 3, ... must be taken that the sum may be 66?

Solution: To solve this problem we apply the formula for the sum of the first n terms of an arithmetic progression. The formula states:

$$S_n = \frac{n}{2}[2a + (n - 1)d], \text{ where}$$

S_n = sum of the first n terms

n = number of terms
a = first term

d = common difference

We are given all of the above information except n. Therefore, by substituting for S_n, a, and d, we can solve for n. We are given that S_n = 66, a = - 9, and d = 3,

since - 9 + 3 = - 6, - 6 + 3 = - 3, ...

Hence, $\frac{n}{2}$ [- 18 + (n - 1)3] = 66.

Now, multiplying both sides of the equation by 2 we obtain: n [-18+ (n - 1)3] = 132; and simplifying the expression in brackets, we have: n (- 18 + 3n - 3) = 132, or n(3n - 21) = 132. Therefore, we have:

$3n^2$ - 21n = 132, and dividing each term by 3 we obtain:

n^2 - 7n - 44 = 0; factoring we have,

(n - 11)(n + 4) = 0;

therefore, n = 11 or - 4.

We can reject the negative value because there cannot be a negative number of terms in the sequence, and therefore, 11 terms must be taken so that the sum of the terms is 66.

We can check this by taking 11 terms of the series. Doing this we have:

- 9, - 6, - 3, 0, 3, 6, 9, 12, 15, 18, 21;

the sum of which is 66.

• **PROBLEM** 30–16

How many terms of the sequence 26, 21, 16, ... must be taken to amount to 74?

Solution: To solve this problem we apply the formula for the sum of the first n terms of an arithmetic progression. The formula states:

S = $\frac{n}{2}$ [2a + (n - 1)d] , where

S = sum of the first n terms

n = number of terms

a = first term

d = common difference

We are given all of the above information except n. Therefore, by substituting for S, a, and d, we can solve for n. We are given that S = 74, a = 26, and d = - 5, since 26 - 5 = 21, 21 - 5 = 16, ...

Hence, 74 = $\frac{n}{2}$ [2(26) + (n - 1)(- 5)] , or

310

$$\frac{n}{2} [52 + (n - 1)(- 5)] = 74.$$

Simplifying, and multiplying both sides of the equation by 2, we obtain:

$$\frac{n}{2} (52 - 5n + 5) = 74$$

$$n (52 - 5n + 5) = 148$$

$$n (- 5n + 57) = 148$$

$$- 5n^2 + 57n = 148, \text{ or}$$

$$5n^2 - 57n + 148 = 0; \text{ factoring we obtain:}$$

$$(n - 4)(5n - 37) = 0;$$

therefore, $n = 4$ or $\frac{37}{5}$.

We can readily reject the value $\frac{37}{5}$, since it is not possible to have $7 \frac{2}{5}$ terms. Thus, 4 terms of the sequence must be added to amount to 74.

We can check this by adding the four terms, 26, 21, 16, 11, and observing that the sum is indeed 74.

• **PROBLEM** 30–17

Insert 4 arithmetic means between 1 and 36.

Solution: The terms between any two given terms of a progression are called the means between these two terms. Inserting 4 arithmetic means between 1 and 36 requires an arithmetic progression (A.P.) of the form 1, ___, ___, ___, ___, 36. Using the formula, $\ell = a + (n - 1)d$, for the nth term, or last term, of an A.P., where a = first term of the progression, d = common difference, n = number of terms, $\ell = n^{th}$ term or last term, we can determine d. Knowing the common difference, d, we can obtain the means by adding d to each preceding number after the first.

$a = 1, \ell = 36$, and n = 6 since there will be six terms

$\ell = a + (n - 1)d$

$36 = 1 + 5d$

$5d = 35$

$d = 7$

The arithmetic means are: 1+7, (1+7)+7, (1+7+7)+7, (1+7+7+7)+7; that is, 8, 15, 22, and 29. The arithmetic progression is 1, 8, 15, 22, 29, 36.

• **PROBLEM** 30–18

Insert five arithmetic means between 13 and 31.

311

<u>Solution:</u> In an arithmetic progression, the terms between any two other terms are called the arithmetic means between the two given terms. An arithmetic progression is a sequence of numbers where each is derived from the preceeding one by adding a constant quantity to it. The constant quantity is called the common difference. The first term of the A.P. is designed by a and the common difference by d. We express the terms of the series:

Term of the Series	1	2	3	4	...	n
Value of the Series	$a_1 = a$	$a_2 = a+d$	$a_3 = a_2 +d$ $= (a+d)+d$ $= a+2d$	$a_4 = a_3 +d$ $= a+3d$	...	$a_n =$ $a+(n-1)d$

We are concerned with seven terms here: the first term, five arithmetic means, and the last term. In order to find the arithmetic means, we need to find the common difference, d. (We know a, which is 13.) The seventh term, $31 = a + (n-1)d = 13(7-1)d = 13 + 6d$. Thus,

$$31 = 13 + 6d$$
$$18 = 6d$$
$$d = 3$$

Consequently the five arithmetic means are

$$a_2 = 13 + 3 = 16, \ a_3 = 19, \ a_4 = 22, \ a_5 = 25, \ a_6 = 28.$$

• **PROBLEM** 30–19

Insert 20 arithmetic means between 4 and 67.

<u>Solution:</u> 'Arithmetic means' are all the terms that fall between any two given terms in an arithmetic progression. The two given terms are called the extremes. Thus, in this example, including the extremes, the number of terms will be 22; so that we have to find a sequence of 22 terms in A.P., of which 4 is the first and 67 the last.

Let d be the common difference; then, since the general nth term of an A.P. $= a + (n - 1)d$, and 67 is the 22nd term, we have:

$67 = a + 21d,$ a = first term.

Since the first term is 4 we obtain:

$4 + 21d = 67.$ Solving for d we find:

$$21d = 63$$
$$d = 3.$$

Thus, the sequence is,

4, 4 + 3, (4 + 3) + 3, ...   or

4, 7, 10, 13, ..., 67

and the 20 required means are,

7, 10, 13, 16, 19, 22, 25, 28, 31, 34, 37, 40, 43, 46, 49,

52, 55, 58, 61, 64.

• PROBLEM 30–20

Determine the first four terms and 12th term of the arithmetic progression generated by F(x) = 2x + 3.

Solution: Find the terms of the progression by letting x = 1, 2, 3, ... etc.

1st term = F(1) = 2(1) + 3 = 5

2nd term = F(2) = 2(2) + 3 = 7

3rd term = F(3) = 2(3) + 3 = 9

4th term = F(4) = 2(4) + 3 = 11

12th term = F(12) = 2(12) + 3 = 27

The common difference, d, is found by subtracting one term from the one that immediately follows it.

The first term is denoted by a.

Note: For this progression a = 5 and d = 2. The coefficient of x in the linear function will always be the common difference for the arithmetic progression.

• PROBLEM 30–21

If an arithmetic progression is generated by the linear function F(x) = -3x + 14, what is the first term? What is the 15th term? What is the common difference?

Solution: 1st term = F(1) = - 3 + 14 = 11

15th term = F(15) = - 3(15) + 14 = - 31

common difference = d = - 3, the coefficient of the linear term.

The coefficient of x in a linear function will always be the common difference, d. To verify that d = - 3, find the second term and subtract the first term from it.

• PROBLEM 30–22

The sum of three numbers in arithmetic progression is 27, and the sum of their squares is 293; find them.

Solution: Let a be the middle number, d the common difference: then the three numbers are a - d, a, a + d.

Since the sum of the three numbers is 27 we have:

a - d + a + a + d = 27; or 3a = 27. Hence, a = 9, and the three numbers are 9 - d, 9, 9 + d.

Now, since the sum of the squares of the numbers is 293, we can use the following equation to solve for d:

313

$$(9 - d)^2 + 9^2 + (9 + d)^2 = 293.$$

Squaring, we obtain:

$$(81 - 18d + d^2) + (81) + (81 + 18d + d^2) = 293$$

$$2d^2 + 243 = 293$$

$$2d^2 = 50$$

$$d^2 = 25$$

$$d = \sqrt{25} = \pm 5.$$

Therefore, the three numbers are:

$9 \pm 5, 9, 9 \pm 5$ or

$4, 9, 14.$

• **PROBLEM** 30–23

The sums of n terms of two arithmetic progressions are in the ratio of 7n + 1 : 4n + 27; find the ratio of their 11th terms.

Solution: Let the first term and common difference of the two sequences be a_1, d_1, and a_2, d_2 respectively.

The sum of the first n terms of an arithmetic progression is given by the formula:

$$S = \frac{n}{2} [2a + (n - 1)d] .$$

Since the sums of the two given progressions are in the ratio $\frac{7n + 1}{4n + 27}$ we have:

$$\frac{\frac{n}{2} [2a_1 + (n - 1)d_1]}{\frac{n}{2} [2a_2 + (n - 1)d_2]} = \frac{7n + 1}{4n + 27} , \text{ or}$$

$$\frac{2a_1 + (n - 1)d_1}{2a_2 + (n - 1)d_2} = \frac{7n + 1}{4n + 27} .$$

Now, using the fact that the nth term of an A.P. = a + (n - 1)d, we find

11th term = a + (11 - 1)d = a + 10d.

Therefore, the ratio of the 11th terms of our two progressions is:

$$\frac{a_1 + 10d_1}{a_2 + 10d_2} .$$

Now, we want to transform the ratio of the sums into the above ratio of the 11th terms. We can do this by dividing each term in the following proportion by 2:

$$\frac{2a_1 + (n - 1)d_1}{2a_2 + (n - 1)d_2} = \frac{7n + 1}{4n + 27} .$$

Doing this we obtain:

$$\frac{a_1 + \frac{(n - 1)}{2} d_1}{a_2 + \frac{(n - 1)}{2} d_2} = \frac{\frac{7n}{2} + \frac{1}{2}}{\frac{4n}{2} + \frac{27}{2}} .$$

Now, to obtain the ratio on the left of the equal sign in the form $\dfrac{a_1 + 10d_1}{a_2 + 10d_2}$, we must have: $\dfrac{n - 1}{2} = 10$, or $n - 1 =$

20; therefore, $n = 21$. Substituting this value in our proportion we obtain:

$$\frac{a_1 + \left(\frac{21 - 1}{2}\right) d_1}{a_2 + \left(\frac{21 - 1}{2}\right) d_2} = \frac{\frac{7(21)}{2} + \frac{1}{2}}{\frac{4(21)}{2} + \frac{27}{2}} \qquad \text{or,}$$

$$\frac{a_1 + 10d_1}{a_2 + 10d_2} = \frac{\frac{147}{2} + \frac{1}{2}}{\frac{84}{2} + \frac{27}{2}} = \frac{\frac{148}{2}}{\frac{111}{2}} = \frac{148}{2} \cdot \frac{2}{111} = \frac{148}{111} .$$

Now, since both numerator and denominator are divisible by 37, we find that the desired ratio is 4 : 3 or $\frac{4}{3}$.

• **PROBLEM** 30–24

If S_1, S_2, S_3, ... S_p are the sums of n terms of an arithmetic progression whose first terms are 1, 2, 3, 4, ... and whose common differences are 1, 3, 5, 7, ... respectively, find the value of

$$S_1 + S_2 + S_3 + ... S_p$$

Solution: We can find S_1, S_2, S_3, ..., S_p by applying the formula for the sum of the first n terms of an arithmetic progression. The formula states:

$$S = \frac{n}{2} [2a + (n - 1)d] , \text{ where}$$

S = the sum

n = the number of terms

a = the first term

d = the common difference

Thus, for S_1, a = 1 and d = 1, we have:

$$S_1 = \frac{n}{2} [2(1) + (n - 1)1] = \frac{n}{2} (2 + n - 1) =$$

315

$$\frac{n}{2}(n + 1) = \frac{n(n + 1)}{2} .$$

For S_2, $a = 2$ and $d = 3$; thus,

$$S_2 = \frac{n}{2}[2(2) + (n - 1)3] = \frac{n}{2}(4 + 3n - 3) =$$

$$\frac{n}{2}(3n + 1) = \frac{n(3n + 1)}{2} .$$

For S_3, $a = 3$ and $d = 5$; thus

$$S_3 = \frac{n}{2}[2(3) + (n - 1)5] = \frac{n}{2}(6 + 5n - 5) =$$

$$\frac{n}{2}(5n + 1) = \frac{n(5n + 1)}{2} .$$

Now, to find a and d for S_p we notice that a relation exists between the sum and the first term, and the sum and the common difference. For S_1, the first term is 1, and the difference 1, or $2(1) - 1$. For S_2, the first term is 2, and the difference 3, or $2(2) - 1$. For S_3, the first term is 3, and the difference 5, or $2(3) - 1$. Similarly, for S_p, the first term is p, and the common difference is $(2p - 1)$. Thus,

$$S_p = \frac{n}{2}[2p + (n - 1)(2p - 1)]$$

$$= \frac{n}{2}[2p + (2pn - 2p - n + 1)] = \frac{n}{2}(2pn - n + 1).$$

Factoring n from the first two terms in the parentheses we have:

$$\frac{n}{2}[(2p - 1)n + 1].$$

Therefore, the required sum,

$S_1 + S_2 + S_3 + \ldots + S_p$ is:

$$\frac{n(n + 1)}{2} + \frac{n(3n + 1)}{2} + \frac{n(5n + 1)}{2} + \ldots + \frac{n[(2p - 1)n + 1]}{2}$$

Factoring $\frac{n}{2}$ from each term, we obtain:

$$\frac{n}{2}[(n + 1) + (3n + 1) + (5n + 1) + \ldots (\{2p - 1\}n + 1)]$$

Now, since we are adding 1, p times, we can write:

$$\frac{n}{2}[(n + 3n + 5n + \ldots + \{2p - 1\}n) + p].$$

Factoring n from the terms in the parentheses, we obtain:

$$\frac{n}{2} [n(1 + 3 + 5 + \ldots + \{2p - 1\}) + p].$$

Let us now examine the terms of the above series: $1 + 3 + 5 + \ldots + (2p - 1)$. Notice that we can apply the formula for the sum of the first n terms of an arithmetic progression, which states the following:

$$S = \frac{n}{2} [2a + (n - 1)d] = \frac{n}{2}(a + \ell).$$

In our case it is more efficient to use the form $S = \frac{n}{2}(a + \ell)$, where S = the sum

$$n = \text{the number of terms}$$

$$a = \text{first term}$$

$$\ell = \text{last term}$$

We know that $n = p$, $a = 1$, $\ell = (2p - 1)$. Thus,

$$S = \frac{p}{2} (1 + 2p - 1) \quad \text{or,} \quad S = \frac{p}{2} (2p) = p^2.$$

Therefore,

$$S_1 + S_2 + S_3 + \ldots + S_p = \frac{n}{2}[n(1 + 3 + 5 + \ldots$$

$$\ldots + \{2p - 1\}) + p] =$$

$$\frac{n}{2} \left[n(p^2) + p \right]. \quad \text{Factoring p from both terms}$$

in the brackets we obtain: $\frac{n}{2} [p (np + 1)] =$

$$\frac{np}{2} (np + 1).$$

Note: It is of interest to observe that in the formula for the sum of n terms of an A.P.,

$$S = \frac{n}{2} [2a + (n - 1)d] = \frac{n}{2}(a + \ell),$$

we can easily derive the first formula, $\frac{n}{2} [2a + (n - 1)d]$, from the second, $\frac{n}{2} (a + \ell)$, as follows:

Since n = the number of terms, and ℓ = last term, then we can use the fact that: $\ell = a + (n - 1)d$. Substituting this value for ℓ we obtain:

$$\frac{n}{2}(a + \ell) = \frac{n}{2} [a + (a + \{n - 1\}d)]$$

$$= \frac{n}{2} [2a + (n - 1)d],$$

which is precisely our first formula.

INDEX

Numbers on this page refer to **PROBLEM NUMBERS**, not page numbers

Numbers on this page refer to **PROBLEM NUMBERS**, not page numbers

Coefficients, 14-7
Coin problems, 26-8, 26-9
Common logarithms, 21-27
Commutative law:
 of addition, 14-10, 26-10
 of multiplication, 5-13,
 21-43
Complement, 3-5, 3-6
Completing the square, 15-22
 to 15-26, 17-13
Complex fractions, 5-3, 5-8
Conditional equations, 15-1
Conditional inequalities, 17-12
Conics, 18-1 to 18-17
Conjugate, 7-12
 complex conjugate, 7-11
Consecutive integers, 26-10
 to 26-12
 even numbers, 26-11
 odd numbers, 26-10
Constant functions, 11-12
Constraints, 12-14
Conversions, decimal and
 fractional, 22-1 to 22-6
Correspondence, rule of, 9-8
Cost problems, 29-1 to 29-5
Critical values, 17-10
Cubes:
 difference of two, 14-12,
 14-28
 sum of two, 14-13, 14-14
Cubic equations, 20-5

Decimal, 22-6, 22-7
 repeating, 22-3 to 22-7
Denominators, 1-11, 5-2, 5-3,
 5-5 to 5-9, 5-11 to 5-14,
 14-22 to 14-28, 22-2, 28-1
Diagonals:
 of rectangles, 23-1
 of rhombus, 23-4, 23-5
Difference of two squares,
 7-15, 14-8, 14-20, 14-22
Digit problems, 26-6, 26-7
Digits, of a number, 26-6
Directrix, 18-8
Discriminant, 16-18, 16-19,

18-6, 19-5
Distance, 24-1, 24-2, 24-4,
 24-5
Distance formula, 18-10, 18-11,
 24-1
Distributive law, 1-4, 1-6,
 1-9, 5-1, 5-9, 5-13, 6-7,
 7-5, 7-6, 7-13, 7-16, 8-2,
 8-4, 8-5, 9-7, 10-5, 10-8,
 10-16, 11-9, 12-6, 12-7,
 14-1, 14-10, 19-3, 25-3
Dividend, 8-11
Divisor, 8-11
Domain, 9-3, 9-8, 9-11, 18-4

Elimination, method of, 13-1
Ellipses, 18-12
 graphing, 18-9 to 18-16
Equations, 20-1
 conditional, 15-1
 cubic, 20-5
 equivalent, 1-9
 exponential, 21-34 to 21-43
 formation of, 20-4
 fractional, 10-7
 general linear, 11-5
 in one variable, 20-1
 linear, 10-1 to 10-16, 11-6,
 13-8
 logarithmic, 21-34 to 21-43
 of degree greater than two,
 20-1 to 20-6
 solving, 10-2, 10-10, 10-13,
 10-16, 15-6, 15-7, 15-17,
 20-3
 with radicals, 10-14, 15-15,
 15-18 to 15-21
Equations of:
 circles, 18-9 to 18-11
 ellipses, 18-12
 hyperbolas, 18-13 to 18-16
 lines, 11-1, 11-3 to 11-11,
 11-14, 11-16 to 11-18, 18-6
 the tangent, 18-6
Equivalent inequalities, 12-7
Exponential and logarithmic
 functions, 21-34 to 21-43

319

Numbers on this page refer to **PROBLEM NUMBERS**, not page numbers

Numbers on this page refer to **PROBLEM NUMBERS**, not page numbers